Y0-EIJ-768

HOLLYWOOD
OCT 0 4 2001

DISCARDED BY
MEMPHIS PUBLIC LIBRARY

The Incredible Internet Guide to Pop Music

By James R. Flowers Jr.

Facts on Demand PRESS

©2001 James R. Flowers Jr. &
Facts on Demand Press
PO Box 27869
Tempe, AZ 85285-7869
(800) 929-3811
www.incredibleguides.com

Facts on Demand
PRESS

The Incredible Internet Guide® to Pop Music

©2001 by James R. Flowers Jr. and Facts on Demand Press
PO Box 27869
Tempe, AZ 85285-7869
(800) 929-3811

ISBN 1-889150-24-X
Cover Design by Robin Fox & Associates
Edited by James R. Flowers Jr.

Cataloging-in-Publication Data
    Flowers, James R. (James Robert), 1973-
        The incredible Internet guide to pop music / by James R. Flowers Jr. -- 1st ed.
        p. cm. -- (Incredible Internet guides)
        Includes index.
        ISBN: 1-889150-24-X

        1. Popular music--Computer network resources. 2. Web sites--Directories. I. Title. II. Title: Pop music III. Series.

    ML3470.F56 2001   025.06'78164
                          QBI01-200079

All rights reserved. Printed in the United States of America. No part of this book may be used or reproduced in any form or by any means, or stored in a database or retrieval system without the prior written permission of the publisher, except in the case of brief quotations embodied in critical articles or reviews. Making copies of any part of this book for any purpose other than your own personal use is a violation of United States copyright laws. Entering any of the contents into a computer for mailing list or database purposes is strictly prohibited unless written authorization is obtained from Facts on Demand Press or BRB Publications, Inc.

The Incredible Internet Guide Series is a registered trademark ® of BRB Publications Inc. Artwork used in *The Incredible Internet Guide to Adventurous & Unusual Travel* is found online on the Internet using web search tools and is intended as examples only. Screen capture images are author property, purchased using an ISP for hire, and found using web tools accessed by the author.
This book is sold as is, without warranty of any kind, either express or implied, respecting the contents of this book, including but not limited to implied warranties for the book's quality, performance, completeness, merchantability, or fitness for any particular purpose. Reasonable care has been taken in the preparation of this text. The book is sold with the understanding that neither the author or publisher provides counseling, advocate or legal advice, nor recommends the suitability of any course of action suggested or implied by a web site listed herein. That any web sites presented herein is a "Must See" or "Editor's Choice" implies only to the quality of its presentation or convenience of its onsite navigation as determined by the author, and does not imply or infer any other result. Neither the authors, the publisher nor its dealers or distributors shall be liable to the purchaser or any other person or entity with respect to any liability, loss, risk or damage (financial, personal, or otherwise) caused or alleged to be caused directly or indirectly by the use and/or application of any of the contents of this book. Readers with specific questions or comments regarding a web site's content must contact the web site owner, author or administrator. Except for technical corrections and suggestion only URLs (with no comments), *The Incredible Internet Guides* author or publisher will not read or forward unsolicited reader comments.

Dedication

To future pop star
Samual Bliven
for being Scooby,
Henry Anderson,
and Honey Child. --
but most of all,
for always being himself.

Contents

Introduction i

The Categories iii

Artist Index

For the music celebrities listed below, we have grouped sites into these categories:

Official E-mail Address, Official Web Site(s), Articles, Audio, Discussion Sites, E-Mail Services, Ecards, FAQs, Galleries, Links, Lyrics, Merchandise, News, Reference, Software, Top Sites, TV Schedules, Video, Wallpapers, Webrings

98 Degrees	1
Aaliyah	7
Alanis Morissette	11
A-Teens	17
Backstreet Boys	19
BBMak	25
Björk	27
Blink 182	31
Boyzone	35
Britney Spears	39
Celine Dion	47
Cher	53
Christina Aguilera	59
Creed	65
Destiny's Child	69

Dixie Chicks 73
Eminem 79
Enrique Iglesias 85
Faith Hill 89
Fiona Apple 93
Foo Fighters 99
Goo Goo Dolls 105
Hanson 109
Janet Jackson 113
Jennifer Lopez 119
Jessica Simpson 125
Jewel 131
Lauryn Hill 135
Lenny Kravitz 139
LFO 143
Lil' Kim 147
Macy Gray 151
Madonna 155
Mandy Moore 165
Marc Anthony 169
Mariah Carey 173
Matchbox Twenty 179
'N Sync 183
Nirvana 191
No Doubt 195
Oasis 199
O-Town 203
Pearl Jam 205
Pink 209
Red Hot Chili Peppers 213
Ricky Martin 217
Santana 223
Sarah McLachlan 227
Savage Garden 231
Shania Twain 237
Sheryl Crow 243
Smashing Pumpkins 247
Sting 253
Stone Temple Pilots 257
Sugar Ray 263
TLC 267

Toni Braxton 271
Westlife 275
Whitney Houston 281
Will Smith 285

Official Sites of Other Musicians   289

More Music Resources   317

Listening to Internet Radio   325

Introduction

The Internet Has Changed Music

The advent of the Internet has changed virtually every aspect of the music industry. Now, we can find out about new artists by clicking on a link. We can listen to sample sounds before we buy. We can watch the videos online that we never seem to catch on MTV. We can even listen to radio around the world. The possibilities are endless.

In the August 2000 issue of *Yahoo! Internet Life*, Alanis Morissette said that the "most promising development" of the Internet "is the millions of different ways I can express who I am as a creator." She goes on to say that "Pretty much any idea I come up with is now feasible."

At the end of 2000, tallies of Yahoo's and Lycos' most popular search terms came up with the same top search -- Britney Spears. Other musicians, such as 'N Sync and the Backstreet Boys also appeared at the top of these lists. What does this mean? It means that music fans everywhere are turning to the Internet to express their interests and further them. Rather than cutting out pictures and hanging them on the wall, today's music fans are writing articles, compiling facts, sharing gossip, and they're doing it all online. They're crowding chat rooms, launching mailing lists, and even creating fan fiction. But with so much activity, it can be difficult to find the best stuff. Enter *The Incredible Internet Guide to Pop Music*!

This book is designed to help you find what you are looking for fast. Whether you want Madonna electronic greeting cards, Eminem discussion groups or Cher wallpaper -- it's all here!

What You Should Know

Pop music is different things to different people. For the purposes of this book, pop music refers to "popular music" that has found its way onto the top *Billboard* charts. Now, we can't possibly hope to cover every artist who's ever had a hit. So, we've limited ourselves to sixty top artists, most of whom have had multiple hits in the past few years.

I can hear it now. Where's Kid Rock? What about Mya? There is no end to the number of people we could cover, and there are only so many pages in a book. However, we have included two chapters ("Official Sites of Other Musicians" and "More Music Resources") both of which are designed to help you find similar sites for other artists.

I can't find a web page -- what's wrong?

There are a number of things you should be aware of, which this book has no control over. First, some web sites simply "die" off – disappear. Also, web sites do change addresses – they move around. Generally, the webmaster will set up a link that takes you to the new location, but not always.

Some sites are only accessible through their main page. One way to try to find a site that won't open is to "truncate" the URL. This is accomplished by deleting the last section of the address. For example, if www.incredibleguides.com/pop would not open for you, then try using only www.incredibleguides.com as the address. Once you are at the "main page" or an "index page," you should then be able to use links to navigate to the specific page you need.

How do you write to us?

We'd certainly like to hear from you, and we'd be especially interested in hearing about anything new or original regarding pop music and the Internet, if briefly stated. You may e-mail us with URLs of sites you feel should be included in future revisions. We're not too excited about web pages that consist mainly of links to other sites. There are plenty of those already. Additionally, if you find an error in this edition of the *Incredible Internet Guide to Pop Music,* feel free to e-mail us a correction.

Our e-mail address is jflowers@incredibleguides.com.

Sorry, we cannot respond to all e-mail, but we especially like to hear good ideas and good words about pop music and our book.

Visit the *Incredible Internet Guides* online

Visit the web site for the *Incredible Internet Guide Series* at www.incredibleguides.com. You will find free e-mail addresses as well as information on other titles in the series, including the *Incredible Internet Guide to Scandals & Conspiracies, Incredible Internet Guide to Adventurous & Unusual Travel* and *Incredible Internet Guide to Howard Stern.*

The Categories

Throughout this book we use categories to make finding what you want a lot easier. The categories were developed based on the function of the web sites we've included. Some pages allow you to send an electronic greeting card; others offer access to a chat room or the latest news; still more have multiple purposes. We've grouped the sites based on the purpose of them so that before you log on, you know what you're getting. Take a minute to familiarize yourself with our categories, before you go online...

E-Mail

You can imagine how much fan mail the artists in this book receive. So it is no surprise that very few offer an "official" e-mail address. Nonetheless, for those artists that offer an e-mail address, we have included it within these pages.

Official Site

With the giant rumor mill that is the Internet, it's a good idea to go "straight to the horse's mouth." Almost every successful musician has an official web site. Although you may see some sites in this book with the word "official" in their title, only those listed under this heading have been verified as truly official web sites of the stars.

Articles

Sites in this category function as an archive of news articles and/or interviews of the artist. Some offer a wide range of articles, while others offer a select yet worthy few. For more articles, see the "News" section.

Audio

Whether it's MP3, Real Audio, Windows Media, WAV or MIDI, all of the sites in this category offer audio files of some kind. You may or may not be able to download, but you will be able to listen. Plug-ins and/or players may be required to listen to the files found on these sites. For the Real Player, visit www.real.com. *For an MP3 player, visit* www.winamp.com. *You can also search* www.hotfiles.com *for other players.*

Discussion

In addition to individual chat rooms and message boards, each Discussion section includes Yahoo! Clubs and Groups. Each Yahoo! Club offers chat, message boards, galleries, links and more. Groups are essentially mailing lists, but they have a lot of other features, including chat, files and links.

E-Mail Services

Sick of having a boring e-mail address? The sites in this category will give you the opportunity to change your e-mail address and pay tribute to your favorite pop star at the same time.

Ecards

Ecards, also known as electronic greeting or post cards, are becoming more commonplace. Sending an online greeting is simple. You choose the image you want to send, type in the e-mail address you want to send it to as well as your own return address, write your personal message, and click send. Most of the pop stars in this book have fan sites that allow you to send a greeting that includes a picture of them.

FAQs

Nagging questions about the artists in this book are often answered in the form of a Frequently Asked Questions (FAQ) file. These documents often clear up myths about the band, dispel rumors, and give you essential background information as well as trivia.

Galleries

Perhaps one of the most popular reasons to use the Internet is to find a picture of something you like. Well, pop stars are no exception. Pictures of these celebrities are in abundance. Use the sites in this category to start your own collection.

Links

This book could not possibly list every single site devoted to each of the artists. However, we can give you a few links that will lead you to more sites. Most celebrities have Top 50, Top 20, etc. list devoted to them. The method by which sites receive "top" status is somewhat questionable, but nonetheless, these lists do provide excellent links.

Lyrics

No more losing sleep trying to figure out what the words are in the second verse of your favorite song. If the lyric is truly questionable, check more than one of the sites in this category. Or do what I do, watch MTV with closed captioning.

Merchandise

Out-of-print, bootlegs, collectors' items, official t-shirts, etc. -- these are the kinds of things you can find for sale or simply on display at the sites in this category.

News

The sites in this category will keep you up-to-date and in-the-know. Some of the sites in this category will even deliver the latest news about your favorite musician direct to your e-mailbox. If not, try www.ananova.com. Ananova e-mails news about many topics, including pop stars.

Reference

How many albums has a particular artist released? When was he born? How are her album sales? These questions and many more can be answered by visiting the sites in this category.

Software

Software can include any or all of the following: wallpaper, desktop themes, fonts, icons, hotbars, WinAmp skins, other skins, cursors, screensavers and more. Sites that are exclusively one type of software are listed under the category that applies ("Wallpaper" or "Themes" etc.) A lot of the sites that are listed in this category accept submissions, so if you have some great wallpaper you've created or some other piece of fan-based software, why not share it with the Web?

Top Sites

The sites in this category are among the best web sites devoted to a particular artist. Most of them offer a wide array of items, including galleries, news, message boards, etc. If any of their "subpages" are of particular interest, they will appear under other categories as well.

TV Schedule

Don't miss a thing! The sites in this category are designed to assist the fan in finding his or her favorite star on television. These schedules cover everything from talk show appearances to feature film roles.

Video

Music videos have become an art form. Use these sites to view videos as well as recordings of live performances. Plug-ins or players may be required.

Wallpapers

Change that boring desktop background to showcase your favorite star! These sites bring you the best in pop star wallpaper.

Webrings

Round and round you go, where you stop nobody knows! Use the webrings in this category to sample a variety of sites that focus on a particular artist.

98 Degrees

SUPER SINGLES "Give Me Just One Night" | "I Do Cherish You" | "Because of You"

Official Site

98Degrees.Com
www.98degrees.com

Articles

98DegreesMusic.Com: Articles
www.98degreesmusic.com/GroupFax/article.htm

Jam! Showbiz: Music: 98 Degrees
www.canoe.ca/JamMusicArtistsN/98degrees.html

Nothing But 98 Degrees: Articles
www.the98degrees.com/multimedia/articles/index.html

Audio

98Degrees.Org: Audio
www.98degrees.org/audio/index.html

Discussion

98Degrees.Org: Message Board
www.98degrees.org/interact/index.html

Yahoo! Clubs: Crazy Love for 98 Degrees
http://clubs.yahoo.com/clubs/crazylovefor98degrees

Yahoo! Clubs: Fever Forever for 98 Degrees
http://clubs.yahoo.com/clubs/feverforeverfor98degrees

Yahoo! Clubs: Hot Ninety 8 Degrees
http://clubs.yahoo.com/clubs/hotninety8degrees

Yahoo! Clubs: Official 98 Degrees Club
http://clubs.yahoo.com/clubs/official98degreesclub

Yahoo! Groups: 98 Degrees 24-7
http://groups.yahoo.com/group/98_Degrees_24-7

Yahoo! Groups: 98-Degrees
http://groups.yahoo.com/group/98-Degrees

Ecards

98DegreesFan.Org: Postcards
www.98degreesfan.org/pages/postcards/index.htm

98DegreesMusic.Com: Postcards
www.98degreesmusic.com/Interactive/cards.htm

Nothing But 98 Degrees: Postcards
www.the98degrees.com/postcards/index.html

Galleries

98DegreesFan.Org: Galleries
www.98degreesfan.org/pics/index.htm

Nothing But 98 Degrees: Galleries
www.the98degrees.com/pictures/index.html

Games

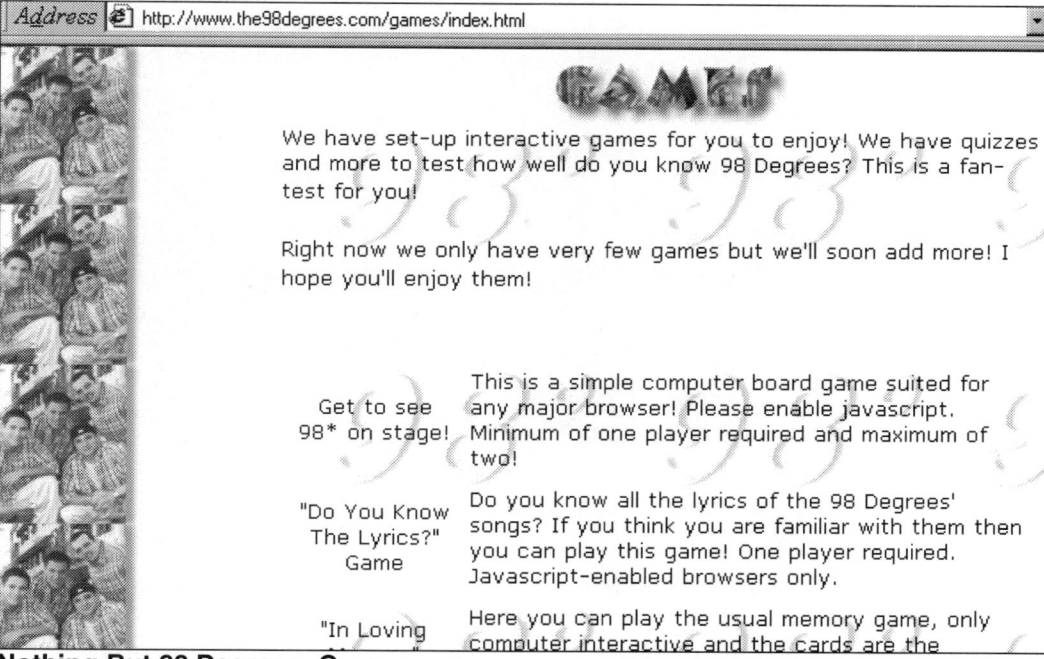

Nothing But 98 Degrees: Games
www.the98degrees.com/games/index.html

Links

Mosiqa Top 100 98 Degrees Sites
www.top.mosiqa.com/98degrees

Lyrics

98 Degrees 2001: Lyrics
www.98degrees2001.com/lyrics.html

98DegreesFan.Org: Lyrics
www.98degreesfan.org/pages/lyrics/index.htm

Nothing But 98 Degrees: Lyrics
www.the98degrees.com/multimedia/lyrics/index.html

Merchandise

98 Degrees Official Store
www.98degreesstore.com

98DegreesMusic.Com: Trading Center
http://pub28.bravenet.com/classified/show.asp?usernum=2337868878&cpv=1

News

98Degrees.Org: News
www.98degrees.org/news.html

98DegreesFan.Org: News
www.98degreesfan.org/pages/news/index.htm

Reference

All Music Guide: 98 Degrees
http://allmusic.com/cg/x.dll?p=amg&sql=198|DEGREES

People Magazine Profiles: 98 Degrees
http://people.aol.com/people/pprofiles/98degrees

Rock on the Net: 98 Degrees
www.rockonthenet.com/artists-n/98degrees_main.htm

Wall of Sound: 98 Degrees
http://wallofsound.go.com/artists/98degrees

Software

Artist Desktop Themes: 98 Degrees
http://artistdesktopthemes.com/gb/d/98_degrees.dt.1.html

Celebrity Desktop: 98 Degrees
www.celebritydesktop.com/musicians/98_degrees

Top Sites

98 Degrees - All Access
www.98degreesallaccess.com

98 Degrees - Still Rising
www.geocities.com/luv98djeff

98 Degrees by Design
http://aztec-princess.com/98degrees

98 Degrees Keep It Hot & Steamy
http://kiss.to/hotsteamy98

98 Degrees on the Net
www.98deg.com

98Degrees.Org
www.98degrees.org

98DegreesFan.Org
www.98degreesfan.org

98DegreesMusic.Com
www.98degreesmusic.com

Heat It Up Online
www.geocities.com/angelof98degrees

Hot 98 Degrees
www.hot98degrees.com

Love 98 Degrees
http://devoted.to/98degrees

Nothing But 98 Degrees
www.the98degrees.com

TV Schedule

98Degrees.Org: TV Appearances
www.98degrees.org/tv.html

Video

98Degrees.Org: Video
www.98degrees.org/videos.html

98DegreesMusic.Com: Mutlimedia
www.98degreesmusic.com/Sightssounds/media.htm

MTV.Com: 98 Degrees
http://98-degrees.mtv.com

Nothing But 98 Degrees: Video
www.the98degrees.com/multimedia/videos/index.html

Wallpapers

98DegreesFan.Org: Wallpapers
www.98degreesfan.org/pages/wall/index.htm

Webrings

1st Unofficial 98 Degrees Web Ring
http://nav.webring.yahoo.com/hub?ring=hot98degrees&list

98 Degrees Cyberfans
http://nav.webring.yahoo.com/hub?ring=98degres&list

98 Degrees Fan Association
http://nav.webring.yahoo.com/hub?ring=98dfa&list

98 Degrees Lovers
http://nav.webring.yahoo.com/hub?ring=98degreeslovers&list

The 98 Degrees Web Ring
http://nav.webring.yahoo.com/hub?ring=98ring&list

Official Site | **Aaliyah**

aaliyah

SUPER SINGLES "Try Again" | "Are You That Somebody" | "Back And Forth"

Official Site

Atlantic Artists / Aaliyah
www.atlantic-records.com/frames/Artists_Music/main.html?artistID=51

Audio

Aaliyah Online: Audio
www.aaliyahonline.com/audio.html

Discussion

Aaliyah Online: Message Board
http://boards.eesite.com/board.cgi?boardset=aaliyah

Yahoo! Clubs: Aaliyah
http://clubs.yahoo.com/clubs/aaliyah

Yahoo! Clubs: Aaliyah's Hot Spot
http://clubs.yahoo.com/clubs/aaliyahshotspot

Yahoo! Clubs: Are You That Somebody?
http://clubs.yahoo.com/clubs/areyouthatsomebody

Galleries

A List Celebrities: Aaliyah
www.the-alist.org/Aaliyah

Aaliyah Online: Photo Galleries
www.aaliyahonline.com/gallery.html

Capital A: Photos
www.angelfire.com/hiphop/CapitalA/photo.html

Yahoo! Clubs: Aaliyah Pictures
http://clubs.yahoo.com/clubs/aaliyahpictures

News

Entertainment Sleuth: Aaliyah
http://e.sleuth.com/details.asp?Entity=4940

Reference

All Music Guide: Aaliyah
http://allmusic.com/cg/x.dll?p=amg&sql=1AALIYAH

Internet Movie Database: Aaliyah
http://us.imdb.com/Name?Aaliyah

Rock on the Net: Aaliyah
www.rockonthenet.com/artists-a/aaliyah_main.htm

Wall of Sound: Aaliyah
http://wallofsound.go.com/artists/aaliyah

Software

Celebrity Desktop: Aaliyah
www.celebritydesktop.com/musicians/aaliyah

Top Sites

100% Aaliyah
www.geocities.com/SunsetStrip/Concert/5692

101% Aaliyah
www.angelfire.com/rnb/101percentaaliyah

Aaliyah - Hot Like Fire
www.angelfire.com/ca/klove/liyah.html

Aaliyah 4 Eva
www.angelfire.com/nv/aaliyah4eva

Aaliyah 4 Life
www.expage.com/aaliyah4life

Aaliyah Heaven
www.geocities.com/aaliyahheaven

Aaliyah Online
www.aaliyahonline.com

Aaliyah Plays It Cool
www.geocities.com/SunsetStrip/Palladium/7966

Aaliyah v. 2.0
www.angelfire.com/al/liyah

Aaliyah, Eternally
http://eternallyaaliyah.cjb.net

Aaliyah's Millennium
http://lovely.as/aaliyah

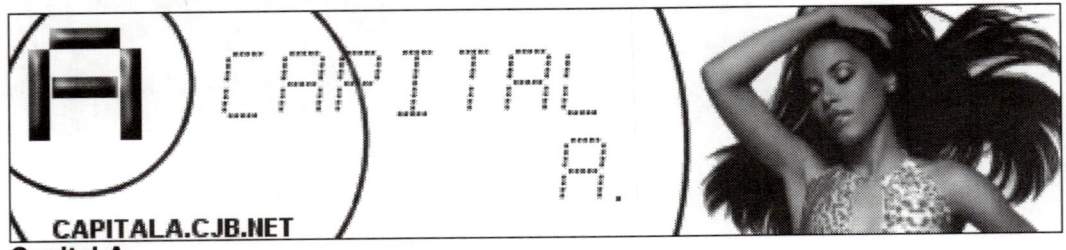

Capital A
www.capitala.cjb.net

The Aaliyah Experience
www.angelfire.com/ar/AaliyahsSpot

Video

Aaliyah Online: Video
www.aaliyahonline.com/videos.html

Aaliyah Plays It Cool: Videos
www.geocities.com/SunsetStrip/Palladium/7966/videos.html

Alanis Morissette

Super Singles "Ironic" | "Thank You" | "You Oughta Know"

Official Sites

Alanis
www.alanis.com

AlanisMorissette.Com
www.alanismorissette.com

Articles

AlanisDirect: Articles
www.musicfanclubs.org/alanis/articles.html

Canoe: Alanis Morissette News Archive
www.canoe.ca/JamMusicAlanisNews/home.html

dotmusic: Alanis Morissette
www.dotmusic.com/artists/AlanisMorissette

Jam! Showbiz: Music: Alanis Morissette
www.canoe.com/JamMusicAlanisNews

Audio

AlanisMP3.Com
www.alanismp3.com

MP3.Com: Alanis Morissette
www.mp3.com/AlanisMorissette

Discussion

Alanis Morissette Network: Chat Room
www.alanischat.com

Alanis Morissette Network: Message Board
www.alanistalk.com

AlanisDirect: Discussion Forum
www.musicfanclubs.org/forums/alanis.html

JAM - Just Alanis Morissette: Message Board
www.alanis-morissette.com/cgi-bin/ubb/Ultimate.cgi

Yahoo! Clubs: Alanis Morissette
http://clubs.yahoo.com/clubs/alanismorissette

Yahoo! Clubs: Alanis Morissette 2000
http://clubs.yahoo.com/clubs/alanismorissette2000

Yahoo! Clubs: Planet Alanis
http://clubs.yahoo.com/clubs/planetalanis

Yahoo! Groups: alanis-fans
http://groups.yahoo.com/group/alanis-fans

Galleries

AtPictures.Com: Alanis Morissette
www.atpictures.com/alanis

Totally Alanis Photo Page
http://hometown.aol.com/rdtrap

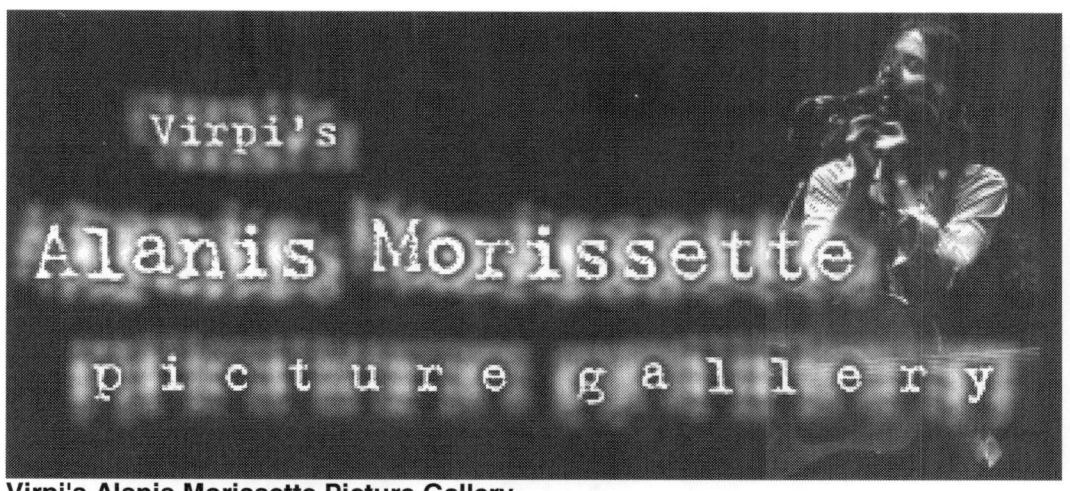

Virpi's Alanis Morissette Picture Gallery
www.geocities.com/SunsetStrip/3223

Lyrics

JAM - Just Alanis Morissette: Lyrics
www.alanis-morissette.com/jam_lyrics

News

Alanis Morissette Network: News
www.alanismorissette.net/news

Entertainment Sleuth: Alanis Morissette
http://e.sleuth.com/details.asp?Entity=3128

Reference

All Music Guide: Alanis Morissette
http://allmusic.com/cg/x.dll?p=amg&sql=1ALANIS|MORISSETTE

Internet Movie Database: Alanis Morissette
http://us.imdb.com/Name?Alanis+Morissette

Rock on the Net: Alanis Morissette
www.rockonthenet.com/artists-m/alanismorissette_main.htm

Wall of Sound: Alanis Morissette
http://wallofsound.go.com/artists/alanismorissette

What You Oughta Know
www.canoe.ca/JamMusicAlanis

Software

Celebrity Desktop: Alanis Morissette
www.celebritydesktop.com/musicians/alanis_morissette

Cinema Desktop Themes: Alanis Morissette
www.cinemadesktopthemes.com/st/m/alanis_morisette.dt.1.html

Top Sites

Alanis!
www.geocities.com/SunsetStrip/9052

Alanis Morissette - One World In Her Pocket
www.geocities.com/SunsetStrip/9052

Alanis Morissette Network
www.alanismorissette.net

Alanis World
http://morissette1.hypermart.net

AlanisDirect
www.musicfanclubs.org/alanis

Crussader's Alanis Morissette Site
www.geocities.com/SunsetStrip/Alley/1845

Definitely Alanis Morissette
www.istnet.net.au/~cawdor

Eric's Guide to Alanis Morissette
http://members.aol.com/ashzero/alanis.htm

Fan Appreciation Site - Alanis Morissette
http://alanisdg.tripod.com

House of Alanis
www.geocities.com/SunsetStrip/Stage/5454

Intellectual Intercourse
www.sgi.net/alanis

JAM - Just Alanis Morissette
www.alanis-morissette.com

Queen of Intimidation - Dana's Alanis Morissette Site
http://members.aol.com/am69dana

The Alanis Connection
www.rebel-tech.com/alanis/alanis-connection.html

VH1 Fan Club: Alanis Morissette
www.vh1.com/fanclubs/main/996.jhtml

Z.Com: Alanis
http://alanis.z.com

Video

The Alanis Connection: Video Archives
www.rebel-tech.com/alanis/videos.html

Wallpapers

Fan Appreciation Site - Alanis Morissette: Wallpapers
http://alanisdg.tripod.com/alaniswall.html

Webrings

THE ALANIS MORISSETTE LINK EXCHANGE

Alanis Morissette Link Exchange
http://nav.webring.yahoo.com/hub?ring=alanisnow&list

Jagged Little Ring
http://nav.webring.yahoo.com/hub?ring=jaggedring&list

The Original Alanis Ring
http://nav.webring.yahoo.com/hub?ring=alanis&list

A-Teens

SUPER SINGLES "Mama Mia" | "Dancing Queen"

Official Site

A-Teens
www.a-teens.com

Discussion

Yahoo! Clubs: A-Teens Online Fan Club
http://clubs.yahoo.com/clubs/ateensonlinefanclub

Yahoo! Clubs: Super ATEENS
http://clubs.yahoo.com/clubs/superateens

Yahoo! Clubs: The Super Troupers
http://clubs.yahoo.com/clubs/thesupertroupers

Yahoo! Clubs: The Way HOTT Ateens
http://clubs.yahoo.com/clubs/thewayhottateens

Yahoo! Groups: A-Teens2
http://groups.yahoo.com/group/A-Teens2

E-Mail

A-Teens.Net (yourname@a-teens.net)
www.a-teens.net

Reference

All Music Guide: A-Teens
http://allmusic.com/cg/x.dll?p=amg&sql=1A|TEENS

Top Sites

AllFans.Org: A-Teens
http://ateens.allfans.org

American A-Teens Wherehouse
http://gurlpages.com/hypergirl13/abbateens.html

A-Teens Fan Asylum
www.fanasylum.com/a-teens

A-Teens Fans Place
www.geocities.com/vince404_99/Ateens/mainpage.html

A-Teens Super Site
www.angelfire.com/pop/mammamia

A-Teens.Net
www.a-teens.net

Concealed Attractions
www.geocities.com/katiet2498

David's A-Teens Site
www.expage.com/ateensarethebest

Backstreet Boys

SUPER SINGLES "Shape of My Heart" | "Show Me The Meaning of Being Lonely" | "Larger Than Life" | "All I Have to Give" | "Quit Playing Games (With My Heart)"

Official Site

Backstreet Boys - Official Site
www.backstreetboys.com

Articles

Canoe: Backstreet Boys News Archive
www.canoe.ca/JamBackstreetBoys/home.html

dotmusic: Backstreet Boys
www.dotmusic.com/artists/BackstreetBoys

Jam! Showbiz: Music: Backstreet Boys
www.canoe.com/JamBackstreetBoys

Discussion

Backstreet Boys - Official Site: Mailing List
www.backstreetboys.com/interact/default.asp

Backstreet Boys Club
www.backstreetboysclub.com

Yahoo! Clubs: Backstreet Boys 3000
http://clubs.yahoo.com/clubs/backstreetboys3000

Yahoo! Clubs: Backstreet Boys Official Club
http://clubs.yahoo.com/clubs/backstreetboysofficialclub

Yahoo! Clubs: Backstreet Boys Pride Club
http://clubs.yahoo.com/clubs/backstreetprideclub

Yahoo! Groups: BackstreetBand
http://groups.yahoo.com/group/BackstreetBand

Yahoo! Groups: BackstreetMultimedia
http://groups.yahoo.com/group/BackstreetMultimedia

Yahoo! Groups: BSBsBackStreetTeam
http://groups.yahoo.com/group/BSBsBackStreetTeam

Yahoo! Groups: thebackfire
http://groups.yahoo.com/group/thebackfire

Yahoo! Groups: TheBackstreetZone
http://groups.yahoo.com/group/TheBackstreetZone

Ecards

Backstreet Boys World: eCards
www.backstreetboysworld.com/fanzone/eCards/index.shtml

Links

Backstreet Boys X-Change Internet Guide
www.gorkypark.com/bsb

FanGuide Top Backstreet Boys Sites
www.fanguide.com/autorankm/bsb

Mosiqa Top 100 Backstreet Boys Sites
www.top.mosiqa.com/bsb

Lyrics

Backstreet Boys Lyrics
http://bsblyrics.tripod.com

Merchandise

Backstreet Project
www.backstreetproject.com

Official Backstreet Boys Store
http://bsbdirect.com

News

backstreet boys news

Backstreet Boys News
www.backstreetboysnews.com

Entertainment Sleuth: Backstreet Boys
http://e.sleuth.com/details.asp?Entity=4945

Reference

All Music Guide: Backstreet Boys
http://allmusic.com/cg/x.dll?p=amg&sql=1BACKSTREET|BOYS

People Magazine Profiles: Backstreet Boys
http://people.aol.com/people/pprofiles/backstreet

Rock on the Net: Backstreet Boys
www.rockonthenet.com/artists-b/backstreetboys_main.htm

Wall of Sound: Backstreet Boys
http://wallofsound.go.com/artists/backstreetboys

Yahoo! Web Celeb: Backstreet Boys
http://features.yahoo.com/webceleb/backstreet

Software

Artist Desktop Themes: Backstreet Boys
http://artistdesktopthemes.com/gb/b/backstreet_boys.dt.1.html

Celebrity Desktop: Backstreet Boys
www.celebritydesktop.com/musicians/backstreet_boys

Top Sites

10,000 Promises - A Backstreet Boys Fan Site
www.fansitez.com/bsb

AllBackstreet.Net
http://allbackstreet.net

Always Backstreet
www.averageangel.com/bsb

B-S-B.Com
http://b-s-b.com

Backstreet Angels
http://backstreetangels.com

Backstreet Boys World
www.backstreetboysworld.com

Backstreet Delight
www.envy.nu/bsbdelight

Backstreet Net
www.backstreetnet.com

Backstreet Zone
www.backstreetzone.com

BackstreetBoys.Nu
http://backstreetboys.nu

BSBFanNet
www.bsbfan.net

Eyes of Stone
www.eyesofstone.net

VH1 Fan Club: Backstreet Boys
http://backsteet-boys.vh1.com

Video

Backstreet Boys - Official Site: Videos
www.backstreetboys.com/videos/default.asp

MTV.Com: Backstreet Boys
http://backstreet-boys.mtv.com

Webrings

Backstreet Boys Webring
http://nav.webring.yahoo.com/hub?ring=getdown&list

Backstreet's Backstreet Boys Webring
http://nav.webring.yahoo.com/hub?ring=backstreetrng&list

The Backstreet Boys All @ccess
http://nav.webring.yahoo.com/hub?ring=bsb4&list

The Backstreet Project Ring by dogwars
[Join Now | Ring Hub | Random | << Prev | Next >>]

The Backstreet Project Ring
http://nav.webring.yahoo.com/hub?ring=thebackstreetpro&id=1&hub

BBMak

SUPER SINGLES "Back Here" | "Still On Your Side"

Official Site

BBMak's Official Site
www.bbmak.co.uk

Discussion

Yahoo! Groups: BBMak
http://groups.yahoo.com/group/BBMak

Yahoo! Groups: BBMak Street Team
http://groups.yahoo.com/group/BBMak_Street_Team

Lyrics

A Night Out With BBMak: Lyrics
www.stas.net/bbmak2000/lyrics/lyrics.html

News

Entertainment Sleuth: BBMak
http://e.sleuth.com/details.asp?Entity=4941

Reference

All Music Guide: BBMak
http://allmusic.com/cg/x.dll?p=amg&sql=1BBMAK

Top Sites

BBMak Blvd
www.bbmakblvd.com

BBMak.nu
www.bbmak.nu

BBMakOnline.Net
www.bbmakonline.net

Hollywood Records: BBMak
www.bbmakfan.com

KT's BBMak Page
www.geocities.com/ktsbbmakpage

Starry Skies
www.geocities.com/bmakb

Top 20 BBMak Sites
http://members.hostedscripts.com/top.cgi?user=bbmaktop20

Wallpapers

BBMak Wallpapers
www.sailingfornsync.com/bbmak/multi/wallpapers/index.html

Webrings

BBMak Central Official Webring
http://nav.webring.yahoo.com/hub?ring=bbmakcentral&list

bjork

SUPER SINGLES "All Is Full of Love" | "Human Behavior" | "It's Oh So Quiet" | "Big Time Sensuality"

Articles

dotmusic: Björk
www.dotmusic.com/artists/Bjork

Jam! Showbiz: Music: Björk
www.canoe.ca/JamMusicArtistsB/bjork.html

The Iceberg Archives
http://ebweb.tuwien.ac.at/ortner/tia/index.html

Audio

Björk - The Ultimate Intimate: Audio
http://bjork.intimate.org/audio

Discussion

Yahoo! Clubs: All Is Full of Björk
http://clubs.yahoo.com/clubs/allisfullofbjork

Yahoo! Clubs: Björk
http://clubs.yahoo.com/clubs/bjork

Yahoo! Clubs: Björk & Sugarcubes Symposium
http://clubs.yahoo.com/clubs/bjorkandsugarcubessymposium

Yahoo! Clubs: Björk CyberGalaxy Club
http://clubs.yahoo.com/clubs/bjorkcybergalaxyclub

Yahoo! Groups: Army of Björk
http://groups.yahoo.com/group/army_of_bjork

Yahoo! Groups: Björk
http://groups.yahoo.com/group/bjork

FAQs

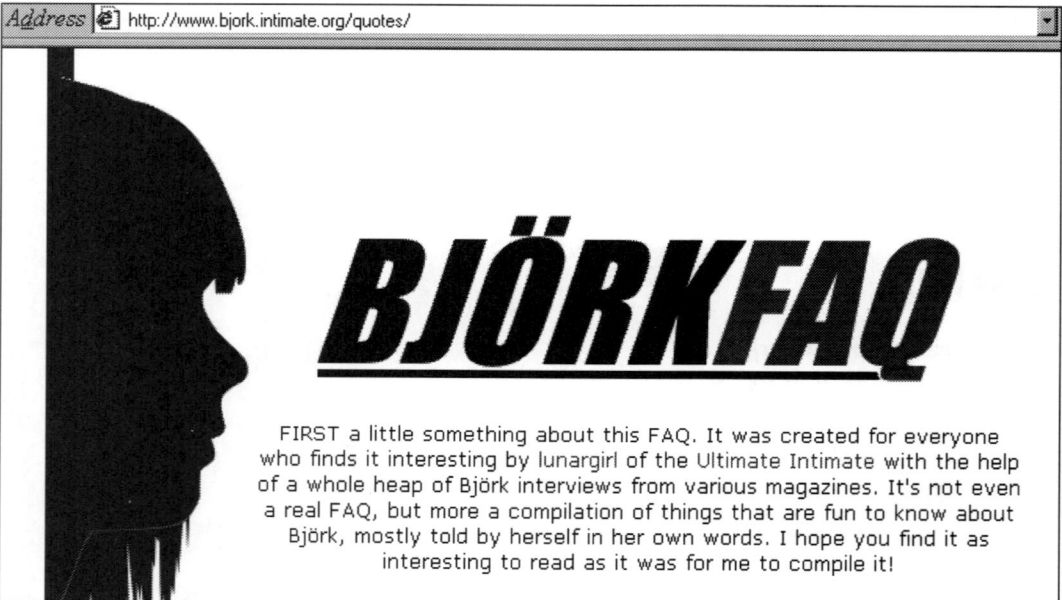

Address http://www.bjork.intimate.org/quotes/

BJÖRKFAQ

FIRST a little something about this FAQ. It was created for everyone who finds it interesting by lunargirl of the Ultimate Intimate with the help of a whole heap of Björk interviews from various magazines. It's not even a real FAQ, but more a compilation of things that are fun to know about Björk, mostly told by herself in her own words. I hope you find it as interesting to read as it was for me to compile it!

Björk - The Ultimate Intimate: FAQs
http://bjork.intimate.org/quotes

The Björk FAQ
www.sugarcube.net/b-faq

Galleries

Björk - The Ultimate Intimate: A Beautiful View
www.intimate.org/bjork/pictures

Lyrics

Björk - The Ultimate Intimate: Lyric Library
www.intimate.org/bjork/lyrics

Merchandise

Björk Direct
http://bjorkdirect.com

News

Entertainment Sleuth: Björk
http://e.sleuth.com/details.asp?Entity=432

Mr. Showbiz Celebrities: Björk
http://mrshowbiz.go.com/people/bjork

Reference

All Music Guide: Björk
http://allmusic.com/cg/x.dll?p=amg&sql=1BJORK

People Magazine Profiles: Björk
http://people.aol.com/people/pprofiles/bjork

Rock on the Net: Björk
www.rockonthenet.com/artists-b/bjork_main.htm

Wall of Sound: Björk
http://wallofsound.go.com/artists/bjork

Software

Celebrity Desktop: Björk
www.celebritydesktop.com/musicians/bjork

Top Sites

Björk - Shape of a Girl
www.angelfire.com/ia/tommr/bjork.html

Björk - The Ultimate Intimate
http://bjork.intimate.org

Björk Art Gallery
http://bjork.intimate.org/art

Björk Land
www.bjorkland.com

Only Björk
www.onlybjork.com

Jun Kit | Björk
www.geocities.com/bjorkfanatica

Video

Björk - The Ultimate Intimate: Videos
http://bjork.intimate.org/realvideo

Unofficial Björk Video Archive
http://ebweb.tuwien.ac.at/ortner/bjork.html

Wallpapers

the Björk wallpaper depot

The Björk Wallpaper Depot
http://wallpapers.intimate.org

Webrings

Björk Ring
http://nav.webring.yahoo.com/hub?ring=bjork&list

Blink 182

Super Singles "All the Small Things" | "What's My Age Again" | "Man Overboard"

Official Site

blink182
www.blink182.com

Discussion

Blink 182 Channel - IRC Chat
www.blink182channel.com

E-Mail Services

Blink182Mail.Com (yourname@blink182mail.com)
www.blink182mail.com

Galleries

PopFolio: Blink-182
www.popfolio.com/blink182.htm

Links

Mosiqa Top 100 Blink 182 Sites
www.top.mosiqa.com/blink182

Lyrics

Blink182Now.Com: Lyrics
http://geocities.com/blink182girl_hotpants/lyrics.html

Merchandise

LoserKids.Com - Official Store
http://loserkids.com

News

Channel Blink 182: News
www.cb182.com/news.html

Entertainment Sleuth: Blink 182
http://e.sleuth.com/details.asp?Entity=4917

Reference

All Music Guide: Blink-182
http://allmusic.com/cg/x.dll?p=amg&sql=1BLINK|182

Wall of Sound: Blink-182
http://wallofsound.go.com/artists/blink182

Software

Channel Blink 182: WinAmp Skins
www.cb182.com/skins.html

Top Sites

A-Blink-182-Site
www.a-blink182-site.com

Blink 1-82
http://blink1-82.hypermart.net

Blink 182 Live
www.blink182live.com

Blink 182 Resources
www.blink182resources.com

blink one eighty two
www.estein.com/blink182

Blink-182.net
www.blink-182.net

Blink182Now.Com
www.blink182now.com

Blink182Palace.Com
www.blink182palace.com

Channel Blink 182
www.cb182.com

Cool Blink 182 Page
www.geocities.com/SunsetStrip/Mezzanine/7739/frames.html

Hill's Blink 182 Page
www.duderanch.de

Kyle's Blink 182 Page
www.geocities.com/SunsetStrip/Studio/5661

Loser Kids 182
www.loserkids182.com

Man Overboard - A Blink 182 Site
www.man-overboard182.com

Mike's Blink 182 Page
www.geocities.com/SunsetStrip/Amphitheatre/7913/index.html

Punk 182
www.punk182.com

The Enema Strikes Back
www.theenemastrikesback.com

World of Blink
http://worldofblink.tripod.ca

Video

Blink 182 Live: Media
www.freemagix.com/~blink182/media/media.htm

Wallpapers

Channel Blink 182: Wallpapers
www.cb182.com/wallpapers.html

Webrings

Blink-182
http://nav.webring.yahoo.com/hub?ring=blink&list

ChuChi's blink 182 Webring
http://nav.webring.yahoo.com/hub?ring=blink182_ratm&list

The Unofficial Blink 182 Webring
http://nav.webring.yahoo.com/hub?ring=ablink182ring&list

Boyzone

Super Singles "You Needed Me" | "I Love the Way You Love Me" | "Everday I Love You"

Articles

dotmusic: Boyzone
www.dotmusic.com/artists/Boyzone

Audio

Boyzone Sound Galleries
http://members.spree.com/boyzone/sounds

Discussion

Yahoo! Clubs: Boyzone
http://clubs.yahoo.com/clubs/boyzone

Yahoo! Clubs: The Boyzone Ultima 12 to 16
http://clubs.yahoo.com/clubs/theboyzoneultima12to16

Yahoo! Clubs: The Stephen Gately Chat Zone
http://clubs.yahoo.com/clubs/stephengatelychatzone

Yahoo! Clubs: The Unofficial Boyzone in the US
http://clubs.yahoo.com/clubs/theunofficialboyzoneintheus

Yahoo! Groups: -boyzone-
http://groups.yahoo.com/group/-boyzone-

Yahoo! Groups: Boyzone Fans
http://groups.yahoo.com/group/Boyzone_fans

E-Mail

iLoveBoyzone.com (yourname@iloveboyzone.com)
www.iloveboyzone.com

Galleries

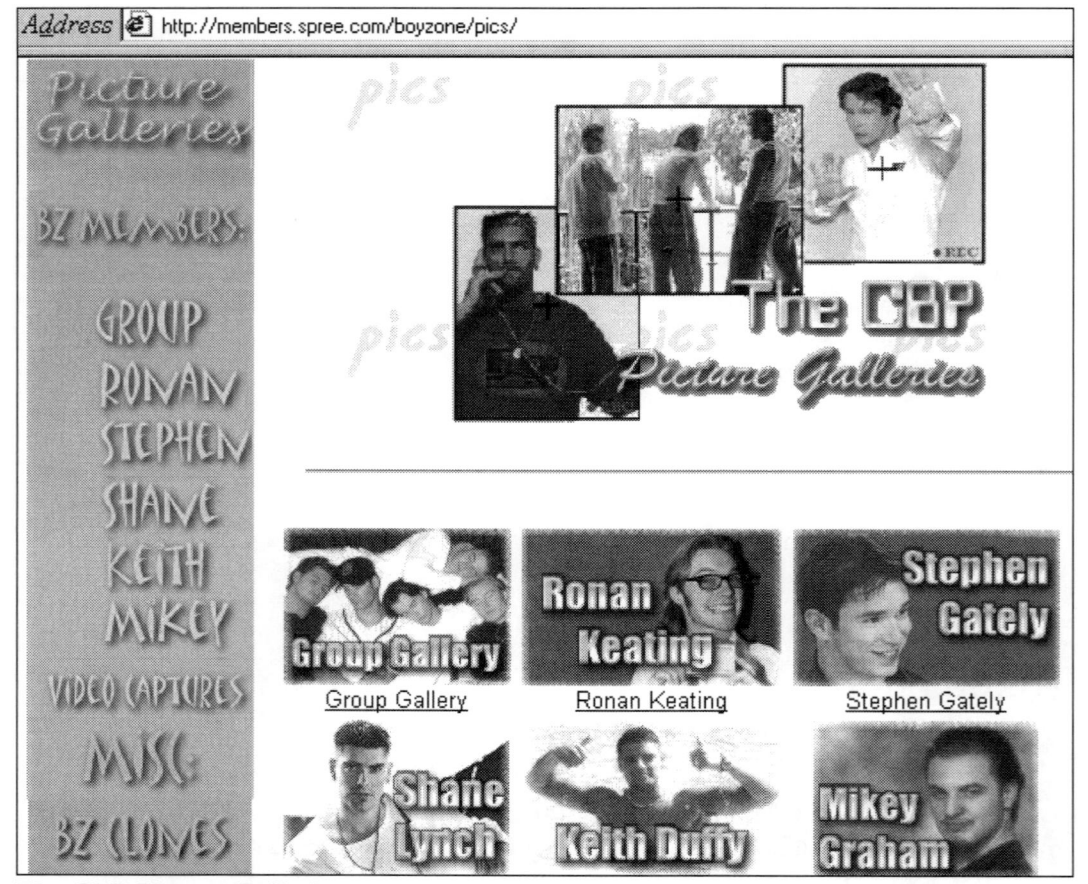

The CBP Picture Galleries
http://members.spree.com/boyzone/pics

Links

Mosiqa Top 100 Boyzone Sites
www.top.mosiqa.com/boyzone

Lyrics

Boyzone Lyrics Galleries
http://members.spree.com/boyzone/lyrics

Reference

All Music Guide: Boyzone
http://allmusic.com/cg/x.dll?p=amg&sql=1BOYZONE

Software

Boyzone Windows Stuff
http://members.spree.com/boyzone/winstuff

Celebrity Desktop: Boyzone
www.celebritydesktop.com/musicians/boyzone

Top Sites

All That I Need
http://members.tripod.com/~Ericamr

Boyzone Fan Zone
www.geocities.com/broadway/Stage/8938/bz.html

Boyzone Fans
www.boyzonefans.com

Boyzone Paradise
www.boyzoneparadise.com

Isa's Boyzone Site
www.boyzonelove.com

The Boyz Behind Boyzone
www.boyzbehindboyzone.cjb.net

Video

All That I Need: Videos
http://members.tripod.com/~Ericamr/videoi.html

Boyzone Videos
http://members.spree.com/boyzone/interactive/bzvideos.html

Wallpapers

Boyzone Wallpaper
http://members.spree.com/boyzone/winstuff/wallpaper.html

Webrings

Boyzone Key Ring
http://nav.webring.yahoo.com/hub?ring=desxbz&id=188&hub

Britney Spears

SUPER SINGLES "Stronger" | "Lucky" | "Oops...I Did It Again" | "Crazy" | "Sometimes" "Baby One More Time" | "From the Bottom of My Broken Heart"

E-mail

britney@peeps.com

Official Site

BritneySpears.Com
www.britneyspears.com

Articles

dotmusic: Britney Spears
www.dotmusic.com/artists/britneyspears

Audio

BritneySpears.Org: Multimedia
www.britneyspears.org/multimedia.html

Discussion

Britney Addicts R Us
www.geocities.com/SouthBeach/1780/index.html

Britney Spears Portal
www.britneyspearsportal.com

BritneySpears.Org: Forum
www.efgforum.com/cgi-bin/forumdisplay.cgi?action=topics&number=2

Club Britney Spears: Message Board
www.messagefriends.com/talk/mtllupoli.html

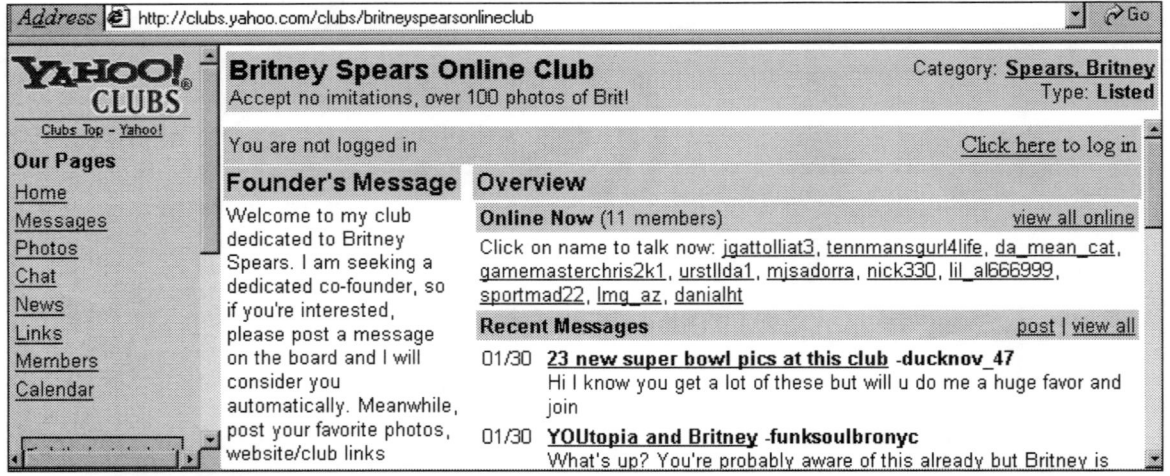

Yahoo! Clubs: Britney Spears Online Club
http://clubs.yahoo.com/clubs/britneyspearsonlineclub

Yahoo! Clubs: Britney Spears Picture Palace
http://clubs.yahoo.com/clubs/britneyspearspicturepalace

Yahoo! Clubs: Britney Spears The Golden Girl
http://clubs.yahoo.com/clubs/britneyspearsthegoldengirl

Yahoo! Clubs: Britney Spears Unofficial Club
http://clubs.yahoo.com/clubs/britneyspearsunofficialclub

Yahoo! Groups: TeamCBS
http://groups.yahoo.com/group/TeamCBS

Yahoo! Groups: Weekends-With-Brit
http://groups.yahoo.com/group/Weekends-With-Brit

Ecards

Club Britney Spears: Ecards
http://geocities.com/clubbritneyspearscom/E-cards.html

E-Mail Services

Britney Spears Mail (yourname@britneyspearsmail.com)
www.britneyspearsmail.com

Britney.To (yourname@britney.to)
http://britney.to

Fan Art

The Britney Spears Painting Site
www.a1britneyspears.com

Galleries

4BritneySpearsPictures.Com
www.4britneyspearspictures.com

A List Celebrities: Britney Spears
www.the-alist.org/BritneySpears

Absolute Pictures: Britney Spears
www.absolutepictures.com/s/spears_britney

AnthemPop: Britney Spears
www.anthempop.com/britneyspears/pictures.html

AtPictures.Com: Britney Spears
www.atpictures.com/britney

Beautfiul Celebrities: Britney Spears
www.beautifulcelebrities.com/britney_spears_pics.html

PopFolio: Britney Spears
www.popfolio.com/britneyspears.htm

Unlimited Britney Spears: Photos
www.angelfire.com/mi/britneyunofficial/pics.html

Links

Britney Spears Links
www.britneyspearslinks.com

Britney Spears Top 40 @ ThinkCelebs.com
www.thinkcelebs.com/britney

FanGuide Top Britney Spears Sites
www.fanguide.com/autorankm/britney

Mosiqa Top 100 Britney Spears Sites
http://top100.mosiqa.com/britney

Lyrics

Britney Spears Lyrics
http://members.xoom.com/Helo_/BritneySpears.htm

Lyrix Engine: Britney Spears
http://lyco.hypermart.net/browse.pl/cat.30/s.Britney_Spears

Merchandise

Britney Spears Online Store
www.signaturessuperstars.com/artists/pop/britneyspears/index.html

Britney Spears Store!
http://britneystore.artistdirect.com

News

Abstracts.Net: Britney Spears
www.abstracts.net/britney-spears

BritneySpears.Org
www.britneyspears.org

Entertainment Sleuth: Britney Spears
http://e.sleuth.com/details.asp?Entity=4183

Mr. Showbiz Celebrities: Britney Spears
http://mrshowbiz.go.com/people/britneyspears

Wall of Sound: Britney Spears News
http://wallofsound.go.com/artists/britneyspears/content/news.html

Reference

All Music Guide: Britney Spears
http://allmusic.com/cg/x.dll?p=amg&sql=1BRITNEY|SPEARS

Britney Spears Foundation
www.britneyspearsfoundation.com

Internet Movie Database: Britney Spears
http://us.imdb.com/Name?Britney+Spears

People Magazine Profiles: Britney Spears
http://people.aol.com/people/pprofiles/bspears

Rock on the Net: Britney Spears
www.rockonthenet.com/artists-s/britneyspears_main.htm

Wall of Sound: Britney Spears
http://wallofsound.go.com/artists/britneyspears

Yahoo! Web Celeb: Britney Spears
http://features.yahoo.com/webceleb/britney

Software

Artist Desktop Themes: Britney Spears
http://artistdesktopthemes.com/st/s/britney_spears.dt.1.html

Britney Spears Cursors from Comet Systems
http://britneyspearscursors.cometsystems.com

Celebrity Desktop: Britney Spears
www.celebritydesktop.com/musicians/britney_spears

Cinema Desktop Themes: Britney Spears
www.cinemadesktopthemes.com/st/s/britney_spears.dt.1.html

Top Sites

101Britney.Com
www.101britney.com

Absolute Britney
www.britneyspears.co.uk

AllBritney.Com
www.allbritney.com

Britney Central
www.britney-central.com

Britney Land
http://reach.to/britney

Britney Spears 2k
www.britney-spears.fsnet.co.uk

Britney Spears Addiction
www.britneyspearsaddiction.com

Britney Spears Café
www.britneyspearscafe.com

Britney Spears Central
www.britneyspearscentral.com

Britney Spears House
http://home.no.net/bspearsh

Britney Spears Shrine
www.antibritneyspears.com

Britney Spears To You!
www.britneytoyou.com

Britney Spears UK Web Site
www.ukbritney.tv

Britney Web
www.britneyweb.de/spears.html

Britney Zone
www.britneyzone.com

Britney.Com
www.britney.com

Britney-Shares.Com
www.britney-shares.com

BritneySpears.ac
http://britneyspears.ac

Club Britney Spears
www.clubbritneyspears.com

Rich's Britney Page
www.brit-spears.ic24.net

Society for Future Husbands of Britney Spears
www.sfhbs.com

The Beat of Britney
www.britneyspearslive.com

Unlimited Britney Spears
www.angelfire.com/mi/britneyunofficial

VH1 Fan Club: Britney Spears
www.vh1.com/fanclubs/main/501686.jhtml

TV Schedule

TV Now: Britney Spears
www.tv-now.com/stars/britney.html

Video

BritneySpears.Org: Multimedia
www.britneyspears.org/multimedia.html

BritneyVideo.Com
www.britneyvideo.com

Launch.Com: Britney Spears
www.launch.com/music/artistpage/1,4391,1037731,00.html

MTV.Com: Britney Spears
http://britney-spears.mtv.com

Wallpapers

Britney Spears House: Wallpapers
http://home.no.net/bspearsh/Galleries/our_wallpapers.htm

Britney Web: Wallpapers
www.britneyweb.de/wall.html

Britney-Shares.Com: Goodies
www.britney-shares.com/goodies.html

Webrings

Base Britney Banner Exchange
www.topsa.com/bp

Britney Spears Club
http://nav.webring.yahoo.com/hub?ring=b_spears_club&list

Britney Spears Webring
http://nav.webring.yahoo.com/hub?ring=megamatt&list

The Original Britney Spears Ring
http://nav.webring.yahoo.com/hub?ring=spearsring&list

Celine Dion

SUPER SINGLES "That's the Way It Is" | "My Heart Will Go On" | "I'm Your Angel"

E-mail

CelineOnline.Com: Write Celine
www.celinedion.net/community_write.html

Official Site

CelineOnline.Com - The Official Celine Dion Web Site
www.celineonline.com

Articles

Canoe: Celine Dion News Archive
www.canoe.ca/JamMusicCelineDion/home.html

Celine Screen: Articles
http://members.aol.com/Docnoid/articles.html

dotmusic: Celine Dion
www.dotmusic.com/artists/CelineDion

Jam! Showbiz: Music: Celine Dion
www.canoe.com/JamMusicCelineDion

Discussion

Celine Dion Fans ICQ List
http://home6.swipnet.se/%7Ew-61372/icqlist/icqlist2.html

Celine Dion Internet Fan Club
http://members.nbci.com/celinedion5/cdifc.html

Celine Dion Music Newsgroup
alt.music.celine-dion

Celine Dion Pictures Newsgroup
alt.binaries.pictures.celine-dion

Yahoo! Clubs: Celine
http://clubs.yahoo.com/clubs/celine

Yahoo! Clubs: Celine Dion Millennium
http://clubs.yahoo.com/clubs/celinedionmillennium

Yahoo! Clubs: Celine Dion Official Fan Club
http://clubs.yahoo.com/clubs/celinedionofficialfanclub

Yahoo! Groups: naturalwoman1
http://groups.yahoo.com/group/naturalwoman1

Yahoo! Groups: The Heart of Celine Club
http://groups.yahoo.com/group/celine_atw

Yahoo! Groups: The Heart of Celine Mailing List
http://groups.yahoo.com/list/theheartofceline/info.html

FAQs

CelineOnline.Com: FAQ
www.celinedion.net/news_celinefaq.html

Galleries

Absolute Pictures: Celine Dion
www.absolutepictures.com/d/dion_celine

Celine Live!: Photos
http://members.chello.nl/~r.lecluse/PHOTOS.htm

Marc's Celine Dion Site: Galleries
www.wow.net/teen/celine/galleries.html

Links

Mosiqa Top 100 Celine Dion Sites
www.top.mosiqa.com/celine

Top 219 Celine Dion Sites
www.top219.org/celine

Lyrics

The Power of Celine: Lyrics
www.geocities.com/tpocnat/lyrics/index.html

Merchandise

Celine Dion Online Store
www.signaturessuperstars.com/artists/pop/celinedion

News

Celine Screen: News
http://members.aol.com/Docnoid/news.html

Entertainment Sleuth: Celine Dion
http://e.sleuth.com/details.asp?Entity=1205

The Power of Celine: News
www.geocities.com/tpocnat/news

Reference

All Music Guide: Celine Dion
http://allmusic.com/cg/x.dll?p=amg&sql=1CELINE|DION

People Magazine Profiles: Celine Dion
http://people.aol.com/people/pprofiles/cdion

Rock on the Net: Celine Dion
www.rockonthenet.com/artists-d/celinedion_main.htm

Wall of Sound: Celine Dion
http://wallofsound.go.com/artists/celinedion

Software

Artist Desktop Themes: Celine Dion
http://artistdesktopthemes.com/st/d/celine_dion.dt.1.html

Celebrity Desktop: Celine Dion
www.celebritydesktop.com/musicians/celine_dion

Celine Live!: Screensavers & WinAmp Skins
http://members.chello.nl/~r.lecluse/DOWNLOAD.htm

Cinema Desktop Themes: Celine Dion
www.cinemadesktopthemes.com/st/d/celine_dion.dt.1.html

Top Sites

Celine!
www.geocities.com/SunsetStrip/Backstage/6550/celine.html

Celine Central
www.celinecentral.com

Celine Dion Forever
http://members.aol.com/nicolasguerreau

Celine Live!
http://welcome.to/celinelive

Celine Screen
http://members.aol.com/Docnoid/index.html

Celine's Music
www.celinesmusic.com

Celine, Planetary Star
http://perso.club-internet.fr/bberizzi

Celine, You Are the Music of My Heart
http://amourceline.cjb.net

Cudacke Dees' Celine Dion Home Page
www.geocities.com/TimesSquare/Alley/5184/celinedion.html

Everything Celine
http://listen.to/everythingceline

Marc's Celine Dion Site
www.wow.net/teen/celine

Passion Celine Dion
www.celine-dion.net

Re: Celine
www.angelvoice.net/celine

Salem's Realm
http://salemsrealm1.homestead.com

The Celine Star
www.celinestar.org.uk

The Power of Celine
www.geocities.com/tpocnat/index.html

VH1 Fan Club: Celine Dion
http://celine-dion.vh1.com

Video

Celine Dion Rare Video Clips
http://members.aol.com/elee1997

Marc's Celine Dion Site: Video Clips
www.wow.net/teen/celine/video.html

Webrings

A Celine Dion Webring
http://nav.webring.yahoo.com/hub?ring=celine&list

Power of Celine
http://nav.webring.yahoo.com/hub?ring=powerofceline&list

That's The Way It Is - A Celine Dion Webring
http://nav.webring.yahoo.com/hub?ring=dionceline&list

cher

SUPER SINGLES "Believe" | "Strong Enough" | "One by One"

Official Site

Cher's Official Web Site
www.cher.com

Articles

Cher World: Interviews
www.cherworld.com/interviews

dotmusic: Cher
www.dotmusic.com/artists/Cher

Audio

Cher World: Multimedia
www.cherworld.com/multimedia

Discussion

The Ultimate Cher Home Page: Discussion Forum
http://pub22.bravenet.com/forum/show.asp?usernum=1856982987&cpv=1

Yahoo! Clubs: Cher
http://clubs.yahoo.com/clubs/cher

Yahoo! Clubs: Cher Online
http://clubs.yahoo.com/clubs/cheronline

Yahoo! Groups: Cher
http://groups.yahoo.com/group/Cher

Yahoo! Groups: Cher Believe
http://groups.yahoo.com/group/-Cher_Believe

Ecards

Cher Glamour: Greeting Cards
www.geocities.com/rickdes/cgbw3.html

Cher World: Ecards
www.cherworld.com/ecards

Galleries

Absolute Pictures: Cher
www.absolutepictures.com/c/cher/index.html

Cher City: Pictures
www.geocities.com/broadway/4662/pictures.html

Cher Photo Gallery
http://members.tripod.com/lmlask

Everything Cher: Photo Galleries
www.everythingcher.com/pages/galindex.htm

Links

10 Most Dazzling Cher Sites
www.topsitelists.com/hollywood/rachelflax/topsites.html

Cher - Best 30 Sites
www.topsitelists.com/bestsites/justplaincher/topsites.html

Lyrics

Cher City: Lyrics
www.geocities.com/broadway/4662/lyrics.html

One by One - Cher Lyrics Resource
www.geocities.com/so_bazaar/Cher

The Ultimate Cher Home Page: Lyrics
http://home4.swipnet.se/~w-49555/cher/lyrics.htm

Merchandise

Cher - The Official Store
http://cherdirect.com

CherShop.Com
www.chershop.com

News

Cher World: News
www.cherworld.com/news

Entertainment Sleuth: Cher
http://e.sleuth.com/details.asp?Entity=793

Just Plain Cher: News
www.justplaincher.com/news.htm

Reference

All Music Guide: Cher
http://allmusic.com/cg/x.dll?p=amg&sql=1CHER

Internet Movie Database: Cher
http://us.imdb.com/Name?Cher

People Magazine Profiles: Cher
http://people.aol.com/people/pprofiles/cher

Rock on the Net: Cher
www.rockonthenet.com/artists-c/cher_main.htm

Wall of Sound: Cher
http://wallofsound.go.com/artists/cher

Software

Artist Desktop Themes: Cher
http://artistdesktopthemes.com/st/c/cher_cher.dt.1.html

Celebrity Desktop: Cher
www.celebritydesktop.com/musicians/cher

Top Sites

Cher - Strong Enough
http://cherstrongenough.homestead.com

Cher City
www.chercity.cjb.net

Cher Dedication
www.cher.org.uk

Cher Glamour
www.geocities.com/rickdes

Cher World
www.cherworld.com

Cher, Just Cher
www.angelfire.com/tx/cherbarbie

CherFans.Org
www.cherfans.org

Everything Cher
www.everythingcher.com

Just Plain Cher
www.justplaincher.com

Paradise Is Here - A Tribute to Cher
www.geocities.com/westhollywood/4983

Simply Cher
www.angelfire.com/tn/KarensPage

The Magic of Cher
http://geocities.com/allornothingnow2000

The Power of Cher
www.angelfire.com/nc2/ThePowerofCHER

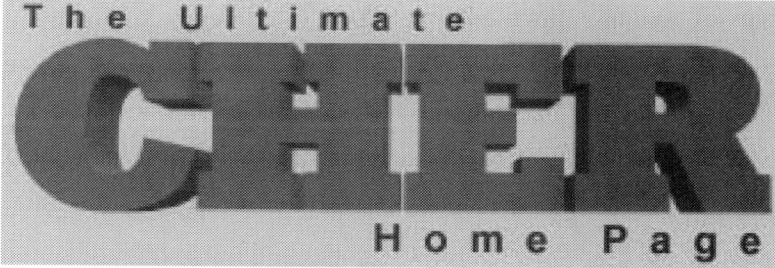

The Ultimate Cher Home Page
http://home4.swipnet.se/~w-49555/cher

The Unofficial Cher Site
http://music.acmecity.com/lyric/336/index.html

VH1 Fan Club: Cher
http://cher.vh1.com

TV Schedule

TV Now: Cher
www.tv-now.com/stars/cher.html

Video

Cher World: Multimedia
www.cherworld.com/multimedia

Wallpapers

Cher - The Wallpaper Collection
   www.geocities.com/cherwp

Cher City: Downloads
   www.geocities.com/broadway/4662/download.html

Cher World: Wallpapers
   www.cherworld.com/wallpapers

Webrings

Cher Ring
   http://nav.webring.yahoo.com/hub?ring=cherb&list

The Cher Webring
   http://nav.webring.yahoo.com/hub?ring=cher&list

Official Site | Christina Aguilera

christina aguilera

SUPER SINGLES "Come On Over" | "What a Girl Wants" | "Genie in a Bottle"

Official Site

Christina Aguilera Official Web Site
www.christina-a.com

Articles

Christina Aguilera 2000: Interviews & Articles
www.geocities.com/ChristinaAguilera2k/Articles.htm

dotmusic: Christina Aguilera
www.dotmusic.com/artists/ChristinaAguilera

Jam! Showbiz: Music: Christina Aguilera
www.canoe.ca/JamMusicArtistsA/aguilera_christina.html

Audio

AllStarz.Org: Christina Aguilera: Audio
www.allstarz.org/christina/audio.html

The Christina Connection: Audio
http://connection.christina-aguilera.net/audio.html

Discussion

Christina Aguilera 2000 @ ezboard.com
http://pub17.ezboard.com/bchristinaaguilera2000

The Christina Aguilera Boards
http://christinaboards.cjb.net

Yahoo! Clubs: Christina Aguilera Club
http://clubs.yahoo.com/clubs/christinaaguileraclub

Yahoo! Clubs: Christina Aguilera Unofficial Fan Club
http://clubs.yahoo.com/clubs/christinasunofficialfanclub

Yahoo! Clubs: ChristinaAguilera
http://clubs.yahoo.com/clubs/christinaaguilera

Yahoo! Groups: Aguilera
http://groups.yahoo.com/group/Aguilera

Yahoo! Groups: Christina Aguilera
http://groups.yahoo.com/group/Christina_Aguilera

Yahoo! Groups: Christina-Aguilera
http://groups.yahoo.com/group/christina-aguilera

E-Mail Services

Christina Aguilera Mail (yourname@christinaaguileramail.com)
www.christinaaguileramail.com

Galleries

4ChristinaAguileraPictures.Com
www.4christinaaguilerapictures.com

A List Celebrities: Christina Aguilera
www.the-alist.org/ChristinaAguilera

Absolute Pictures: Christina Aguilera
www.absolutepictures.com/a/aguilera_christina1

AllStarz.Org: Christina Aguilera: Pictures
www.allstarz.org/christina/pictures.htm

AtPictures.Com: Christina Aguilera
www.atpictures.com/aguilera

Babe Central: Christina Aguilera
www.thebabecentral.com/aguilera.html

Beautfiul Celebrities: Christina Aguilera
www.beautifulcelebrities.com/christina_aguilera_pics.html

Christina Aguilera 2000: Pictures
www.geocities.com/ChristinaAguilera2k/Pics.htm

Superb Christina Aguilera
www.superbcelebrities.com/christina_aguilera/gallery1.htm

The Christina Aguilera Picture Site
www.christinaaguilera.hotresume.net

The Christina Connection: Photos
http://connection.christina-aguilera.net/photos.html

Links

Christina Aguilera Top 40 @ ThinkCelebs.com
www.thinkcelebs.com/chris/index.html

FanGuide Top Christina Aguilera Sites
www.fanguide.com/autorankm/christina

GenieNet
http://genienet.christina-aguilera.net

Mosiqa Top 100 Christina Aguilera Sites
www.top.mosiqa.com/christina

Top 50 Christina Aguilera Sites
http://christina-aguilera.virtualave.net/topsites/topsites.html

Lyrics

AllStarz.Org: Christina Aguilera: Lyrics
www.allstarz.org/christina/lyrics.html

Christina Aguilera 2000: Lyrics
www.geocities.com/ChristinaAguilera2k/Lyrics.htm

The Christina Aguilera Zone: Lyrics
www.geocities.com/aguilerath/lyric.html

Merchandise

TheChristiniaStore.Com
www.thechristinastore.com

News

Abstracts.Net: Christina Aguilera
www.abstracts.net/christina-aguilera

Entertainment Sleuth: Christina Aguilera
http://e.sleuth.com/details.asp?Entity=33

The Christina Connection: News Mailing List
www.angelfire.com/celeb/christinaconnection/news.html

Reference

All Music Guide: Christina Aguilera
http://allmusic.com/cg/x.dll?p=amg&sql=1CHRISTINA|AGUILERA

Internet Movie Database: Christina Aguilera
http://us.imdb.com/Name?Christina+Aguilera

People Magazine Profiles: Christina Aguilera
http://people.aol.com/people/pprofiles/caguilera

Rock on the Net: Christina Aguilera
www.rockonthenet.com/artists-a/christinaaguilera.htm

Wall of Sound: Christina Aguilera
http://wallofsound.go.com/artists/christinaaguilera

Software

Artist Desktop Themes: Christina Aguilera
http://artistdesktopthemes.com/st/a/christina_aguilera.dt.1.html

Celebrity Desktop: Christina Aguilera
www.celebritydesktop.com/musicians/christina_aguilera

Themes

Cinema Desktop Themes: Christina Aguilera
www.cinemadesktopthemes.com/st/a/christina_aguilera.dt.1.html

Top Sites

AllStarz.Org: Christina Aguilera
www.allstarz.org/christina

Christina Aguilera
www.christinaaguilera-genieinabottle.com

Christina Aguilera 2000
www.christinaaguilera2k.com

Christina Aguilera C2K
http://christinaaguilerac2k.cjb.net

Christina Aguilera Web
www.christinaaguilera-web.com

ChristinaAguilera.Org
www.christinaaguilera.org

Click2Music: Christina Aguilera
www.click2music.com/christina

Come On Over - The Cliquey
www.christinaaguilera.org/comeonoverclique/index.html

Cool Christina
www.angelfire.com/pop/coolchristina

Soul Diva
http://diva.christinaaguilera.org

The Christina Aguilera Zone
www.geocities.com/aguilerath

The Christina Connection
http://connection.christina-aguilera.net

Unofficial Christina Aguilera Web Site
www.geocities.com/christina_aguilera1439

VH1 Fan Club: Christina Aguilera
http://christina-aguilera.vh1.com

Voice of a Genie
www.voiceofagenie.cjb.net

TV Schedule

The Christina Connection: TV Alerts
http://connection.christina-aguilera.net/tvalerts.html

Video

AllStarz.Org: Christina Aguilera: Video
www.allstarz.org/christina/video.html

MTV.Com: Christina Aguilera
http://christina-aguilera.mtv.com

Wallpapers

AllStarz.Org: Christina Aguilera: Wallpaper
www.allstarz.org/christina/wallpaper.html

Cool Christina: Backgrounds
www.angelfire.com/pop/coolchristina/Backgrounds.html

Webrings

Christina Aguilera Webring
http://nav.webring.yahoo.com/hub?ring=caguilera&list

Christina in a Bottle
http://nav.webring.yahoo.com/hub?ring=christinabottle&list

Creed

SUPER SINGLES "With Arms Wide Open" | "Higher" | "One" | "My Own Prison"

Official Site

Creednet - The Official Web Site of Creed
www.creednet.com

Audio

Creed 4 Ever: Downloads
www.geocities.com/y2aroon/downloads.htm

Creednet: Audio Clips
www.creednet.com/audio/index.html

Discussion

Creed Worldwide Online Fan Club
www.creedworldwide.com

Creednet: Forums
http://209.61.167.176/cgi-bin/Ultimate.cgi

Yahoo! Clubs: Creed Net
http://clubs.yahoo.com/clubs/creednet

Yahoo! Clubs: With Arms Wide Open
http://clubs.yahoo.com/clubs/witharmswideopen

Yahoo! Groups: Creed
http://groups.yahoo.com/group/creed

Ecards

Creednet: Postcards
www.creednet.com/postcards/photos/index.html

FAQs

Creednet: Official FAQ
www.creednet.com/webdocs/faq.htm

Galleries

Creed 4 Ever: Photos
www.geocities.com/y2aroon/photos.htm

Creednet: Photo Gallery
www.creednet.com/photos/index.html

Links

Creed Top 100 Web Sites
www.creedtop100.com

Mosiqa Top 100 Creed Sites
http://topsites.mosiqa.com/creed

Lyrics

Creed 4 Ever: Lyrics
www.geocities.com/y2aroon/lyrics.htm

Creednet: Lyrics
www.creednet.com/lyrics/lyricsfrm.htm

Mailing Lists

Creednet: Discussion List
www.creednet.com/discussion/discussion.htm

News

Creednet: Enews
www.winduplist.com/ls/signups/enews/creed_enews.asp

Entertainment Sleuth: Creed
http://e.sleuth.com/details.asp?Entity=4927

Reference

All Music Guide: Creed
http://allmusic.com/cg/x.dll?p=amg&sql=1CREED

Rock on the Net: Creed
www.rockonthenet.com/artists-c/creed.htm

Wall of Sound: Creed
http://wallofsound.go.com/artists/creed

Software

Artist Desktop Themes: Creed
http://artistdesktopthemes.com/gb/c/creed.dt.1.html

Celebrity Desktop: Creed
www.celebritydesktop.com/musicians/creed

Top Sites

Creed 4 Ever
www.creed4ever.com

Creed-Fan.Com
www.creed-fan.com

Creed Never Die
http://creed0084.cjb.net

Creeds Own Prison
http://creedsownprison.cjb.net

Creed World
www.creedworld.co.uk

CreedOnline.Com
www.creedonline.com

Faceless - A Tribute to the Music of Creed
http://facelessman.cjb.net

My Own Prison
http://creed.netfirms.com

SilverBleuz
http://members.tripod.com/silverbleuz

Torn - A Creed Fan's Source
www.creed-torn.com

VH1 Fan Club: Creed
www.vh1.com/fanclubs/main/1243.jhtml

Zero to Sixty - A Creed Page
www.fromzerotosixty.com

Video

Creednet: Video Clips
www.creednet.com/video/index.html

MTV.Com: Creed
http://creed.mtv.com

Webrings

The Creed Ring
http://nav.webring.yahoo.com/hub?ring=creedring&list

The Original Creed Webring
http://nav.webring.yahoo.com/hub?ring=creedwebring&list

destiny's child

SUPER SINGLES "Independent Women" | "Say My Name" | "Jumpin' Jumpin' " | "Bills Bills Bills"

Official Site

DestinysChild.Com
www.destinyschild.com

Articles

dotmusic: Destiny's Child
www.dotmusic.com/artists/DestinysChild

Jam! Showbiz: Music: Destiny's Child
www.canoe.ca/JamMusicArtistsD/destinychild.html

Audio

DestinysChild.Com: Audio
www.destinyschild.com/musicFr.html

Discussion

Yahoo! Clubs: dchild
http://clubs.yahoo.com/clubs/dchild

Yahoo! Clubs: Destiny's Child Fan Club
http://clubs.yahoo.com/clubs/destinyschildfanclub

Yahoo! Clubs: Destiny's Child Fans
http://clubs.yahoo.com/clubs/destinyschildfans

Yahoo! Clubs: Destiny's Child Platinum 2g
http://clubs.yahoo.com/clubs/destinychildplatinum2g

Yahoo! Groups: 1destinyschildgroup
http://groups.yahoo.com/group/1destinyschildgroup

Galleries

AtPictures.Com: Destiny's Child
www.atpictures.com/destiny

Destiny's Divas: Galleries
www.geocities.com/destinysdivas/Gallery.html

PopFolio: Destiny's Child
www.popfolio.com/destinychild.htm

Merchandise

TheStore@SonyMusic.Com: Destiny's Child
http://thestore.sonymusic.com/thestore/music.asp?talent_id=36433

News

Destiny's Divas: News
www.geocities.com/destinysdivas/News.html

DestinysChild.Com: E-Mail List
www.destinyschild.com/emailFr.html

Entertainment Sleuth: Destiny's Child
http://e.sleuth.com/details.asp?Entity=4942

Reference

All Music Guide: Destiny's Child
http://allmusic.com/cg/x.dll?p=amg&sql=1DESTINYS|CHILD

People Magazine Profiles: Destiny's Child
http://people.aol.com/people/pprofiles/destinys

Rock on the Net: Destiny's Child
www.rockonthenet.com/artists-d/destinyschild.htm

Wall of Sound: Destiny's Child
http://wallofsound.go.com/artists/destinyschild

Software

Artist Desktop Themes: Destiny's Child
http://artistdesktopthemes.com/gb/d/destiny_child.dt.1.html

Celebrity Desktop: Destiny's Child
www.celebritydesktop.com/musicians/destinys_child

Top Sites

Destiny's Capital
www.destinyscapital.com

Destiny's Child - Final Destin-ation
http://homes.acmecity.com/music/riff/466

Destiny's Divas
   www.destinysdivas.com

Destiny's Planet
   http://destinysplanet.cjb.net

Jon Blaze - Destiny's Child
   http://jbdc.cjb.net

The Destiny's Child Dimension
   www.thedcdimension.com

Video

Destiny's Divas: Video
   www.geocities.com/destinysdivas/Video.html

MTV.Com: Destiny's Child
   http://destinys-child.mtv.com

Wallpapers

The Destiny's Child Dimension: Downloads
   www.thedcdimension.com/downloads.html

DIXIE CHICKS

Super Singles "Ready to Run" | "Wide Open Spaces" | "Goodbye Earl"

Official Site

Official Dixie Chicks Web Site
www.dixiechicks.com

The Official Dixie Chicks Web Site
www.dixiechicks.com/indexF.html

Articles

Jam! Showbiz: Music: Dixie Chicks
www.canoe.ca/JamMusicArtistsD/dixie_chicks.html

Liz's Dixie Chicks Page: Articles
www.geocities.com/Nashville/7402/article.html

Audio

Dixie Chicks Central: Audio
www.dixiechickscentral.com/audio.html

Official Dixie Chicks Web Site: Audio
www.dixiechicks.com/av/audio.html

Unofficial Dixie Chicks Site: Audio Clips
www.dixiechicksfans.com/audio.html

Discussion

ChicksFeet.Com: Boards
www.chicksfeet.com/cgi-local/bbs/YaBB.pl

Dixie Chicks Fans Net Directory
http://come.to/dixiechicks

Dixie Chicks Post Office
www.dixiechicks.com/cgi-bin/ultimate.cgi

Unofficial Dixie Chicks Site: Message Board
http://pub32.ezboard.com/bdixiechicksmessageboard

Yahoo! Clubs: All Dixie Chicks
http://clubs.yahoo.com/clubs/alldixiechicks

Yahoo! Clubs: Fans of Dixie Chicks
http://clubs.yahoo.com/clubs/fansofdixiechicks

Yahoo! Clubs: The Dixie Chicks
http://clubs.yahoo.com/clubs/thedixiechicks

Yahoo! Groups: Dixie Chicks
http://groups.yahoo.com/list/dixiechicks

Ecards

Dixie Chicks Fly World: E-Greeting Cards
www.geocities.com/dixiechicksflyworld/cards.html

Unofficial Dixie Chicks Site: Postcards
www.dixiechicksfans.com/postcards.html

Fan Art

Dixie Chicks Fly World: Artwork Gallery
www.geocities.com/dixiechicksflyworld/art.html

kbchick's Dixie Chick's Art Gallery
www.angelfire.com/country/DixieChicksFans/drawings.html

FAQs

Dixie Chicks eGroup FAQ
www.dixiechicksfaq.com

Not Just Whistlin' Dixie: FAQ
http://members.tripod.com/whistlingdixie/faq.htm

Galleries

All Inclusive Dixie Chicks Page: Pictures
www.dixiechicks.mixedsignal.net/pictures.html

Dixie Chicks Fly World
www.dixiechicksflyworld.com

PopFolio: Dixie Chicks
www.popfolio.com/dixiechicks.htm

Unofficial Dixie Chicks Site: Photo Gallery
www.dixiechicksfans.com/gallery.html

Yahoo! Clubs: Dixie Chicks Pics
http://clubs.yahoo.com/clubs/dixiechickspics

Games

Chicks Games
www.angelfire.com/country/DixieChicksFans/games.html

Lyrics

Unofficial Dixie Chicks Site: Lyrics
www.dixiechicksfans.com/lyrics.html

Merchandise

iMusic County Showcase: Dixie Chicks
http://imusic.artistdirect.com/showcase/country/dixiechicks.html

News

Entertainment Sleuth: Dixie Chicks
http://e.sleuth.com/details.asp?Entity=5743

Liz's Dixie Chicks Page: News
www.geocities.com/Nashville/7402/news.html

Reference

All Music Guide: Dixie Chicks
http://allmusic.com/cg/x.dll?p=amg&sql=1DIXIE|CHICKS

People Magazine Profiles: Dixie Chicks
http://people.aol.com/people/pprofiles/dixiechicks

Rock on the Net: Dixie Chicks
www.rockonthenet.com/artists-d/dixiechicks.htm

Wall of Sound: Dixie Chicks
http://wallofsound.go.com/artists/dixiechicks

Software

Celebrity Desktop: Dixie Chicks
www.celebritydesktop.com/musicians/dixie_chicks

Top Sites

All Inclusive Dixie Chicks Page
www.dixiechicks.mixedsignal.net

Chicks From Dixie
www.chicksfromdixie.com

ChicksFeet.Com
www.chicksfeet.com

CMT - Dixie Chick's Fly Tour
www.dixiechicksfly.com

Dixie Chickdom
www.geocities.com/Nashville/Opry/3740

Dixie Chicks Central
www.dixiechickscentral.com

Dixie Chicks Online
www.dixiechicksonline.com

DixieLand
http://dixiemutt.cjb.net

Laura's Dixie Chicks Page
www.geocities.com/Nashville/6918/dixiechicks.html

Liz's Dixie Chicks Page
www.geocities.com/Nashville/7402/index.html

Not Just Whistlin' Dixie
http://members.tripod.com/whistlingdixie

Sin-Wagon.Com - Lissa's Dixie Chicks Page
www.sin-wagon.com

The Dixie Chicks' Shack
http://members.tripod.com/LuvbugKAT/Chicks.html

The Roost
www.geocities.com/Nashville/Ranch/1751

Unofficial Dixie Chicks Site
www.dixiechicksfans.com

VH1 Fan Club: Dixie Chicks
http://dixie-chicks.vh1.com

You Know You're A Dixie Chicks Fan When…
www.angelfire.com/country/DixieChicksFans

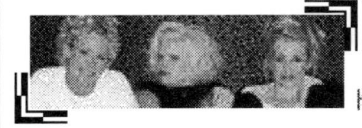

Whitney's Dixie Chicks Page
www.geocities.com/Nashville/Opry/5727

Video

Dixie Chicks Central: Video
www.dixiechickscentral.com/video.html

Official Dixie Chicks Web Site: Video
www.dixiechicks.com/av/video.html

Wallpapers

Dixie Chicks Fly World: Wallpaper
www.geocities.com/dixiechicksflyworld

Unofficial Dixie Chicks Site: Wallpaper
www.dixiechicksfans.com/wallpaper.html

Webrings

The Dixie Chicks Webring
http://nav.webring.yahoo.com/hub?ring=dixiechicks&list

Eminem

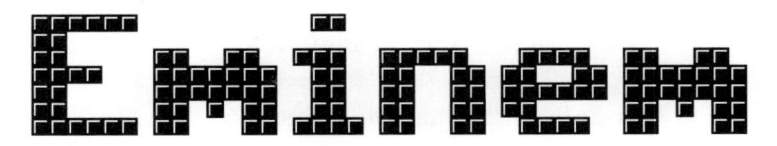

SUPER SINGLES "Stan" | "The Real Slim Shady" | "My Name Is"

Official Site

Eminem
www.eminem.com

Articles

dotmusic: Eminem
www.dotmusic.com/artists/Eminem

Jam! Showbiz: Music: Eminem
www.canoe.ca/JamMusicArtistsE/eminem.html

Audio

Marshall-Mathers.Net: MP3s
www.marshall-mathers.net/mp3.shtml

Discussion

Eminem Board
www.eminemboard.com

Yahoo! Clubs: Abstrakt EMINEM
http://clubs.yahoo.com/clubs/abstrakteminem

Yahoo! Clubs: Eminem Fan Zone
www.eminemclub.com

Yahoo! Clubs: Shady Underground
http://clubs.yahoo.com/clubs/shadyunderground

Yahoo! Clubs: Slim Shady 2000
http://clubs.yahoo.com/clubs/slimshady2000

Yahoo! Clubs: The Official Eminem Club
http://clubs.yahoo.com/clubs/theofficialeminemclub

Yahoo! Clubs: The Shady Bunch
http://clubs.yahoo.com/clubs/theshadybunch

Yahoo! Clubs: Ultimate Eminem
http://clubs.yahoo.com/clubs/ultimateeminem

Yahoo! Groups: crazyshady
http://groups.yahoo.com/group/crazyshady

Yahoo! Groups: eminem
http://groups.yahoo.com/group/eminem

E-Mail Services

Eminem World: Free E-Mail (yourname@eminemworld.com)
www.eminemworld.com/email.html

Eminem365 (yourname@eminem365.net)
www.eminem365.net

Marshall-Mathers.Net: E-Mail Sign-Up (yourname@marshall-mathers.net)
www.marshall-mathers.net/signup.shtml

Galleries

Absolute Pictures: Eminem
www.absolutepictures.com/e/eminem/index.html

Access Eminem: Pictures
www.topcities.com/music/accesseminem/pictures.html

AtPictures.Com: Eminem
www.atpictures.com/eminem

Eminem Unrestricted: Pictures
www.eminemunrestricted.com/pics.html

Eminem World: Pictures
www.eminemworld.com/pictures.html

Marshall-Mathers.Net: Pictures
www.marshall-mathers.net/pictures.shtml

PopFolio: Eminem
www.popfolio.com/eminem.htm

Links

Eminem Links
www.eminemlinks.com

Eminem Network
www.eminemnetwork.com

Mosiqa Top 100 Eminem Sites
http://top100.mosiqa.com/eminem

Top 25 Eminem Sites
http://new.topsitelists.com/run/eminemonline/topsites.html

Top 50 Eminem Sites
www.eminemsites.com

Lyrics

Eminem World: Lyrics
www.eminemworld.com/lyrics.html

Marshall-Mathers.Net: Lyrics
www.marshall-mathers.net/lyrics.shtml

The Real Shady Site: Lyrics
www.geocities.com/eminem1104/lyrix.html

Merchandise

Eminem Direct - The Official Store
http://eminemdirect.com

News

Abstracts.Net: Eminem
www.abstracts.net/eminem

Eminem World
www.eminemworld.com

Entertainment Sleuth: Eminem
http://e.sleuth.com/details.asp?Entity=5781

Marshall-Mathers.Net: Main
www.marshall-mathers.net/main.shtml

Reference

All Music Guide: Eminem
http://allmusic.com/cg/x.dll?p=amg&sql=1EMINEM

Internet Movie Database: Eminem
http://us.imdb.com/Name?Eminem

People Magazine Profiles: Eminem
http://people.aol.com/people/pprofiles/eminem

Rock on the Net: Eminem
www.rockonthenet.com/artists-e/eminem_main.htm

Wall of Sound: Eminem
http://wallofsound.go.com/artists/eminem

Software

Celebrity Desktop: Eminem
www.celebritydesktop.com/musicians/eminem

Top Sites

123Eminem.Com
www.123eminem.com

Access Eminem
www.accesseminem.com

Cool Eminem
www.cooleminem.com

Eminem 2000 - Slim Shady in Y2k
www.eminem2000.com

Eminem 2001
www.eminem2001.com

Eminem Connection
www.eminemconnection.com

Eminem Crib
http://eminemcrib.8m.com

Eminem Dome
http://eminemdome.cjb.net

Eminem Fan Zone
www.eminemfanzone.com

Eminem Forever
www.eminem-forever.com

Eminem Online
www.eminemonline.com

Eminem Place
www.eminemplace.com

Eminem Planet
www.eminem-planet.com

Eminem Shady World
www.eminemshadyworld.com

Eminem Spot
www.eminemspot.net

Eminem Top Sites
www.eminemtopsites.com

Eminem Universe
www.eminemheaven.com

Eminem Unrestricted
www.eminemunrestricted.com

Eminem World
www.eminemworld.com

EminemFan.Com
www.eminemfan.com

Eminemville
http://www.maxpages.com/eminemville

Marshall-Mathers.Net
www.marshall-mathers.net

Slim Shady Center
http://members.home.net/djrom69

Subject: Eminem
http://subjecteminem.cjb.net

The Real Shady Site
www.eminem2001.net

Tour Dates

Marshall-Mathers.Net: Tour Dates
www.marshall-mathers.net/tourdates.shtml

Video

Marshall-Mathers.Net: MPEGs
www.marshall-mathers.net/mpeg.shtml

MTV.Com: Eminem
http://eminem.mtv.com

The Real Shady Site: Multimedia
www.geocities.com/eminem1104/multi.html

Wallpapers

Eminem World: Wallpaper
www.eminemworld.com/wallpaper.html

Webrings

The Eminem Webring
http://nav.webring.yahoo.com/hub?ring=eminemring&list

Enrique Iglesias

SUPER SINGLES "Be With You" | "Rhythm Divine" | "Bailamos"

Official Site

Enrique Iglesias
www.enriqueiglesias.com

Articles

Jam! Showbiz: Music: Enrique Iglesias
www.canoe.ca/JamMusicArtistsI/iglesias_enrique.html

Audio

Enrique Iglesias: Music
www.enriqueiglesias.com/english/music.html

Discussion

Enrique Iglesias: Enrique Fan Forum
www.enriqueiglesias.com/english/fans.html

Yahoo! Clubs: Bailamos con Enrique
http://clubs.yahoo.com/clubs/bailamosconenrique

Yahoo! Clubs: Enrique Iglesias
http://clubs.yahoo.com/clubs/enriqueiglesias

Yahoo! Clubs: EnriqueandJJIglesias
http://clubs.yahoo.com/clubs/eandjjiglesias

Yahoo! Groups: Enrique Iglesias Realm
http://groups.yahoo.com/group/EnriqueIglesiasRealm

Yahoo! Groups: Enrique-Iglesias
http://groups.yahoo.com/group/enrique-iglesias

E-Mail

Pretty E-Mail: Enrique Iglesias Fans (yourname@enriqueiglesiasfans.com)
www.enriqueiglesiasfans.com

Galleries

Absolute Pictures: Enrique Iglesias
www.absolutepictures.com/i/iglesias_enrique

PopFolio: Enrique Iglesias
www.popfolio.com/enriqueiglesias.htm

Merchandise

Enrique Iglesias - Online Store
www.signaturesuperstars.com/artists/latin/enriqueiglesias/apparel.html

News

Abstracts.Net: Enrique Iglesias
www.abstracts.net/enrique-iglesias

Enrique Online: News
http://silverwing.net/enrique/news

Reference

All Music Guide: Enrique Iglesias
http://allmusic.com/cg/x.dll?p=amg&sql=1ENRIQUE|IGLESIAS

Internet Movie Database: Enrique Iglesias
http://us.imdb.com/Name?Enrique+Iglesias

People Magazine Profiles: Enrique Iglesias
http://people.aol.com/people/pprofiles/eiglesias

Rock on the Net: Enrique Iglesias
www.rockonthenet.com/artists-i/enriqueiglesias_main.htm

Software

Artist Desktop Themes: Enrique Iglesias
http://artistdesktopthemes.com/st/i/enrique_iglesias.dt.1.html

Celebrity Desktop: Enrique Iglesias
www.celebritydesktop.com/musicians/enrique_iglesias

Top Sites

Cosas-De-Enrique.Com
www.cosas-de-enrique.com

Crazy 4 Enrique
www.geocities.com/baby_latina02/Crazy4EnriqueIglesias.html

Enrique Iglesias - Kelly's Personal Page
http://get.to/enrique

Enrique Iglesias Downloads
www.geocities.com/enriqueiglesiasdownloads

Enrique Online
www.enrique-online.com

Simply Enrique
www.geocities.com/simplyenrique

Sunny's Enrique Iglesias Page
www.geocities.com/sunny_dlt/first.html

Tonight We Dance
http://gurlpages.com/cync

Video

MTV.Com: Enrique Iglesias
http://enrique-iglesias.mtv.com

Wallpapers

Enrique Iglesias Downloads: Wallpapers
www.geocities.com/enriqueiglesiasdownloads/wallpaperindex.html

Webrings

Enrique Iglesias Webring
http://nav.webring.yahoo.com/hub?ring=eiglesias&list

Faith Hill

SUPER SINGLES "The Way You Love Me" | "Breathe" | "This Kiss"

Official Site

Faith Hill Official Web Site
www.faithhill.com

Articles

Jam! Showbiz: Music: Faith Hill
www.canoe.ca/JamMusicArtistsH/hill_faith.html

Audio

MP3.Com: Faith Hill
www.mp3.com/faithhill

Discussion

Yahoo! Clubs: Faith Hill
http://clubs.yahoo.com/clubs/faithhill

Yahoo! Clubs: She Took a Piece of Our Heart
http://clubs.yahoo.com/clubs/shestookapieceofourheart

Yahoo! Clubs: The Way You Love Me
http://clubs.yahoo.com/clubs/thewayyouloveme

Yahoo! Clubs: Tim McGraw & Faith Hill Club
http://clubs.yahoo.com/clubs/timmcgrawandfaithhillclub

Yahoo! Groups: Faith Hill
http://groups.yahoo.com/group/Faith_Hill

Ecards

ForeverFaith.Com: Ecards
www.foreverfaith.com/postcards.html

E-Mail

fun2mail.com: Faith Hill Fan (yourname@faithhillfan.com)
www.faithhillfan.com

Galleries

A List Celebrities: Faith Hill
www.the-alist.org/FaithHill

Absolute Pictures: Faith Hill
www.absolutepictures.com/h/hill_faith

Faith Hill Breathes in the UK: Gallery
www.faithhill.org.uk/BreatheUK.data/Components/gallery/indexpage1.htm

Merchandise

Faith Hill Official Web Site: Merchandise
www.faithhill.com/cgi-bin/shop.pl/page=new.htm

News

Entertainment Sleuth: Faith Hill
http://e.sleuth.com/details.asp?Entity=2020

Faith Hill Official Web Site: News
www.faithhill.com/news

Reference

All Music Guide: Faith Hill
http://allmusic.com/cg/x.dll?p=amg&sql=1FAITH|HILL

Internet Movie Database: Faith Hill
http://us.imdb.com/Name?Faith+Hill

People Magazine Profiles: Faith Hill
http://people.aol.com/people/pprofiles/fhill

Rock on the Net: Faith Hill
www.rockonthenet.com/artists-h/faithhill.htm

Wall of Sound: Faith Hill
http://wallofsound.go.com/artists/faithhill

Software

Artist Desktop Themes: Faith Hill
http://artistdesktopthemes.com/st/h/faith_hill.dt.1.html

Celebrity Desktop: Faith Hill
www.celebritydesktop.com/musicians/faith_hill

Top Sites

Advertronic's Gotta Have Faith?
www.advertronic.getserver.com/faith.html

Amy's Faith Hill Page
www.geocities.com/Nashville/Opry/6059/faith.html

Faith Hill Breathes in the UK
www.faithhill.org.uk

Faith Hill Multimedia Site
www.gregreiter.com/faithhill/breathe.htm

Faith Hill's World
www.angelfire.com/tn/TheFaithHillPage

ForeverFaith.Com
www.foreverfaith.com

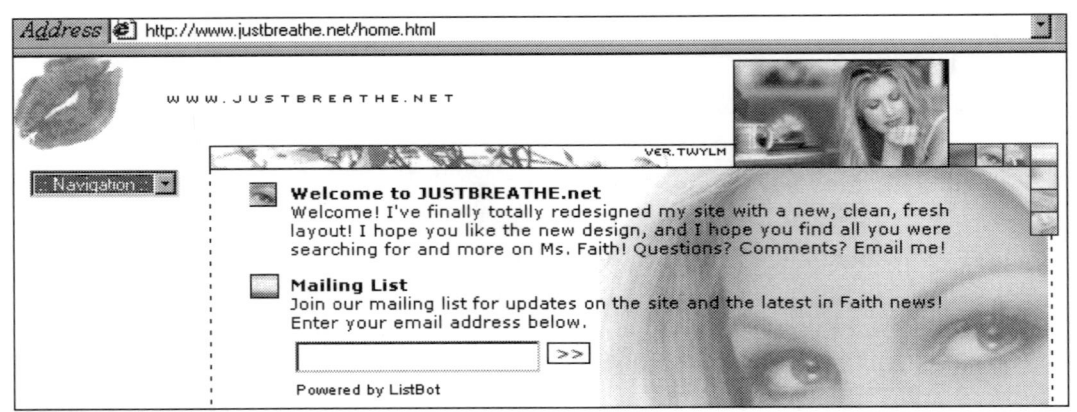

JustBreathe.Net
www.justbreathe.net

Leanne's Faith Hill Gallery
www.geocities.com/Nashville/9796

MgGraws.Com
www.mcgraws.com

VH1 Fan Club: Faith Hill
http://faith-hill.vh1.com

You Gotta Have Faith Hill
http://members.tripod.com/~this_kiss2

Video

Faith Hill Breathes in the UK: Multimedia
www.faithhill.org.uk/multimedia.html

Wallpapers

ForeverFaith.Com: Downloads
www.foreverfaith.com/downloads.html

JustBreathe.Net: Wallpapers
www.justbreathe.net/media/wallpaper.html

Webrings

The Faith Hill Webring
http://nav.webring.yahoo.com/hub?ring=faithhill&list

The Tim McGraw & Faith Hill Webring
http://nav.webring.yahoo.com/hub?ring=mcgrawhill&list

Fiona Apple

SUPER SINGLES "Fast As You Can" | "Criminal" | "Shadow Boxer"

Official Site

Fiona Apple
www.fiona-apple.com

Articles

Jam! Showbiz: Music: Fiona Apple
www.canoe.ca/JamMusicArtistsA/apple_fiona.html

Never is a Promise: Articles, Interviews, Reviews
www.neverisapromise.com/niap/articleshome.htm

This Mind, This Body & This Voice: Articles
http://members.tripod.com/~SuperEddie/articles/fiarticles.html

Audio

Never is a Promise: Audio
www.neverisapromise.com/niap/fa/sounds.html

Discussion

Sony Music's Fiona Apple Message Board
http://bbs.sonymusic.com/wwwthreads.pl?action=list&Board=fionaapple

Yahoo! Clubs: Applelicious
http://clubs.yahoo.com/clubs/applelicious

Yahoo! Clubs: Heavy With Mood
http://clubs.yahoo.com/clubs/heavywithmood

Yahoo! Clubs: To Take Flight
http://clubs.yahoo.com/clubs/totakeflight

Yahoo! Groups: Apple-Addicts
http://groups.yahoo.com/group/apple-addicts

Yahoo! Groups: Fiona Underground
http://groups.yahoo.com/group/fiona_underground

Fan Art

Brilliant As the Moon is Full - Fiona Apple Music Interpretations & Artwork
www.fiproductions.com/apple

Fi Productions
www.fiproductions.com

Sing, Sing Again
www.fiproductions.com/singing

Galleries

Absolute Pictures: Fiona Apple
www.absolutepictures.com/a/apple_fiona

AtPictures.Com: Fiona Apple
www.atpictures.com/fiona

Fiona Rocks: Gallery
http://fionarocks.tripod.com/fiona_gallery.htm

PopFolio: Fiona Apple
www.popfolio.com/apple.htm

Lyrics

Never is a Promise: Lyrics
www.neverisapromise.com/niap/lyrics/lyrics.htm

News

Fiona Apple Online: News
www.fionaappleonline.com/news.htm

Mr. Showbiz Celebrities: Fiona Apple
http://mrshowbiz.go.com/people/fionaapple

Reference

All Music Guide: Fiona Apple
http://allmusic.com/cg/x.dll?p=amg&sql=1FIONA|APPLE

Internet Movie Database: Fiona Apple
http://us.imdb.com/Name?Fiona+Apple

People Magazine Profiles: Fiona Apple
http://people.aol.com/people/pprofiles/fapple

Rock on the Net: Fiona Apple
www.rockonthenet.com/artists-a/fionaapple_main.htm

Wall of Sound: Fiona Apple
http://wallofsound.go.com/artists/fionaapple

Yahoo! Web Celeb: Fiona Apple
http://features.yahoo.com/webceleb/apple

Software

Artist Desktop Themes: Fiona Apple
http://artistdesktopthemes.com/st/a/fiona_apple.dt.1.html

Celebrity Desktop: Fiona Apple
www.celebritydesktop.com/musicians/fiona_apple

Go With Yourself: Downloads
http://gurlpages.com/fiona.apple/downloads.html

Top Sites

And She Said...Fiona Apple Fan Base
www.fiproductions.com/andshesaid

Autumn Days
www.geocities.com/autumndays_fa/main.htm

Feet on the Ground
www.spiritone.com/~buzzd/fa/fiona.html

Fi Productions Adoption Agency (Fiona Apple Clique)
www.geocities.com/fiproductions/adoption

Fiona Apple - The Rigadoon
www.envy.nu/therigadoon/ent.html

Fiona Apple - The Way Things Are
www.thewaythingsare.cjb.net

Fiona Apple Online
www.fionaappleonline.com

Fiona Has Wings
www.fionahaswings.com

Fiona Rocks
http://fionarocks.tripod.com

FionaApple.co.uk
www.fionaapple.co.uk

Go With Yourself
http://gurlpages.com/fiona.apple/index.html

In the Blue of My Oblivion
www.fiproductions.com/blueoblivion

Limp - Will My Eyes Be Closed or Open?
http://limp.port5.com

Looking for a Little Hope
http://littlehope.netfuze.com

Never is a Promise
www.neverisapromise.com

Perfectly Windy Sky
www.perfectlywindysky.net

Sleep to Dream
http://devoted.to/sleeptodream

Soulful Songmaker
http://icing.simplenet.com/FionaPage/index.html

Sullen Girl
http://blok.org/fiona

The Way Things Are
www.thewaythingsare.cjb.net

The Woman
http://tornumbilical.nu/fiona

This Mind, This Body & This Voice
http://members.tripod.com/~SuperEddie/fionavoice.html

Under the Waves
http://members.aol.com/zooberries/fiona/utw.htm

VH1 Fan Club: Fiona Apple
http://fiona-apple.vh1.com

Wicked Garden
www.envy.nu/therigadoon/wickedgarden.html

Video

Limp - Will My Eyes Be Closed or Open?: Video Stills
http://limp.port5.com/b/video

Never is a Promise: Video
www.neverisapromise.com/niap/fa/videos.html

Webrings

Apple Bites
    http://nav.webring.yahoo.com/hub?ring=fionapple&list

Tidal - The Fiona Apple Webring
    http://nav.webring.yahoo.com/hub?ring=fionaao&list

FOO FIGHTERS

SUPER SINGLES "Learn to Fly" | "Everlong" | "Monkey Wrench" | "This Is a Call"

Official Site

FooFighters.Com
www.foofighters.com

Articles

Jam! Showbiz: Music: Foo Fighters
www.canoe.ca/JamMusicArtistsF/foo.html

Audio

UNTITLED: MIDI
www.hoching.com/foofighter/midi.shtml

Discussion

The Foo Fighters @ EzBoard.com
http://server5.ezboard.com/bthefoofightersmessageboard

There's Nothing Left to Lose (TNLTL.Com) : Message Boards
http://forums.tnltl.com

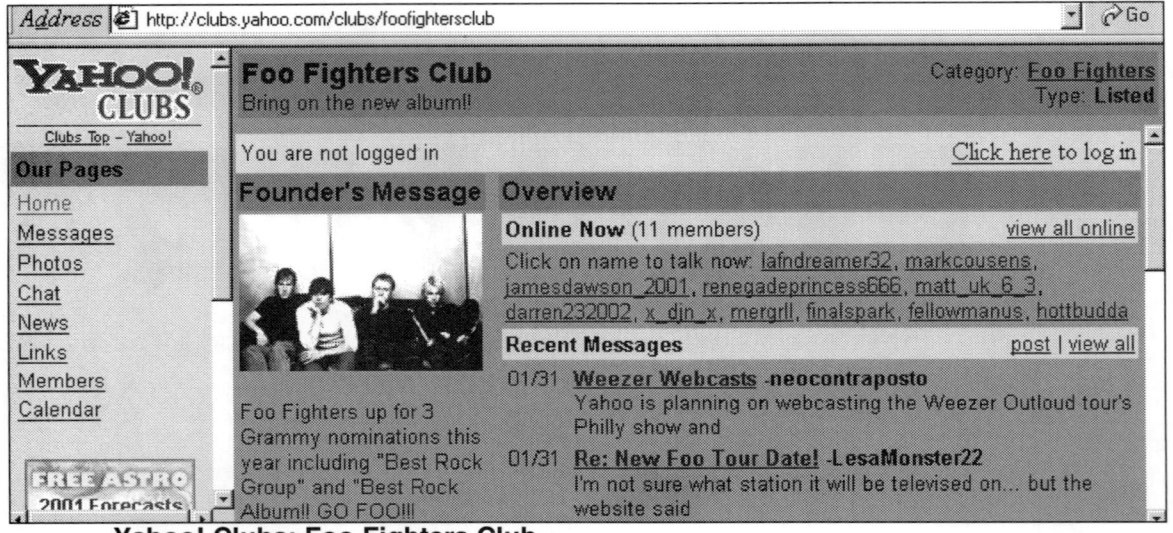

Yahoo! Clubs: Foo Fighters Club
http://clubs.yahoo.com/clubs/foofightersclub

Yahoo! Clubs: Foo Fighters Fans
http://clubs.yahoo.com/clubs/foofightersfans

Yahoo! Groups: foofighter2108
http://groups.yahoo.com/group/foofighter2108

Fan Art

I'll Stick Around - A Foo Fighters Art Page
www.tiac.net/users/daveread/foo

Galleries

Stacked Actors: Pics
www.angelfire.com/rock/foonet/pictures.html

Links

Foo Fighters Top 50
www.foofighters.com/top50/top50.html

Lyrics

Foo Fighters Central: Lyrics
www.foofighterscentral.org.uk/media/lyrics/lyricsmainleft.htm

There's Nothing Left to Lose (TNLTL.Com) : Lyrics
http://24.157.14.57/foofighters/lyrics

Merchandise

Foo Fighters Direct - The Official Store for Foo Gear
www.foofighters.com/store/index.html

News

Entertainment Sleuth: Foo Fighters
http://e.sleuth.com/details.asp?Entity=4951

Foo Fighters Central: News
www.foofighterscentral.org.uk/newsmain.htm

Reference

All Music Guide: Foo Fighters
http://allmusic.com/cg/x.dll?p=amg&sql=1FOO|FIGHTERS

Wall of Sound: Foo Fighters
http://wallofsound.go.com/artists/foofighters

Software

Celebrity Desktop: Foo Fighters
www.celebritydesktop.com/musicians/foo_fighters

Foo Fighters Downloads @ Aurora
http://216.97.12.249/aurora/downloads

Top Sites

Click2Music: Foo Fighters
www.click2music.com/foofighters

Flying Foo
http://members.tripod.com/flyingfoo/foo.html

Foo Attack
www.geocities.com/earnestolee/efooattaq.htm

Foo Fighters Central
www.foofighterscentral.org.uk

Foo Fighters Live Guide
www.foofighters-live.com

Foo Maniacs
http://home.beseen.com/internet/flufcat/foomaniacs.index.html

Footos - The Fresh Fighter!
www.dave-grohl.com

Foozy - A Fun Load of Foo
www.geocities.com/Area51/Corridor/8580/foo.html

Generator
http://kobain.hypermart.net/foo

Running With the Foo
www.runningwiththefoo.com

Stacked Actors
www.stackedactors.com

The Borrowed Cloud
www.geocities.com/the_borrowed_cloud

The Monkey Wrench
www.themonkeywrench.homestead.com

There's Nothing Left to Lose (TNLTL.Com) - A Foo Fighters Fan Site
www.tnltl.com

UNTITLED - aFooFightersPage
www.hoching.com/foofighter

VH1 Fan Club: Foo Fighters
http://foo-fighters.vh1.com

Walking After You
www.walkingafteryou.com

Video

MTV.Com: Foo Fighters
http://foo-fighters.mtv.com

The Monkey Wrench: Videos
www.pokeythelittlepuppy.homestead.com/videos.html

There's Nothing Left to Lose (TNLTL.Com) : Videos
http://24.157.14.57/foofighters/video

Wallpapers

UNTITLED: Wallpapers
www.hoching.com/foofighter/walls.shtml

Webrings

Foo Fighters Webring
http://nav.webring.yahoo.com/hub?ring=foofighter&list

Footos - The Official Foo Fighters Webring
http://nav.webring.yahoo.com/hub?ring=footos&list

Goo Goo Dolls

SUPER SINGLES "Broadway" | "Black Balloon" | "Slide" | "Iris" | "Name"

Official Site

Goo Goo Dolls
www.googoodolls.com

Articles

Jam! Showbiz: Music: Goo Goo Dolls
www.canoe.ca/JamMusicArtistsG/googoo_dolls.html

The Goo Hive
www.geocities.com/SunsetStrip/Vine/5378

Discussion

Yahoo! Clubs: A Club Called Goo Goo Dolls
http://clubs.yahoo.com/clubs/aclubcalledgoogoodolls

Yahoo! Clubs: Goo Goo Dolls Official Club
http://clubs.yahoo.com/clubs/googoodollsofficialclub

Yahoo! Clubs: Hopelessly Devoted to Goo
http://clubs.yahoo.com/clubs/hopelesslydevotedtogoo

Yahoo! Groups: AllEyesOnMe
http://groups.yahoo.com/group/AllEyesOnMe

Yahoo! Groups: goo-goo-dolls
http://groups.yahoo.com/group/goo-goo-dolls

Ecards

The Black & White World: Send a Goo Postcard!
www.angelfire.com/nd/amigone/postcard.html

Links

Top 30 Goo Sites
http://members.sitegadgets.com/g2drzznk/topsites.html

Lyrics

Abstract Goo: Lyrics
www.geocities.com/SunsetStrip/7881/googoodolls/albums.html

News

Okay 6 Goo's News
www.angelfire.com/music/ok6googoodolls/goosnews.htm

Reference

All Music Guide: Goo Goo Dolls
http://allmusic.com/cg/x.dll?p=amg&sql=1GOO|GOO|DOLLS

Rock on the Net: Goo Goo Dolls
www.rockonthenet.com/artists-g/googoodolls_main.htm

Wall of Sound: Goo Goo Dolls
http://wallofsound.go.com/artists/googoodolls

Software

Celebrity Desktop: Goo Goo Dolls
www.celebritydesktop.com/musicians/goo_goo_dolls

Top Sites

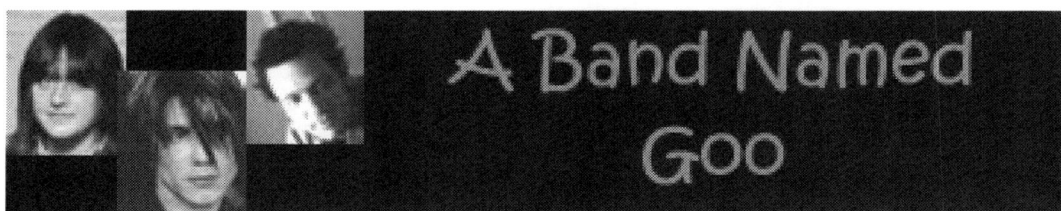

A Band Named Goo
www.devolution.net/googoodolls

Abstract Goo
www.geocities.com/SunsetStrip/7881/googoodolls

Dizzy Goo
http://go.to/dizzygoo

Dizzy Up the Boys
http://dutb.tripod.com

Forever Goo
http://members.tripod.com/amchan/ggd.html

Goo Goo Land
http://clik.to/goo

Gootopia
http://gootopia.homestead.com/main.html

Okay 6 Goo Goo Dolls
www.angelfire.com/music/ok6googoodolls

Rain'z SlideLand
www.angelfire.com/nt/raindrops4/gooindex.html

The Black & White World
www.angelfire.com/bc/dizzy

VH1 Fan Club: Goo Goo Dolls
http://goo-goo-dolls.vh1.com

World of Goo
www.musicfanclubs.org/googoodolls

Video

Forever Goo: Videos & Sounds
http://members.tripod.com/amchan/videos.html

Wallpapers

A Band Named Goo: Wallpapers
www.devolution.net/googoodolls/wallpapers.html

Webrings

All-Goo! The Ultimate Goo Goo Dolls Webring
http://nav.webring.yahoo.com/hub?ring=rockongoo&list

Goo Goo Dolls Sites Webring
http://nav.webring.yahoo.com/hub?ring=googoo_dolls&list

Hanson

SUPER SINGLES "This Time Around" | "If Only" | "Weird" | "MMMBop"

Official Site

HANSONLINE
www.hansonline.com

Articles

Jam! Showbiz: Music: Hanson
www.canoe.ca/JamMusicArtistsH/hanson.html

Discussion

Hanson Fan Newsgroup
alt.fan.hanson

Yahoo! Clubs: Hanson (Over 40,000 members)
http://clubs.yahoo.com/clubs/hanson

Yahoo! Clubs: Hanson Angels Place
http://clubs.yahoo.com/clubs/hansonangelsplace

Yahoo! Clubs: Hanson MOE Tell
http://clubs.yahoo.com/clubs/hansonmoetell

Yahoo! Clubs: HansonWorld
http://clubs.yahoo.com/clubs/hansonworld

Yahoo! Clubs: Hcrazy
http://clubs.yahoo.com/clubs/hcrazy

Yahoo! Groups: -hanson-
http://groups.yahoo.com/group/-hanson-

Fan Art

Masterpiece of Hanson
http://homepages.go.com/~monitwin1/Masterpiece.htm

The Art of Albertane
http://members.tripod.com/biko77/hanson.html

Fan Fiction

Hanson Horizon
www.hansonhorizon.com

Galleries

Hanson House: Articles & Scans
http://hansonhouse.com/articles.htm

Yahoo! Groups: Hanson-Pics-Daily
http://groups.yahoo.com/group/hanson-pics-daily

Lyrics

Kangarooland's Hanson Web Site: Lyrics
http://kangarooland.com/hanson/lyrics

News

Entertainment Sleuth: Hanson
http://e.sleuth.com/details.asp?Entity=5282

Reference

All Music Guide: Hanson
http://allmusic.com/cg/x.dll?p=amg&sql=1HANSON

People Magazine Profiles: Hanson
http://people.aol.com/people/pprofiles/hanson

Rock on the Net: Hanson
www.rockonthenet.com/artists-h/hanson_main.htm

Wall of Sound: Hanson
http://wallofsound.go.com/artists/hanson

Software

Celebrity Desktop: Hanson
www.celebritydesktop.com/musicians/hanson

Top Sites

ALH2 - Adults Like Hanson Too!
http://alh2.www2.50megs.com

Hanson - Live
www.musicfanclubs.org/hanson

Hanson Hangout
http://hansonhangout.netfirms.com

Hanson House
http://hansonhouse.com

Hanson in Clay-O-Vision
www.clayvision.net/hanson/hansonfanart.htm

Hanson Planet
www.idv8.com/hansonplanet

It's Pretty Wild
www.itsprettywild.com

Kangarooland's Hanson Web Site
http://kangarooland.com/hanson

KidMMMBop's Hanson Page
www.kidmmmbop.com

Video

Hanson House: Video Clips
http://hansonhouse.com/video.htm

Webrings

-hanson
http://nav.webring.yahoo.com/hub?ring=hanson11&list

The Hanson Hotel Webring
http://nav.webring.yahoo.com/hub?ring=hansonhotel&list

Janet Jackson

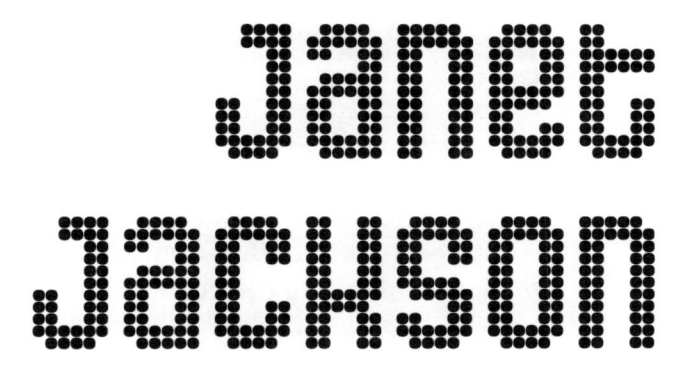

SUPER SINGLES "Doesn't Really Matter" | "I Get Lonely" | "Together Again" | "That's the Way Love Goes" | "Escapade" | "Black Cat" | "Miss You Much"

Official Site

Janet
www.janet-jackson.com

Articles

dotmusic: Janet Jackson
www.dotmusic.com/artists/JanetJackson

Jam! Showbiz: Music: Janet Jackson
www.canoe.ca/JamMusicArtistsJ/jackson_janet.html

Discussion

Janet Talk
http://jtalk.cjb.net

Yahoo! Clubs: Janet
http://clubs.yahoo.com/clubs/janet

Yahoo! Clubs: Janet Jackson Hangout
http://clubs.yahoo.com/clubs/janetjacksonhangout

Yahoo! Clubs: Nasty Girl 2000
http://clubs.yahoo.com/clubs/nastygirl2000

Yahoo! Groups: Janet-Jackson
http://groups.yahoo.com/group/Janet-Jackson

Yahoo! Groups: JanetsVelvetZone
http://groups.yahoo.com/group/JanetsVelvetXone

Fan Clubs

Miss Janet International Fan Club
http://miss-janet.com

Galleries

Absolute Pictures: Janet Jackson
www.absolutepictures.com/j/jackson_janet

PopFolio: Janet Jackson
www.popfolio.com/jacksonjanet.htm

Links

Mosiqa Top 100 Janet Jackson Sites
www.top.mosiqa.com/janet

Lyrics

Forever Janet: Lyrics
http://members.nbci.com/foreverjanet/lyrics.html

Merchandise

Janet Jackson Direct
http://janetjacksondirect.com

News

Entertainment Sleuth: Janet Jackson
http://e.sleuth.com/details.asp?Entity=2184

Mr. Showbiz Celebrities: Janet Jackson
http://mrshowbiz.go.com/people/janetjackson

Yahoo! Groups: THROBline
http://groups.yahoo.com/group/THROBline

Reference

All Music Guide: Janet Jackson
http://allmusic.com/cg/x.dll?p=amg&sql=1JANET|JACKSON

Internet Movie Database: Janet Jackson
http://us.imdb.com/Name?Janet+Jackson

People Magazine Profiles: Janet Jackson
http://people.aol.com/people/pprofiles/celebhomepage/0,3371,54,00.html

Rock on the Net: Janet Jackson
www.rockonthenet.com/artists-j/janetjackson_main.htm

Wall of Sound: Janet Jackson
http://wallofsound.go.com/artists/janetjackson

Software

Celebrity Desktop: Janet Jackson
www.celebritydesktop.com/musicians/janet_jackson

Themes

Cinema Dekstop Themes: Janet Jackson
www.cinemadesktopthemes.com/st/j/janet_jackson.dt.1.html

Top Sites

100% Janet
http://janetjackson.cjb.net

24-J
www.geocities.com/twenty4janet

Empty Space
www.janet.fr.fm

Essence of Janet
http://missjanet.cjb.net

Forever Janet
http://members.nbci.com/foreverjanet

Funky New Agenda
http://fnagenda.virtualave.net

Janet - The Velvet Rope 2218
http://tomo1983.tripod.com

JANET Interactive
www.janet-interactive.com

Janet Planet
http://nav.to/janetboo

Janet World
www.janetworld.com

Janet's Velvet Xone
www.geocities.com/SunsetStrip/4966

Runaway With Janet
www.geocities.com/SunsetStrip/Disco/9310

Strictly Janet
www.geocities.com/SunsetStrip/Stadium/8565/janet.html

The French Janet Connection
www.geocities.com/Hollywood/Theater/9850/index.html

The Funky Janet Web
www.janet.nu

The Japanese Janet Connection
http://drive.to/janet

Velvet Dreams
www.velvet-dreams.de

Webrings

FNA Janet Webring
http://nav.webring.yahoo.com/hub?ring=fnajanet&list

JANET interactive
http://nav.webring.yahoo.com/hub?ring=janetjackson&list

The Velvet Rope Ring
http://nav.webring.yahoo.com/hub?ring=vrope&list

Jennifer Lopez

SUPER SINGLES "Love Don't Cost a Thing" | "Feelin' So Good"
"Waiting for Tonight" | "If You Had My Love"

Official Site

Jennifer Lopez Online
www.jenniferlopez.com

Articles

AllStarz.Org: Jennifer Lopez: Interview Transcripts
www.allstarz.org/jenniferlopez/interview.html

dotmusic: Jennifer Lopez
www.dotmusic.com/artists/JenniferLopez

Audio

JenniferLopez.Net: Audio
http://jenniferlopez.net/jlo/audios.shtml

Discussion

Yahoo! Clubs: Jennifer Lopez Lovers
http://clubs.yahoo.com/clubs/jenniferlopezlovers

Yahoo! Clubs: Jennifer Lopez Pictures
http://clubs.yahoo.com/clubs/jenniferlopezspictures

Yahoo! Clubs: Kyle's Jennifer Lopez Page00
http://clubs.yahoo.com/clubs/kylesjenniferlopezpage00

Yahoo! Clubs: Official Jennifer Lopez Club
http://clubs.yahoo.com/clubs/officialjenniferlopezclub

Yahoo! Groups: jenniferonline
http://groups.yahoo.com/group/jenniferonline

Yahoo! Groups: JennifersWorld
http://groups.yahoo.com/group/JennifersWorld

Yahoo! Groups: RedHotJenniferLopez
http://groups.yahoo.com/group/RedHotJenniferLopez

E-Mail Services

JenniferLopez.Net: E-Mail (yourname@jenniferlopez.net)
http://jenniferlopez.net/jlo/email.shtml

Galleries

4JenniferLopezPictures.Com
www.4jenniferlopezpictures.com

A List Celebrities: Jennifer Lopez
www.the-alist.org/JenniferLopez

Absolute Pictures: Jennifer Lopez
www.absolutepictures.com/l/lopez_jennifer

AllStarz.Org: Jennifer Lopez: Galleries
www.allstarz.org/jenniferlopez/pics.html

AnthemPop: Jennifer Lopez
www.anthempop.com/jenniferlopez/pictures.html

AtPictures.Com: Jennifer Lopez
www.atpictures.com/jennifer

Beautfiul Celebrities: Jennifer Lopez
www.beautifulcelebrities.com/jennifer_lopez_pics.html

Jennifer Lopez Dedication
http://home.tiscalinet.be/Jennifer_Lopez

Jennifer Lopez Pictures Gallery
www.jenniferlopez-all.com

Jennifer Lopez Web: Fotos
www.jenniferlopezweb.com/fotos/foto1.htm

JenniferLopez.Net: Gallery
http://jenniferlopez.net/jlo/gallery.shtml

Totally Jennifer Lopez: Gallery
http://members.nbci.com/_XMCM/foxharther/gallery/index.html

Links

FanGuide Top Jennifer Lopez Sites
www.fanguide.com/autorankm/lopez

Top 219 Jennifer Lopez Sites
www.top219.org/lopez

Lyrics

Jennifer Lopez Fan Site: Lyrics
www.redrival.com/mci/lyrics.htm

Merchandise

JenniferLopez.Net: Online Store
http://jenniferlopez.net/jlo/products.shtml

News

Abstracts.Net: Jennifer Lopez
www.abstracts.net/jennifer-lopez

Entertainment Sleuth: Jennifer Lopez
http://e.sleuth.com/details.asp?Entity=2690

Mr. Showbiz Celebrities: Jennifer Lopez
http://mrshowbiz.go.com/people/jenniferlopez

Reference

All Music Guide: Jennifer Lopez
http://allmusic.com/cg/x.dll?p=amg&sql=1JENNIFER|LOPEZ

Internet Movie Database: Jennifer Lopez
http://us.imdb.com/Name?Jennifer+Lopez

Wall of Sound: Jennifer Lopez
http://wallofsound.go.com/artists/jenniferlopez

Software

Artist Desktop Themes: Jennifer Lopez
http://artistdesktopthemes.com/st/l/jennifer_lopez.dt.1.html

Celebrity Desktop: Jennifer Lopez
www.celebritydesktop.com/actresses/jennifer_lopez

Themes

Cinema Desktop Themes: Jennifer Lopez
www.cinemadesktopthemes.com/st/l/jennifer_lopez.dt.1.html

Top Sites

AllFans.Org: Jennifer Lopez
http://jenniferlopez.allfans.org

AllStarz.Org: Jennifer Lopez
www.allstarz.org/jenniferlopez

Givin' It Her All: Jennifer Lopez
www.angelfire.com/il2/jenlopez

Jennifer Lopez - The New Millennium
www.jenlopeznm.com

Jennifer Lopez Fan Site
www.jenniferlopezclub.com

Jennifer Lopez Latin Soul
http://jlols.cjb.net

Jennifer Lopez on the Net
www.geocities.com/Hollywood/Agency/1288

JenniferLopez.Net
http://jenniferlopez.net

Totally Jennifer Lopez
http://totallyjennifer.cjb.net

VH1 Fan Club: Jennifer Lopez
http://jennifer-lopez.vh1.com

TV Schedule

TV Now: Jennifer Lopez
www.tv-now.com/stars/lopez.html

Video

Jennifer Lopez on the Net: Video
www.geocities.com/Hollywood/Agency/1288/mvideos.html

JenniferLopez: Video
http://jenniferlopez.net/jlo/videos.shtml

MTV.Com: Jennifer Lopez
http://jennifer-lopez.mtv.com

Wallpapers

Jennifer Lopez - Could This Be Love: Wallpaper
http://shinjuku.cool.ne.jp/jenniferlopez/wallpaper.htm

Jennifer Lopez - The New Millennium: Wallpaper
www.jenloznm.com/wallpaper1.html

Jennifer Lopez Dedication: Wallpaper
http://home.tiscalinet.be/Jennifer_Lopez/wallpaper.htm

Webrings

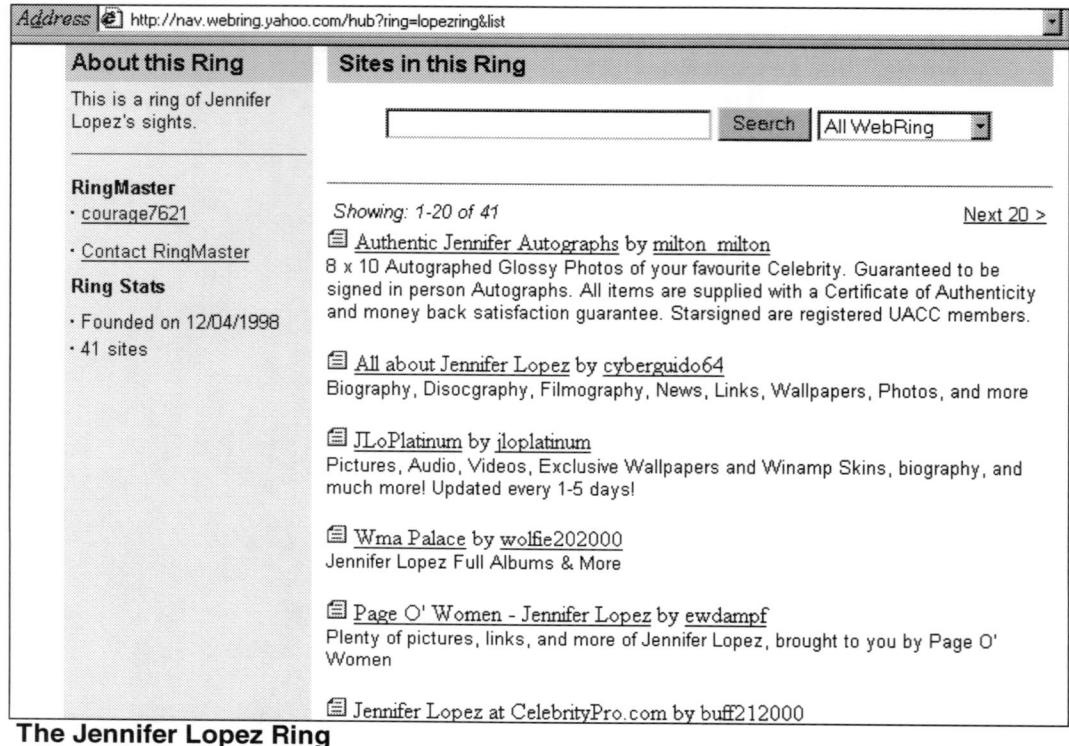

Address: http://nav.webring.yahoo.com/hub?ring=lopezring&list

About this Ring
This is a ring of Jennifer Lopez's sights.

RingMaster
- courage7621
- Contact RingMaster

Ring Stats
- Founded on 12/04/1998
- 41 sites

Sites in this Ring

[Search] [All WebRing]

Showing: 1-20 of 41   Next 20 >

Authentic Jennifer Autographs by milton_milton
8 x 10 Autographed Glossy Photos of your favourite Celebrity. Guaranteed to be signed in person Autographs. All items are supplied with a Certificate of Authenticity and money back satisfaction guarantee. Starsigned are registered UACC members.

All about Jennifer Lopez by cyberguido64
Biography, Disocgraphy, Filmography, News, Links, Wallpapers, Photos, and more

JLoPlatinum by jloplatinum
Pictures, Audio, Videos, Exclusive Wallpapers and Winamp Skins, biography, and much more! Updated every 1-5 days!

Wma Palace by wolfie202000
Jennifer Lopez Full Albums & More

Page O' Women - Jennifer Lopez by ewdampf
Plenty of pictures, links, and more of Jennifer Lopez, brought to you by Page O' Women

Jennifer Lopez at CelebrityPro.com by buff212000

The Jennifer Lopez Ring
http://nav.webring.yahoo.com/hub?ring=lopezring&list

Jessica Simpson

SUPER SINGLES "I Think I'm in Love With You" | "Where You Are" | "I Wanna Love You Forever"

Official Site

Jessica Simpson
www.jessicasimpson.com

Articles

Amazing Jessica: Articles
http://gurlpages.com/amazingjessica/articles.html

Jam! Showbiz: Music: Jessica Simpson
www.canoe.ca/JamMusicArtistsS/simpson_jessica.html

The Girl Behind the Voice: Articles
www.jessica-simpson.org/articles.html

Audio

Amazing Jessica: Lyrics & Audio
http://gurlpages.com/amazingjessica/lyrics.html

JessicaSimpson.Net: Audio
www.jessicasimpson.net/html/music.html

Discussion

Jessica Simpson: Community
http://jessicasimpson.com/communityF.html

JessicaSimpson.Net: Mailing List
www.jessicasimpson.net/html/mail.html

Searching for Jessica: Message Board
http://pub26.ezboard.com/bsearchingforjessicamb

Yahoo! Clubs: All Jessica Simpson
http://clubs.yahoo.com/clubs/alljessicasimpson

Yahoo! Clubs: Jessica Simpson Unofficial Club
http://clubs.yahoo.com/clubs/jessicasimpsonunofficialclub

Yahoo! Clubs: Just Jessica Simpson
http://clubs.yahoo.com/clubs/justjessicasimpson

Yahoo! Clubs: Official Jessica Simpson Club
http://clubs.yahoo.com/clubs/officialjessicasimpsonclub

Yahoo! Groups: Jessica-Simpson
http://groups.yahoo.com/group/Jessica-Simpson

Yahoo! Groups: Jessica-Simpson-Fans
http://groups.yahoo.com/group/Jessica-Simpson-Fans

Ecards

Always Jessica Simpson: Postcards
www.alwaysjessicasimpson.com/postcards.html

Jessica Simpson: Postcards
www.jessicasimpson.com/postcard

Fan Art

The J Spot: Art
www.geocities.com/Paris/Cinema/9470/art.html

FAQs

Jessica Simpson: FAQ
www.jessicasimpson.com/faq

Galleries

A List Celebrities: Jessica Simpson
www.the-alist.org/JessicaSimpson

Absolute Pictures: Jessica Simpson
www.absolutepictures.com/s/simpson_jessica

Always Jessica Simpson: Gallery
www.alwaysjessicasimpson.com/gallery/promotional/index.html

JessicaSimpson.Net: Pictures
www.jessicasimpson.net/whoa_pics/page_01.htm

Searching for Jessica: Gallery
www.geocities.com/jesusgirlangel/gallery.html

The Girl Behind the Voice: Images
www.jessica-simpson.org/images.html

Links

Jessica Awards
http://jess_awards.tripod.com

Jessica Simpson Top 40 @ ThinkCelebs.com
www.thinkcelebs.com/simpson

Mosiqa Top 100 Jessica Simpson Sites
www.top.mosiqa.com/jessica

Lyrics

Always Jessica Simpson: Song Lyrics
www.alwaysjessicasimpson.com/lyrics.html

Amazing Jessica: Lyrics & Audio
http://gurlpages.com/amazingjessica/lyrics.html

Heart of Jessica: Lyrics
www.geocities.com/rosekitty00/lyrics.html

Searching for Jessica: Lyrics
www.geocities.com/jesusgirlangel/lyrics.html

News

Abstracts.Net: Jessica Simpson
www.abstracts.net/jessica-simpson

Entertainment Sleuth: Jessica Simpson
http://e.sleuth.com/details.asp?Entity=4921

Reference

All Music Guide: Jessica Simpson
http://allmusic.com/cg/x.dll?p=amg&sql=1JESSICA|SIMPSON

Internet Movie Database: Jessica Simpson
http://us.imdb.com/Name?Jessica+Simpson

Rock on the Net: Jessica Simpson
www.rockonthenet.com/artists-s/jessicasimpson.htm

Software

Always Jessica Simpson: Fan Stuff
www.alwaysjessicasimpson.com/downloads.html

Artist Desktop Themes: Jessica Simpson
http://artistdesktopthemes.com/st/s/jessica_simpson.dt.1.html

Celebrity Desktop: Jessica Simpson
www.celebritydesktop.com/musicians/jessica_simpson

Top Sites

Ablazingly Jessica
www.jessicasimpson.fsnet.co.uk

Always Jessica Simpson
www.alwaysjessicasimpson.com

Amazing Jessica
http://gurlpages.com/amazingjessica/main.html

Forever Jessica
http://geocities.com/ashlee_hardy

Heart of Innocence
http://clik.to/heartofinnocence

Heart of Jessica
http://heartofjessica.musicpage.com

Jessica Academy
www.geocities.com/jessica_academy

Jessica Online
http://come.to/Jessica_Online

Jessica Simpson Headquarters
www.jessicaheadquarters.net

JessicaSimpson.Net
www.jessicasimpson.net

Searching for Jessica
www.geocities.com/jesusgirlangel/jessicacontents.html

The Girl Behind the Voice
www.jessica-simpson.org

The J Spot
http://jessicasimpson.musicpage.com

The JSimpson Zone
http://geocities.com/jessicazone2000

TV Schedule

The Girl Behind the Voice: TV Alerts
www.jessica-simpson.org/alerts.html

Video

JessicaSimpson.Net: Video
www.jessicasimpson.net/html/video.html

MTV.Com: Jessica Simpson
http://jessica-simpson.mtv.com

Wallpapers

Searching for Jessica: Wallpapers
www.geocities.com/sfj_extra/wallpaper.html

The Girl Behind the Voice: Desktop
www.jessica-simpson.org/desktop.html

Webrings

Jessica Simpson Ring 4 U
http://nav.webring.yahoo.com/hub?ring=jessicasimpson4&list

Sweet Kisses Ring
http://nav.webring.yahoo.com/hub?ring=sweetkisses&list

The Heart of Jessica Webring
http://nav.webring.yahoo.com/hub?ring=heartofjessica&list

Jewel

SUPER SINGLES "Hands" | "You Were Meant for Me" | "Foolish Games" | "Who Will Save Your Soul"

Official Site

JewelJK
www.jeweljk.com

Articles

Jam! Showbiz: Music: Jewel
www.canoe.ca/JamMusicArtistsJ/jewel.html

Audio

Jewel "Audio Only" Page
http://members.aol.com/jewelpage

Discussion

Jewel EveryDay Angels List
www.quackquack.net/jewel

Yahoo! Clubs: Down So Long
http://clubs.yahoo.com/clubs/downsolong

Yahoo! Clubs: Jewel Fan Club
http://clubs.yahoo.com/clubs/jewelfanclub

Yahoo! Clubs: Jewel's Other Angels
http://clubs.yahoo.com/clubs/jewelsotherangels

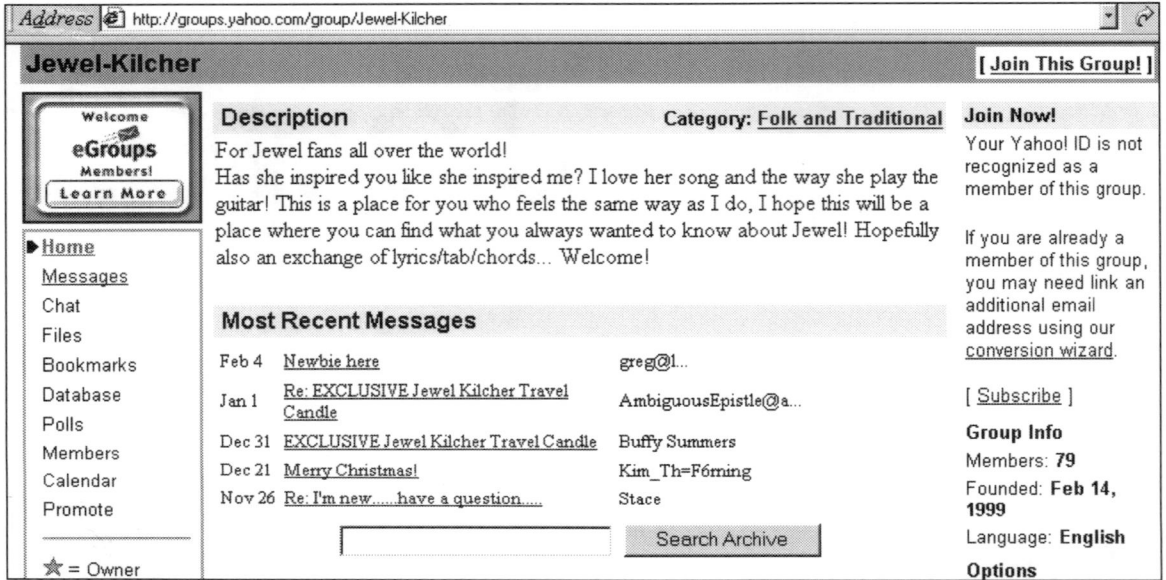

Yahoo! Groups: Jewel-Kilcher
http://groups.yahoo.com/group/Jewel-Kilcher

Ecards

Jewel Postcards
www.fortunecity.com/tinpan/penny/411/jewel/jewel.htm

FAQs

The Official Jewel Kilcher FAQ
www.smoe.org/lists/jewel/angels/faq.html

Galleries

AtPictures.Com: Jewel
www.atpictures.com/jewel

Links

Gerritt's Jewel Links
www.endor.org/jewel/links

Mosiqa Top 100 Jewel Sites
http://top100.mosiqa.com/jewel

Lyrics

Hotel Angel: Lyrics
http://members.nbci.com/hotelangeljk/Lyrics.html

JewelJK: Lyrics
www.jeweljk.com/lowend2/lyrics.html

News

Entertainment Sleuth: Jewel
http://e.sleuth.com/details.asp?Entity=2377

Reference

All Music Guide: Jewel
http://allmusic.com/cg/x.dll?p=amg&sql=1JEWEL

People Magazine Profiles: Jewel
http://people.aol.com/people/pprofiles/celebhomepage/0,3371,63,00.html

Rock on the Net: Jewel
www.rockonthenet.com/artists-j/jewel_main.htm

Wall of Sound: Jewel
http://wallofsound.go.com/artists/jewel

Yahoo! Web Celeb: Jewel
http://features.yahoo.com/webceleb/jewel

Software

Celebrity Desktop: Jewel
www.celebritydesktop.com/musicians/jewel

Top Sites

Alien's Invasion Presents Jewel Kilcher
http://users.cincyol.net/dashton

Everyday Angels - Aaron's Unofficial Jewel Page
www.smoe.org/lists/jewel/angels

Foolish Games
www.foolishgames.com

Gerrit's Jewel Page
www.endor.org/jewel

Hotel Angel
http://members.nbci.com/hotelangeljk

Java Jewel's
http://jewel.de.vu

Jewel Fan Site
www.jewelfansite.com

Jewel Impala
www.jewelkilcher.myweb.nl

Pieces of Jewel
http://jewel.zoonation.com

Planet Jewel
http://jewel.tanweb.com

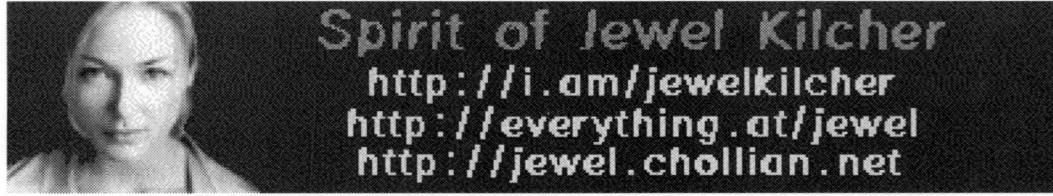

Spirit of Jewel Kilcher
http://jewel.chollian.net

VH1 Fan Club: Jewel
http://jewel.vh1.com

Webrings

Jewel Webring
http://nav.webring.yahoo.com/hub?ring=jewel&list

The Jewel Kilcher Music Ring
http://nav.webring.yahoo.com/hub?ring=jewel1&list

LAURYN HILL

SUPER SINGLES "Everything Is Everything" | "Do Wop (That Thing)" | "Ex-Factor"

Official Sites

LaurynHill.Com - The Official Lauryn Hill Web Site
www.laurynhill.com

Sony Music: Lauryn Hill
www.lauryn-hill.com

Articles

dotmusic: Lauryn Hill
www.dotmusic.com/artists/LaurynHill

Jam! Showbiz: Music: Lauryn Hill
www.canoe.ca/JamMusicArtistsH/hill_lauryn.html

Discussion

Yahoo! Clubs: Hip Hop's Queen Lauryn Hill
http://clubs.yahoo.com/clubs/hiphopsqueenlaurynhill

Yahoo! Clubs: Official Lauryn Hill Fan Club
http://clubs.yahoo.com/clubs/officiallaurynhillfanclub

Yahoo! Clubs: The Lauryn Hill School
http://clubs.yahoo.com/clubs/thelaurynhillschool

Yahoo! Groups: laurynhilllovers
http://groups.yahoo.com/group/laurynhilllovers

Galleries

AnthemPop: Lauryn Hill
www.anthempop.com/laurynhill/pictures.html

AtPictures.Com: Lauryn Hill
www.atpictures.com/lauryn

Lauryn Hill Tribute Page: Pictures
http://home.online.no/~dlysn/pictures.htm

PopFolio: Lauryn Hill
www.popfolio.com/hill.htm

Lyrics

Sony Music: Lauryn Hill: Lyrics
www.lauryn-hill.com/lyrics.html

News

Entertainment Sleuth: Lauryn Hill
http://e.sleuth.com/details.asp?Entity=2022

Reference

All Music Guide: Lauryn Hill
http://allmusic.com/cg/x.dll?p=amg&sql=1LAURYN|HILL

People Magazine Profiles: Lauryn Hill
http://people.aol.com/people/pprofiles/lhill

Rock on the Net: Lauryn Hill
www.rockonthenet.com/artists-h/laurynhill_main.htm

Wall of Sound: Lauryn Hill
http://wallofsound.go.com/artists/laurynhill

Yahoo! Web Celeb: Lauryn Hill
http://features.yahoo.com/webceleb/lauryn

Software

Celebrity Desktop: Lauryn Hill
www.celebritydesktop.com/musicians/lauryn_hill

Top Sites

A Lauryn Hill Fan Page
www.angelfire.com/ab/lauryn

Dedicated to Lauryn Hill
http://listen.to/lauryn-hill

Inspiration - Lauryn Hill
www.geocities.com/lilchills

Lauryn Hill Tribute Page
http://home.online.no/~dlysn/Index.html

Let Lauryn Light Your Fire
http://gurlpages.com/lauryn_hill

New Jersey Online: Spotlight: Lauryn Hill
www.nj.com/spotlight/hill

The Pink Lauryn Hill Site
www.pinklauryn.com

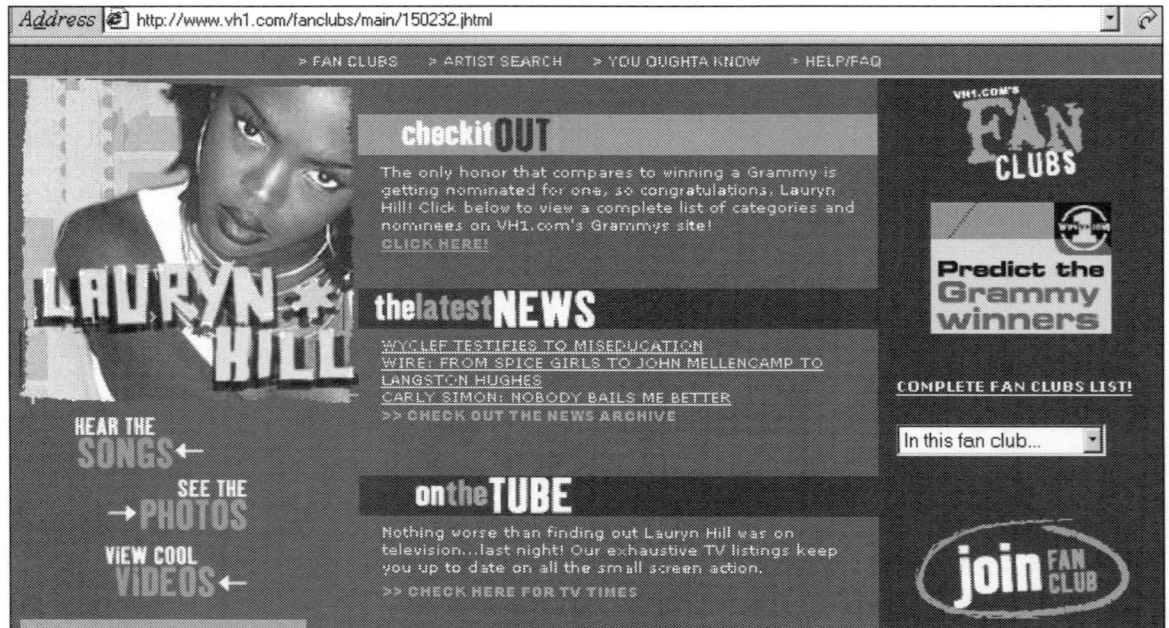

VH1 Fan Club: Lauryn Hill
http://lauryn-hill.vh1.com

Webrings

Lauryn Hill's Webring
http://nav.webring.yahoo.com/hub?ring=laurynhill&list

Lenny Kravitz

SUPER SINGLES "American Woman" | "Are You Gonna Go My Way" | "I Belong to You"

E-Mail

lennyk@virginrecords.com

Official Site

LennyKravitz.Com
www.lennykravitz.com

Audio

Chris' Lenny Kravitz Site
http://shakti.trincoll.edu/~chunt/lenny.html

Discussion

S.O.U.L - Spirit of Universal Love
www.spiritoflove.com
Yahoo! Clubs: Fly Away
http://clubs.yahoo.com/clubs/flyaway

Yahoo! Clubs: Lenny Kravitz
http://clubs.yahoo.com/clubs/lennykravitz

Yahoo! Groups: Lenny-Kravitz
http://groups.yahoo.com/group/lenny-kravitz

Yahoo! Groups: lkfans
http://groups.yahoo.com/group/lkfans

Ecards

Lenny Kr@vitz: Greeting Cards
http://pub7.bravenet.com/postcard/post.asp?usernum=574950489

Galleries

Ben's Lenny Kravitz Site
www.lenny.kravitz.site.nl

PopFolio: Lenny Kravitz
www.popfolio.com/kravitz.htm

Lyrics

Ben's Lenny Kravitz Site: Lyrics
www.lenny.kravitz.site.nl/lyrics/main.html

Merchandise

Lenny Kravitz - The Official Store
http://lennykravitzdirect.com

News

Entertainment Sleuth: Lenny Kravitz
http://e.sleuth.com/details.asp?Entity=2444

Mr. Showbiz Celebrities: Lenny Kravitz
http://mrshowbiz.go.com/people/lennykravitz

Reference

All Music Guide: Lenny Kravitz
http://allmusic.com/cg/x.dll?p=amg&sql=1LENNY|KRAVITZ

Internet Movie Database: Lenny Kravitz
http://us.imdb.com/Name?Lenny+Kravitz

Rock on the Net: Lenny Kravitz
www.rockonthenet.com/artists-k/lennykravitz_main.htm

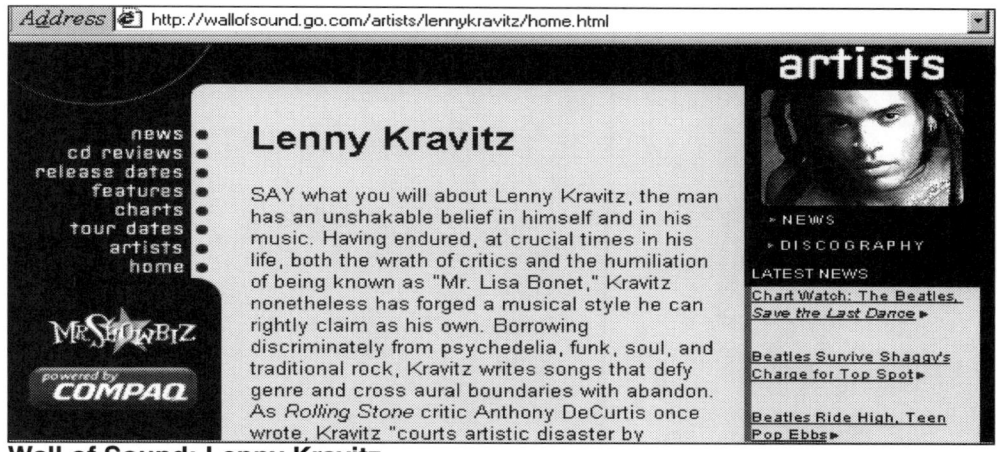

Wall of Sound: Lenny Kravitz
http://wallofsound.go.com/artists/lennykravitz

Top Sites

Ben's Lenny Kravitz Site
www.lenny.kravitz.site.nl

Freedom Train - Tribute to Lenny Kravitz
www.geocities.com/SunsetStrip/Palladium/5536

Lenny Kr@vitz
http://home.planet.nl/~kravitz/home.html

VH1 Fan Club: Lenny Kravitz
http://lenny-kravitz.vh1.com

Webrings

Lenny Kravitz Webring
http://nav.webring.yahoo.com/hub?ring=kravitz&list

LFO

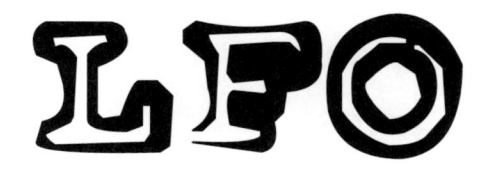

Super Singles "Girl on TV" | "I Don't Wanna Kiss You Goodnight..." | "Summer Girls"

Official Site

Arista Records: LFO
www.aristarec.com/aristaweb/LFO

Articles

LFOonline.Net: Articles & Chats
www.lfoonline.net/trans.html

Discussion

Yahoo! Clubs: LFO
http://clubs.yahoo.com/clubs/lfo

Yahoo! Clubs: LFO The Summer Boys
http://clubs.yahoo.com/clubs/lfothesummerboys

Yahoo! Clubs: LFO's Summer Girls
http://clubs.yahoo.com/clubs/lfossummergirls

Yahoo! Groups: LFO
http://groups.yahoo.com/group/LFO

Yahoo! Groups: LFO Has Got Da Flo
http://groups.yahoo.com/group/LFO_Has_Got_Da_Flo

Galleries

LFOonline.Net: Photos
www.lfoonline.net/photos/photos.html

PopFolio: LFO
www.popfolio.com/lfo.htm

Lyrics

LFO Lyrics
www.expage.com/page/linkpls7

LFOonline.Net: Lyrics
www.lfoonline.net/lyrics.html

Reference

All Music Guide: LFO
http://allmusic.com/cg/x.dll?p=amg&sql=1LFO

People Magazine Profiles: LFO
http://people.aol.com/people/pprofiles/lfo

Top Sites

Click2Music: LFO
www.click2music.com/lfo

Guys on TV
www.angelfire.com/nj2/lytefunkyones

LFO - Then & Now
http://lfo.4ever.cc

LFO Lovers
www.angelfire.com/boybands/LFOlovers

LFO UK
http://lfouk.cjb.net

LFOonline.Net
www.lfoonline.net

Love Jones
http://lfo.isgreat.net

Loungin' Wit LFO
http://gurlpages.com/louginwitlfo

Luvin LFO
www.luvinlfo.isgreat.net

Scooby Snax
www.geocities.com/SunsetStrip/Bass/8725

Unofficial LFO Page
www.geocities.com/richlfocronin

Video

Guys on TV: Video
www.angelfire.com/nj2/lytefunkyones/videos.html

LFOonline.Net: Video
www.lfoonline.net/media.html

Webrings

The LFO Connection
http://geocities.com/lfolinkcollection/ring.html

Top LFO Sites Webring
http://nav.webring.yahoo.com/hub?ring=lfo&list

lil' kim

SUPER SINGLES "How Many Licks" | "No Matter What They Say" | "Not Tonight"

Official Site

Lil' Kim's World
www.lilkim.com

Discussion

Yahoo! Clubs: Lil' Kim
http://clubs.yahoo.com/clubs/lilkim

Yahoo! Clubs: The Lil' Kim Club
http://clubs.yahoo.com/clubs/thelilkimclub

Yahoo! Clubs: The Notorous Kim
http://clubs.yahoo.com/clubs/thenotoriouskim

Yahoo! Groups: Lil Kim
http://groups.yahoo.com/group/Lil_Kim

Yahoo! Groups: LilKim
http://groups.yahoo.com/group/LilKim

Queen B's World: Greeting Cards
http://pub18.bravenet.com/postcard/post.asp?usernum=1503324741

Galleries

Lil' Kim Pictures Page
www.ewsonline.com/badboy/kim/pics.html

Lil' Kim's Domain: Picture Gallery
www.angelfire.com/mo2/first2000/gallerys.html

Lyrics

Lil' Kim's Domain: Lyrics
www.angelfire.com/mo2/first2000/lyrics.html

Reference

All Music Guide: Lil' Kim
http://allmusic.com/cg/x.dll?p=amg&sql=1LIL|KIM

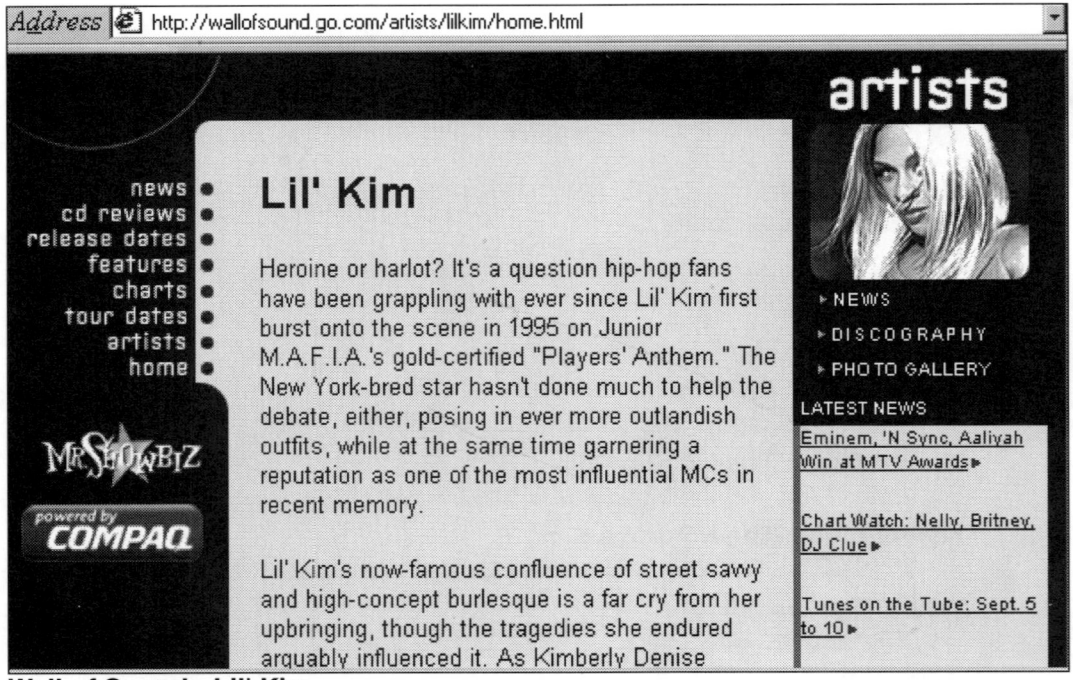

Wall of Sound: Lil' Kim
http://wallofsound.go.com/artists/lilkim

Software

Celebrity Desktop: Lil' Kim
www.celebritydesktop.com/musicians/lil_kim

Top Sites

K.I.M. Millenium
www.kim2g.com

Lil' Kim Queen of Rap
www.lilkimqueenofrap.homestead.com

Lil' Kim Zone
www.lilkimzone.com

Lil' Kim's Domain
www.lilkimsdomain.com

Lil' Kim's Universe
www.lilkim.sexypage.net

Mama Bee
www.mamabee.homestead.com

Queen B's World
http://members.spree.com/entertainment/queenb2k/default.htm

Queen Bitch World
www.queenbitchworld.com

The Lil' Kim Fortress
www.y2kim.net

The Plantinum K.I.M. Web Site
www.lilkim.org

Video

Lil' Kim's Domain: Video Clips
www.angelfire.com/mo2/first2000/video.html

Macy Gray

SUPER SINGLES "Still" | "Do Something" | "I Try"

Official Sites

Macy Gray
www.macygray.com

Macy Gray Official Asia Web Site
www.macygrayasia.com

Articles

Jam! Showbiz: Music: Macy Gray
www.canoe.ca/JamMusicArtistsG/gray_macy.html

Discussion

Yahoo! Clubs: Macy Gray The Best
http://clubs.yahoo.com/clubs/macygraythebest

Yahoo! Clubs: The Macy Gray Centre
http://clubs.yahoo.com/clubs/themacygraycentre

Lyrics

Macy on Words
www.macygrayasia.com/index_words.html

News

Entertainment Sleuth: Macy Gray
http://e.sleuth.com/details.asp?Entity=5789

Reference

All Music Guide: Macy Gray
http://allmusic.com/cg/x.dll?p=amg&sql=1MACY|GRAY

Internet Movie Database: Macy Gray
http://us.imdb.com/Name?macy+gray

People Magazine Profiles: Macy Gray
http://people.aol.com/people/pprofiles/mgray

Rock on the Net: Macy Gray
www.rockonthenet.com/artists-g/macygray.htm

Wall of Sound: Macy Gray
http://wallofsound.go.com/artists/macygray

Software

Celebrity Desktop: Macy Gray
www.celebritydesktop.com/musicians/macy_gray

Top Sites

24/7 Music of Macy Gray
http://members.nbci.com/rock247music/macygray/index.htm

Macy Gray Boulevard Café
http://come.to/macygray

Macy Gray In Style
http://go.to/macygray

Macy Gray Unofficialized
www.geocities.com/macygray00

Macy Net
www.macynet.co.uk

Planet Macy
http://community-2.webtv.net/dharma_love/MacyGray

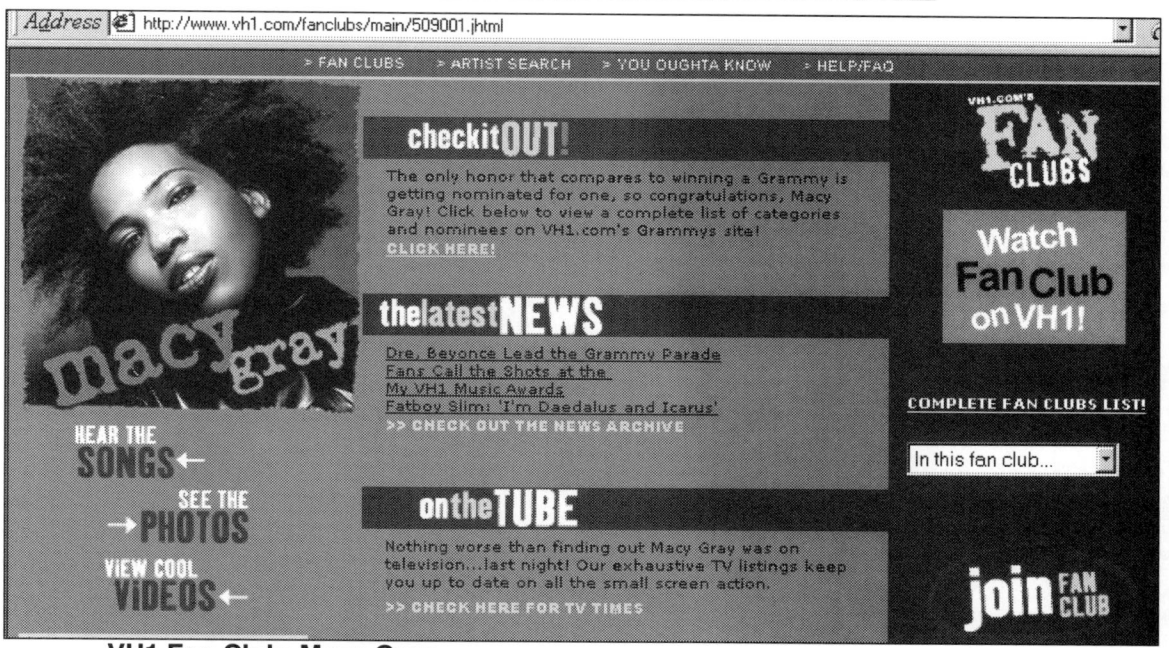

VH1 Fan Club: Macy Gray
http://macy-gray.vh1.com

Video

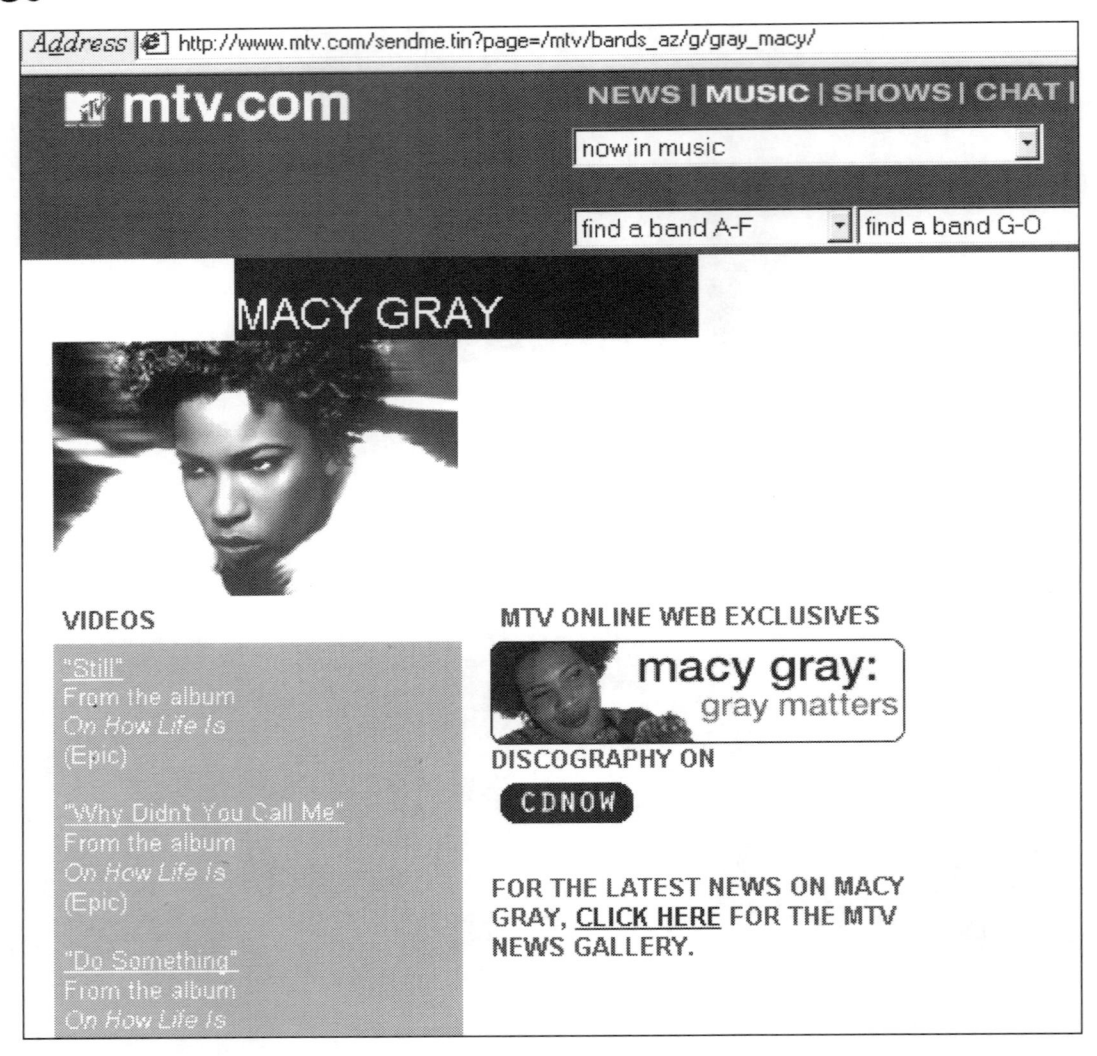

MTV.Com: Macy Gray
   http://macy-gray.mtv.com

MADONNA

SUPER SINGLES "Don't Tell Me" | "Music" | "Beautiful Stranger" | "Ray of Light" | "Power of Goodbye" | "Take a Bow" | "Rain" | "Vogue" | "Like a Prayer" | "Express Yourself" | "Open Your Heart" | "Like a Virgin" | "Lucky Star"

Official Sites

Madonna
www.madonnamusic.com

Warner Brothers Records: Madonna
www.wbr.com/madonna

Articles

Canoe: Madonna News Archive
www.canoe.ca/JamMadonna/home.html

dotmusic: Madonna
www.dotmusic.com/artists/Madonna

Jam! Showbiz: Music: Madonna
www.canoe.com/JamMadonna

The Study of Madonna
www.studyofmadonna.com

Discussion

Alt.Fan.Madonna Newsgroup Members
www.altfanmadonna.com

ICON - Official Madonna Fan Club
http://madonnafanclub.com

ICON: Message Board
www.madonnamusic.com/shared/discus/messages/board-topics.html

Madonna Fan Newsgroup
alt.fan.madonna

Madonna Power: MadonnaChat.Com
www.madonnachat.com

Madonna Power: MadonnaForum.Com
www.madonnaforum.com

Madonna Web Forum
www.madonnawebforum.com

MadonnaChat!
http://madonnachat.cjb.net

MadonnaRama: Chat
www.madonnarama.com/chat.html

Yahoo! Clubs: House of Madonna
http://clubs.yahoo.com/clubs/houseofmadonna

Yahoo! Clubs: Madomination
http://clubs.yahoo.com/clubs/madomination

Yahoo! Clubs: Madonna
http://clubs.yahoo.com/clubs/madonna

Yahoo! Clubs: Madonna Fan Club
http://clubs.yahoo.com/clubs/madonnafanclub

Yahoo! Clubs: The Madonna Haven
http://clubs.yahoo.com/clubs/themadonnahaven

Yahoo! Groups: Madonna Music 4 Me
http://groups.yahoo.com/group/Madonna-Music4Me

Ecards

Inside of Madonna: Postcards
www.inside-madonna.com/card.html

Strike-A-Post Madonna Cards
www.madonnanet.com/cards

E-Mail Services

Another.Com: Madonna Fan (yourname@madonnafan.co.uk)
www.madonnafan.co.uk

Madonna Mail (yourname@madonnamail.com)
www.madonnamail.com

Fan Art

Mad Gal
http://members.nbci.com/thepollution/page3.htm

Galleries

A List Celebrities: Madonna
www.the-alist.org/Madonna

Absolute Pictures: Madonna
www.absolutepictures.com/c/ciccone_madonna

AnthemPop: Madonna
www.anthempop.com/madonna/pictures.html

AtPictures.Com: Madonna
www.atpictures.com/madonna

M & E's Madonna Pictures — The Largest Madonna Gallery on the Net
www.madonnanet.com/madonna

M & E's Madonna Pictures
www.madonnanet.com/madonna

Madonna Art
www.madonna-art.com

Madonna Photo Collection
www.madonnaphotocollection.de

Nina Marie's Madonna Gallery
www.geocities.com/Hollywood/Picture/3673

Games

The Madonna Playground
http://web.singnet.com.sg/~a12345/playgrnd.htm

Links

CECA Madonna Top Sites
www.ceca.de/cecatop/madonna

Mosiqa Top 100 Madonna Sites
www.top.mosiqa.com/madonna

The Best of the Web: Top Madonna Sites
http://new.topsitelists.com/bestsites/tbotw-madonna/topsites.html

Lyrics

All Madonna: Lyrics
www.geocities.com/allmadonna/lyrics/lyrics.html

Pietro's Madonna Pages: Lyrics
http://madonna.excelland.com/lyre.htm

Merchandise

Dial M 4 Madonna
www.dialm4madonna.com

Madonna Catalog
http://madonnacatalog.com

Madonna Collectibles & More
www.madonnacollectibles.com

Madonna Collection
www.madonnacollection.com

Madonna Direct
http://madonnadirect.com

Madonna Merchandise
www.madonnamerchandise.com

Madonna Ultiography - The World Collector's Guide
www.buysellmadonna.com

Official Madonna Store
www.madonnadirect.com

Miscellaneous

Madonna Catalog: Madonna on Saturday Night Live
http://madonnacatalog.com/snl/snl.htm

News

Entertainment Sleuth: Madonna
http://e.sleuth.com/details.asp?Entity=2773

ICON: News
www.madonnafanclub.com/news/main.html

Madonna NewsWatch
http://web.singnet.com.sg/~a12345/news.htm

MadonnaRama
www.madonnarama.com

Madonna's Parlor
www.madonnasparlor.com

Mr. Showbiz Celebrities: Madonna
http://mrshowbiz.go.com/people/madonna

Yahoo! Groups: Madonna Texts
http://groups.yahoo.com/group/madonnatexts

Reference

All Music Guide: Madonna
http://allmusic.com/cg/x.dll?p=amg&sql=1MADONNA

Internet Movie Database: Madonna
http://us.imdb.com/Name?Madonna

People Magazine Profiles: Madonna
http://people.aol.com/people/pprofiles/madonna/vital.html

Rock on the Net: Madonna
www.rockonthenet.com/artists-m/madonna_main.htm

Wall of Sound: Madonna
http://wallofsound.go.com/artists/madonna

Software

Celebrity Desktop: Madonna
www.celebritydesktop.com/musicians/madonna

Cinema Desktop Themes: Madonna
www.cinemadesktopthemes.com/st/m/madonna_madonna.dt.1.html

Top Sites

Aikie's Madonna Pages
http://members.fortunecity.com/jaikie

All Madonna
www.allmadonna.com

AllFans.Org: Madonna
http://madonna.allfans.org

Inside of Madonna
www.inside-madonna.com

Madonna Cosmos
www.madonnacosmos.com

Madonna Dome
   www.madonnadome.com

Madonna Dreamland
   www.madonnadreamland.cjb.net

Madonna Efnet
   www.madonna-efnet.net

Madonna Electronica
   www.madonnanet.com/madoelec

Madonna Extreme
   www.madonnaextreme.com

Madonna Fanatic
   www.madonnafanatic.com

Madonna Fest
   www.madonnafest.com

Madonna Fever
   www.madonnafever.com

Madonna Land
   www.madonnaland.com

Madonna Power
   www.madonnapower.com

Madonna Request
http://go.to/madonnarequest

Madonna Sounds
www.madonnasounds.com

Madonnabilia
www.madonnabilia.com

MadonnaRama
www.madonnarama.com

Madonna's Secret Garden
www.madonnagarden.com

Madonna's World
www.madonnasworld.com

Madonnaville
www.madonnaville.de

MadonnaWeb
http://madonnaweb.com

Miss Boogie Woogie
http://go.to/missboogiewoogie

Pietro's Madonna Pages
http://madonna.excelland.com

Sindri's Madonna Page
www.sindrismadonnapage.com

Temple of Madonna
www.musicfanclubs.org/madonna

The Madonna Centre
http://come.to/MadonnaCentre

The Madonna Network
http://madonnanet.com

VH1 Fan Club: Madonna
http://madonna.vh1.com

Where Life Begins
www.geocities.com/wherelifebegins

TV Schedule

TV Now: Madonna
www.tv-now.com/stars/madonna.html

Video

Madonna TV
http://madonnatv.cjb.net

MTV.Com: Madonna
http://madonna.mtv.com

Wallpapers

Madonna Art
http://digilander.iol.it/pegaso71/madonna.htm

Madonna Desktop Wallpapers
http://madonnawallpaper.freeyellow.com

Madonna Extreme: Wallpapers
www.madonnaextreme.com/graphics/wallpapers.html

Webrings

The Madonna Pictures Webring
http://nav.webring.yahoo.com/hub?ring=madonnapics&list

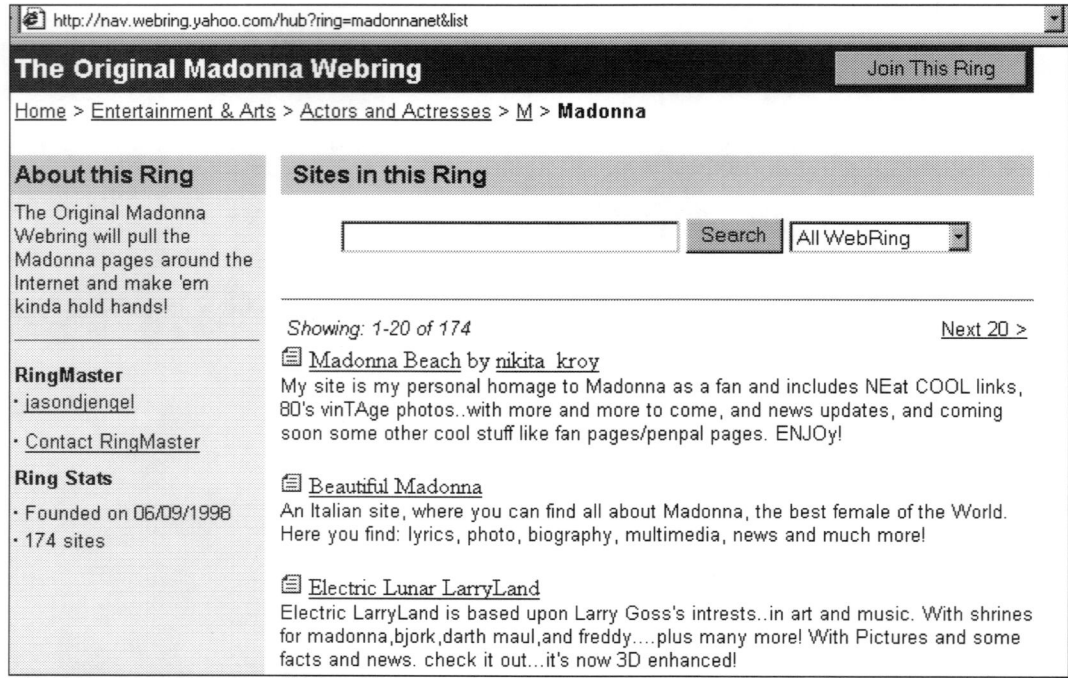

---

http://nav.webring.yahoo.com/hub?ring=madonnanet&list

The Original Madonna Webring   [Join This Ring]

Home > Entertainment & Arts > Actors and Actresses > M > **Madonna**

About this Ring

The Original Madonna Webring will pull the Madonna pages around the Internet and make 'em kinda hold hands!

RingMaster
- jasondjengel
- Contact RingMaster

Ring Stats
- Founded on 06/09/1998
- 174 sites

Sites in this Ring

[   ] [Search] [All WebRing ▼]

Showing: 1-20 of 174   Next 20 >

Madonna Beach by nikita_kroy
My site is my personal homage to Madonna as a fan and includes NEat COOL links, 80's vinTAge photos..with more and more to come, and news updates, and coming soon some other cool stuff like fan pages/penpal pages. ENJOy!

Beautiful Madonna
An Italian site, where you can find all about Madonna, the best female of the World. Here you find: lyrics, photo, biography, multimedia, news and much more!

Electric Lunar LarryLand
Electric LarryLand is based upon Larry Goss's intrests..in art and music. With shrines for madonna,bjork,darth maul,and freddy....plus many more! With Pictures and some facts and news. check it out...it's now 3D enhanced!

The Original Madonna Webring
http://nav.webring.yahoo.com/hub?ring=madonnanet&list

Mandy Moore

SUPER SINGLES "I Wanna Be With You" | "Candy" | "Walk Me Home"

Official Site

Mandy Moore - Official Site
www.mandymoore.com

Audio

AllStarz.Org: Mandy Moore: Audio
www.allstarz.org/mandymoore/audio.htm

Mandy Moore Multimedia: Audio
http://members.home.net/mandymoore/audio.htm

Discussion

Mandy Moore - Official Site: BBS
http://ultimate.infopop.com/~mandy/cgi-bin/Ultimate.cgi?action=intro

Yahoo! Clubs: Mandy Moore Central
http://clubs.yahoo.com/clubs/mandymoorecentral

Yahoo! Clubs: The Forever Mandy Club
http://clubs.yahoo.com/clubs/theforevermandyclub

Yahoo! Clubs: The Official Mandy Moore Club
http://clubs.yahoo.com/clubs/theofficialmandymooreclub

Yahoo! Clubs: The Ultimate Mandy Moore Club
http://clubs.yahoo.com/clubs/theultimatemandymooreclub

Yahoo! Groups: mandymoorenet
http://groups.yahoo.com/group/mandymoorenet

Yahoo! Groups: MandyMooreOfficialStreetTeam
http://groups.yahoo.com/group/MandyMooreOfficialStreetTeam

Yahoo! Groups: Mandy-Shes-So-Real
http://groups.yahoo.com/group/Mandy-Shes-So-Real

Galleries

Absolute Pictures: Mandy Moore
www.absolutepictures.com/m/moore_mandy

AllStarz.Org: Mandy Moore: Galleries
www.allstarz.org/mandymoore/pictures.htm

AtPictures.Com: Mandy Moore
www.atpictures.com/mandy

Beautfiul Celebrities: Mandy Moore
www.beautifulcelebrities.com/mandy_moore_pics.html

Lost in the Crowd - MandyMoore.Org: Picture Gallery
www.mandymoore.org/pictures.html

PopFolio: Mandy Moore
www.popfolio.com/mandymoore.htm

Links

FanGuide Top Mandy Moore Sites
www.fanguide.com/autorankm/mandy

Mandy Moore Top 40 @ ThinkCelebs.com
www.thinkcelebs.com/moore

Mosiqa Top 100 Mandy Moore Sites
www.top.mosiqa.com/mandy

Lyrics

Mandy Moore Multimedia: Lyrics
http://members.home.net/mandymoore/lyrics.htm

Merchandise

Mandy Moore Direct - Official Store
http://mandymooredirect.com

News

Abstracts.Net: Mandy Moore
www.abstracts.net/mandy-moore

Entertainment Sleuth: Mandy Moore
http://e.sleuth.com/details.asp?Entity=4905

Reference

All Music Guide: Mandy Moore
http://allmusic.com/cg/x.dll?p=amg&sql=1MANDY|MOORE

Internet Movie Database: Mandy Moore
http://us.imdb.com/Name?Moore,+Mandy+(II)

People Magazine Profiles: Mandy Moore
http://people.aol.com/people/pprofiles/mmoore

Software

Celebrity Desktop: Mandy Moore
www.celebritydesktop.com/musicians/mandy_moore

Lost in the Crowd - MandyMoore.Org: Downloads
www.mandymoore.org/goodies.html

Top Sites

AllStarz.Org: Mandy Moore
www.allstarz.org/mandymoore

Lost in the Crowd - MandyMoore.Org
www.mandymoore.org

Mandy Moore 4 Always
www.mandymoore4always.org

Mandy Moore Live
www.mandymoorelive.com

Mandy Moore Multimedia
http://members.home.net/mandymoore/index.htm

Mandy Moore UK
www.mandymooreuk.net

MandyMooreFan.Com
www.mandymoorefan.com

MandyMooreNet
www.mandymoorenet.com

Video

AllStarz.Org: Mandy Moore: Video
www.allstarz.org/mandymoore/video.htm

Mandy Moore Multimedia: Videos
http://members.home.net/mandymoore/videos.htm

MandyMooreFan.Com: Video
www.mandymoorefan.com/video.html

MTV.Com: Mandy Moore
http://mandy-moore.mtv.com

Wallpapers

AllStarz.Org: Mandy Moore: Wallpapers
www.allstarz.org/mandymoore/wallpaper.htm

Webrings

The ~Always Mandy~ Webring
http://nav.webring.yahoo.com/hub?ring=alwaysmandy&list

MARC ANTHONY

SUPER SINGLES "I Need to Know" | "You Sang to Me"

Official Site

Marc Anthony's Official Site
http://marcanthonyonline.com

Articles

Jam! Showbiz: Music: Marc Anthony
www.canoe.ca/JamMusicArtistsA/anthony_marc.html

Discussion

Marc Anthony Fans: Message Boards
http://marcanthonyfans.com/cgi-bin/Ultimate.cgi

Marc Anthony's Official Site: Bulletin Board
http://bbs.sonymusic.com/wwwthreads.pl?action=list&Board=marca

Marc Anthony's Official Site: Chat Room
www.marcanthonyonline.com/chat.html

Yahoo! Clubs: Marc Anthony Fan Club
http://clubs.yahoo.com/clubs/marcanthonyfanclub

Yahoo! Clubs: Marc Anthony's Club
http://clubs.yahoo.com/clubs/marcanthonysclub

Yahoo! Clubs: The Best Marc Anthony
http://clubs.yahoo.com/clubs/thebestmarcanthony

Yahoo! Groups: Marc Anthony
http://groups.yahoo.com/group/Marc_Anthony

Galleries

Absolute Pictures: Marc Anthony
www.absolutepictures.com/a/anthony_marc

Marc Anthony Photo Gallery
http://members.aol.com/FaysCookie/marcanthony.html

Merchandise

Marc Anthony - Online Store
www.signaturessuperstars.com/artists/latin/marcanthony/index.html

News

Entertainment Sleuth: Marc Anthony
http://e.sleuth.com/details.asp?Entity=119

Reference

All Music Guide: Marc Anthony
http://allmusic.com/cg/x.dll?p=amg&sql=1MARC|ANTHONY

Internet Movie Database: Marc Anthony
http://us.imdb.com/Name?Marc+Anthony

Internet Movie Database: Mariah Carey
http://us.imdb.com/Name?Mariah+Carey

People Magazine Profiles: Marc Anthony
http://people.aol.com/people/pprofiles/manthony

Rock on the Net: Marc Anthony
www.rockonthenet.com/artists-a/marcanthony.htm

Wall of Sound: Marc Anthony
http://wallofsound.go.com/artists/marcanthony

Top Sites

A Tribute to Marc Anthony
http://members.nbci.com/atributetoma/main.html

Chinese Marc Anthony Fan Site
www.whitejade.com/marcanthonyfan.html

Jenee's Marc Anthony Page
www.geocities.com/Hollywood/Film/8958

Marc Anthony Fan Club
www.marcanthonyfanclub.com

Marc Anthony Fan Page
www.marcanthonyfanpage.com

Marc Anthony Fans
www.marcanthonyfans.com

Marc Anthony Unofficial Home Page
www.marcanthonyweb.com

My Marc Anthony World
www.geocities.com/Hollywood/Club/8198/enter.html

Video

Marc Anthony Unofficial Home Page: Videos
www.marcanthonyweb.com/frameset_videos.html

Wallpapers

My Marc Anthony World: Wallpapers
www.geocities.com/Hollywood/Club/8198/wallpapers.html

Webrings

The Marc Anthony Webring
http://nav.webring.yahoo.com/hub?ring=mawr&list

Mariah Carey

SUPER SINGLES "Heartbreaker" | "Fantasy" | "My All" | "Always Be My Baby" | "Hero"

E-mail

mariahcarey@mariahcarey.org

Official Site

Mariah Carey Official Fan Club
www.mariahcarey-fanclub.com

Official Mariah Carey Tour Site
www.mariahcarey.com

Articles

dotmusic: Mariah Carey
www.dotmusic.com/artists/MariahCarey

Jam! Showbiz: Music: Mariah Carey
www.canoe.ca/JamMusicArtistsC/carey_mariah.html

MariahCarey.Org: Articles
http://mariahcarey.org/reading/articles

Audio

MariahCarey.Org: Mariah Radio
http://mariahcarey.org/radio

Discussion

MariahCarey.Org: Bulletin Board
http://home.mariah-fan.com/commun_v3/scripts/directory.pl

MariahCarey.Org: Mailing List
http://mariahcarey.org/mailinglist

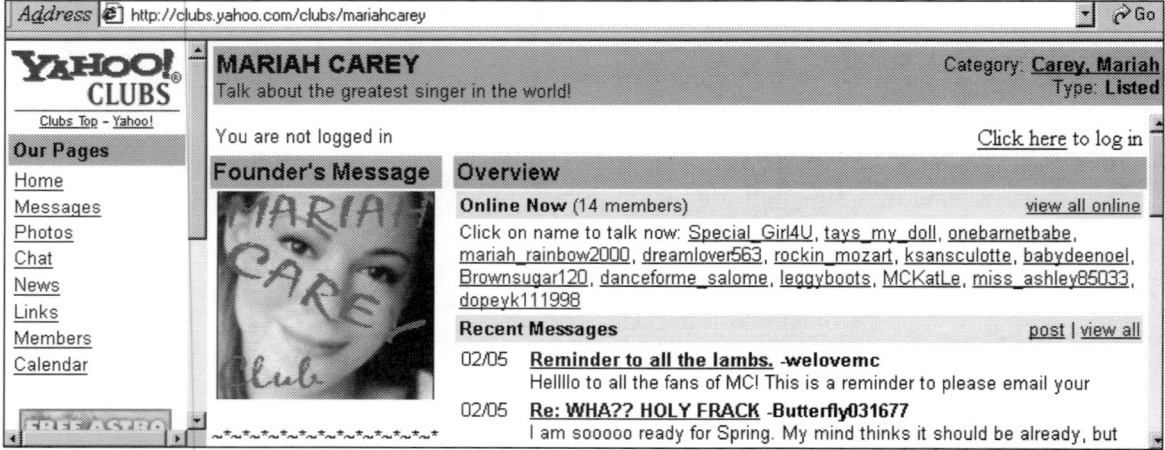

Yahoo! Clubs: Mariah Carey
http://clubs.yahoo.com/clubs/mariahcarey

Yahoo! Clubs: Mariah Carey Fantasy
http://clubs.yahoo.com/clubs/mariahcareyfantasy

Yahoo! Clubs: Rainbow Princess
http://clubs.yahoo.com/clubs/rainbowprincess

Yahoo! Clubs: The Mariah Carey Picture Club
http://clubs.yahoo.com/clubs/themariahcareypictureclub

Yahoo! Groups: mcfire
http://groups.yahoo.com/group/mcfire

Ecards

MariahCarey.Org: Postcards
http://mariahcarey.org/activities/postcards/cardrack.shtml

Galleries

A List Celebrities: Mariah Carey
www.the-alist.org/MariahCarey

Absolute Pictures: Mariah Carey
www.absolutepictures.com/c/carey_mariah

AnthemPop: Mariah Carey
www.anthempop.com/mariahcarey/pictures.html

AtPictures.Com: Mariah Carey
www.atpictures.com/mariah

Beautfiul Celebrities: Mariah Carey
www.beautifulcelebrities.com/mariah_carey_pics.html

MariahCarey.Org: Galleries
http://mariahcarey.org/incentives/photogallery.shtml

Links

Mosiqa Top 100 Mariah Carey Sites
www.top.mosiqa.com/mariah

Lyrics

MariahCarey.Org: Lyrics
http://mariahcarey.org/music/discography.shtml

Merchandise

Mariah Carey Direct
http://mariahdirect.com

News

Abstracts.Net: Mariah Carey
www.abstracts.net/mariah-carey

Entertainment Sleuth: Mariah Carey
http://e.sleuth.com/details.asp?Entity=692

MariahCarey.Org
http://mariahcarey.org

Reference

All Music Guide: Mariah Carey
http://allmusic.com/cg/x.dll?p=amg&sql=1MARIAH|CAREY

People Magazine Profiles: Mariah Carey
http://people.aol.com/people/pprofiles/celebhomepage/0,3371,76,00.html

Rock on the Net: Mariah Carey
www.rockonthenet.com/artists-c/mariahcarey_main.htm

Wall of Sound: Mariah Carey
http://wallofsound.go.com/artists/mariahcarey

Software

Artist Desktop Themes: Mariah Carey
http://artistdesktopthemes.com/st/c/mariah_carey.dt.1.html

Celebrity Desktop: Mariah Carey
www.celebritydesktop.com/musicians/mariah_carey

Cinema Desktop Themes: Mariah Carey
www.cinemadesktopthemes.com/st/c/mariah_carey.dt.1.html

MariahCarey.Org: Desktop Enhancements
http://mariahcarey.org/incentives/desktopenhancements.shtml

Top Sites

All Mariah
www.geocities.com/all_mariah

AllStarz.Org: Mariah Carey
www.allstarz.org/mariahcarey

Fly Like Mariah
www.flylikemariah.pe.ky

I Love Mariah Carey
www.ilovemariahcarey.net

Mariah Carey by Eyetouch
www.geocities.com/yavuzaytac

Mariah Carey Archives
www.mcarchives.com

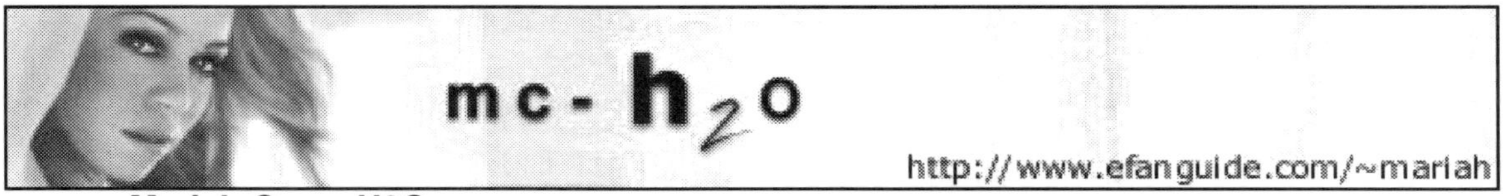

Mariah Carey H2O
www.efanguide.com/~mariah

Mariah Carey Site
http://mariahcareyfile.tripod.com

Mariah Carey X-Girlfriend
www.fansites.nl/mariah

Mariah Carey File
http://mariahcareyfile.tripod.com/english.htm

Mariah Connections
http://mariahconnections.cjb.net

Mariah Land
www.mariahland.net

Mariah Online
www.mariahonline.net

MariahCarey.Org
http://mariahcarey.org

MariahWorld.Com
www.mariahworld.com

MC Place
www.geocities.com/mc_place

Sweet Sweet Mariah Carey
www.mariahcareycentral.com

VH1 Fan Club: Mariah Carey
http://mariah-carey.vh1.com

Video

Mariah Online: Videos
www.mariahonline.net/mvideos.htm

MariahCarey.Org: Video Clips
http://mariahcarey.org/incentives/videoclips.shtml

Wallpapers

AllStarz.Org: Mariah Carey: Wallpapers
www.allstarz.org/mariahcarey/wallpaper.htm

Mariah Carey File: Wallpapers
http://mariahcareyfile.tripod.com/ewallpaper.htm

Mariah Online: Wallpapers
www.mariahonline.net/wallpaper/wallpaper.htm

MC Place: Wallpapers
www.geocities.com/mc_place/wallgeo.htm

Matchbox Twenty

SUPER SINGLES "Bent" | "Push" | "Real World" | "3 A.M."

Official Sites

Matchbox Twenty Fan Club
www.matchboxtwentyfans.com

The Official Matchbox Twenty Web Site
www.matchbox20.com

Articles

Jam! Showbiz: Music: Matchbox 20
www.canoe.ca/JamMusicArtistsM/matchbox20.html

Matchbox 20 Lovers: Articles
http://members.tripod.com/matchbox20-fans/articles.html

Discussion

Yahoo! Clubs: Matchbox 20 Lovers
http://clubs.yahoo.com/clubs/matchbox20lovers

Yahoo! Clubs: MB20's Back 2 Good
http://clubs.yahoo.com/clubs/mb20sback2good

Yahoo! Clubs: The Rest Stop
http://clubs.yahoo.com/clubs/thereststop

Yahoo! Groups: MadSeason
http://groups.yahoo.com/group/MadSeason

Yahoo! Groups: PureMatchbox20
http://groups.yahoo.com/group/PureMatchbox20

Galleries

PopFolio: Matchbox 20
www.popfolio.com/matchbox20.htm

Links

Mosiqa Top 100 Matchbox Twenty Sites
http://topsites.mosiqa.com/mb20

Lyrics

Matchbox 20 Lovers: Lyrics
http://members.tripod.com/matchbox20-fans/lyrics.html

Merchandise

Matchbox Twenty Direct - Official Store
http://matchboxtwentydirect.com

News

Entertainment Sleuth: Matchbox Twenty
http://e.sleuth.com/details.asp?Entity=4919

Reference

All Music Guide: Matchbox Twenty
http://allmusic.com/cg/x.dll?p=amg&sql=1MATCHBOX|TWENTY

Rock on the Net: Matchbox Twenty
www.rockonthenet.com/artists-m/matchbox20.htm

Wall of Sound: Matchbox Twenty
http://wallofsound.go.com/artists/matchbox20

Software

Celebrity Desktop: Matchbox Twenty
www.celebritydesktop.com/musicians/matchbox_20

Top Sites

Black Vulture's Matchbox 20 Web Site
www.matchboxtwentyonline.com

Linda's Matchbox 20 Page
www.angelfire.com/boybands/mb20

Love When You Love
www.lovewhenyoulove.com

Matchbox 20 Lovers
www.matchbox20-fans.com

Matchbox Twenty 4U
http://matchboxtwenty4u.tripod.com

Matchbox Twenty Fan
www.matchboxtwentyfan.com

Rain in Boxes
www.jump.to/mb20

The Real World - Matchbox 20
www.musicfanclubs.org/matchbox20

VH1 Fan Club: Matchbox 20
www.vh1.com/fanclubs/main/746.jhtml

Video

Matchbox 20 Lovers: Video
http://members.tripod.com/matchbox20-fans/video.html

Webrings

Back2TheRestStop
http://nav.webring.yahoo.com/hub?ring=b2trs&list

The First Matchbox 20 Webring
http://nav.webring.yahoo.com/hub?ring=canoly&list

The Unofficial Hang Webring
http://nav.webring.yahoo.com/hub?ring=hang&list

'N SYNC

SUPER SINGLES "This I Promise You" | "It's Gonna Be Me" | "Bye Bye Bye" | "Tearin' Up My Heart"

Official Sites

Jive Records - 'N Sync
www.byebyebye.com

NSYNC.COM - The Official Web Site
www.nsync.com

Articles

Always 'N Sync: Articles
www.always-nsync.com/articles.html

dotmusic: 'N Sync
www.dotmusic.com/artists/NSync

Jam! Showbiz: Music: 'N Sync
www.canoe.ca/JamMusicArtistsN/nsync.html

'N Sync Studio: Transcripts
http://nsyncstudio.com/newsroom/chat.html

Discussion

Nsync Studio: Message Board
http://pub11.ezboard.com/bnsyncstudiodotcommessage

Yahoo! Clubs: Abby's 'N Sync Fan Club
http://clubs.yahoo.com/clubs/abbysnsyncfanclub

Yahoo! Clubs: Crunk 'N Sync 24'7
http://clubs.yahoo.com/clubs/crunknsync247

Yahoo! Clubs: N Touch with 'N Sync
http://clubs.yahoo.com/clubs/ntouchwithnsync

Yahoo! Clubs: 'N Sync Pleasure
http://clubs.yahoo.com/clubs/nsyncpleasure

Yahoo! Clubs: 'N SyncStudioVIPS
http://clubs.yahoo.com/clubs/nsyncstudiovips

Yahoo! Groups: getnsyncdaily
http://groups.yahoo.com/group/getnsyncdaily

Yahoo! Groups: Jens 'N Sync Pix
http://groups.yahoo.com/group/Jens_nsync_pix

Yahoo! Groups: 'N Sync Pics Daily
http://groups.yahoo.com/group/NSYNC_Pics_Daily

Yahoo! Groups: 'N SyncFlow
http://groups.yahoo.com/group/NSyncFlow

Ecards

All Access 'N Sync: Greeting Cards
http://pub38.bravenet.com/postcard/post.asp?usernum=3244081883

'N Sync World: Postcards
http://nsyncworld.com/ecards/index.shtml

E-Mail Services

Awesome E-mail: I Love 'N Sync (yourname@ilovensync.com)
www.ilovensync.com

'N Sync E-Mail (yourname@nsyncemail.com)
www.nsyncemail.com

Fan Art

'N Sync Studio: Fan Art
http://nsyncstudio.com/fan_art

Fan Fiction

Ever After Digital 'N Sync Fan Fics
www.everafter-digital-nsync-fanfics.com

Justin's 'N Sync Fictional Library
www.nsync-fiction.com

'N Sync Imagination
www.nsyncimagination.com

Nsynctified
www.nsynctified.com

Top 100 'N Sync Fan Fiction Sites
http://new.topsitelists.com/bestsites/nsyncfanfiction/topsites.html

Galleries

Absolute Pictures: Justin Timberlake
www.absolutepictures.com/t/timberlake_justin

All Access 'N Sync: Animations
www.angelfire.com/vt/nsync/animations.html

'N Sync Pictures
http://www15.brinkster.com/annebelle/nsyncpics

NsyncFans.Net
www.nsyncfans.net

Links

Mosiqa Top 100 'N Sync Sites
www.top.mosiqa.com/nsync

nso's Top 100 'N Sync Web Sites
http://nso.hypermart.net/lspro.html

'N Sync Top 50
www.nsynctop50.com

Lyrics

'N Sync Studio: Lyrics
http://nsyncstudio.com/lyrics

Merchandise

Always 'N Sync: Trading Post
www.insidetheweb.com/mbs.cgi/mb742640

'N Sync Direct - The Official Store
http://nsyncdirect.com

News

Abstracts.Net: Justin Timberlake
www.abstracts.net/justin-timberlake-nsync

Crunk News
www.crunknews.com

Entertainment Sleuth: 'N Sync
http://e.sleuth.com/details.asp?Entity=4907

'N Sync Base
www.nsyncbase.com

'N Sync Studio: Newsroom
http://nsyncstudio.com/newsroom

NsyncFan.Org
www.nsyncfan.org

Reference

All Music Guide: 'N Sync
http://allmusic.com/cg/x.dll?p=amg&sql=1'N|SYNC

People Magazine Profiles: 'N Sync
http://people.aol.com/people/pprofiles/nsync

Rock on the Net: 'N Sync
www.rockonthenet.com/artists-n/nsync_main.htm

Wall of Sound: 'N Sync
http://wallofsound.go.com/artists/nsync

Yahoo! Web Celeb: 'N Sync
http://features.yahoo.com/webceleb/nsync

Software

Artist Desktop Themes: 'N Sync
http://artistdesktopthemes.com/gb/n/nsync.dt.1.html

Celebrity Desktop: 'N Sync
www.celebritydesktop.com/musicians/nsync

Top Sites

All Access 'N Sync
www.allaccessnsync.com

All 'N Sync
www.allnsync.com

AllFans.Org: 'N Sync
http://nsync.allfans.org

Always 'N Sync
www.always-nsync.com

Digital Rock Starz
www.digitalrockstarz.com

Jen's 'N Sync Haven
www.nsynchaven1.com

'N Sync and Anime
www.nsyncandanime.net

'N Sync Dreams
www.nsync-dreams.com

'N Sync Dreamz
www.angelfire.com/boybands/ndreamz/index.html

'N Sync Fans United
www.nsyncfansunited.com

'N Sync Forever
www.nsync-forever.com

'N Sync Galaxy
www.nsyncgalaxy.com

'N Sync Heaven
www.nsyncheaven.com

'N Sync Hometown
www.nsynchometown.com

'N Sync Nsanity
http://start.at/nsync

'N Sync Studio
http://nsyncstudio.com

'N Sync World
http://nsyncworld.com

Nsyncable
www.nsyncable.com

NsyncDaze.Com
www.nsyncdaze.com

Nsynchronize
www.nsynchronize.com

nwnsync
www.nwnsync.com

The Ultimate 'N Sync Site
www.nsyncforever.com

VH1 Fan Club: 'N Sync
www.vh1.com/fanclubs/main/500956.jhtml

TV Schedule

'N Sync Studio: TV Dates
http://nsyncstudio.com/newsroom/tv.html

Video

'N Sync Studio: Multimedia Videos
http://nsyncstudio.com/multi/video/index.html

Wallpapers

'N Sync Studio: Wallpapers
http://nsyncstudio.com/etc/background

Webrings

Crazy 4 'N Sync Webring
http://nav.webring.yahoo.com/hub?ring=crazy4nsync&list

'N Sync Mania Webring
http://nav.webring.yahoo.com/hub?ring=nsyncmania&list

'N Sync's Got It Webring
http://nav.webring.yahoo.com/hub?ring=shoot&list

Nirvana

SUPER SINGLES "Smells Like Teen Spirit" | "Come As You Are" | "All Apologies" | "Lithium"

Articles

Jam! Showbiz: Music: Nirvana
www.canoe.ca/JamMusicArtistsN/nirvana.html

Audio

The Internet Nirvana Fan Club: Sound Gallery
http://nirvanaclub.com/sounds.htm

Discussion

Nirvana Chat
www.nirvanachat.net

The Internet Nirvana Fan Club: Discussion Forum
http://nirvanaclub.com/cgi-bin/ubbcgi/Ultimate.cgi?action=intro

Yahoo! Clubs: Drain You
http://clubs.yahoo.com/clubs/drainyou

Yahoo! Clubs: Nirvana
http://clubs.yahoo.com/clubs/nirvana

Yahoo! Clubs: Nirvana Lover's Hangout
http://clubs.yahoo.com/clubs/nirvanalovershangout

Yahoo! Groups: nirvana-and-hole
http://groups.yahoo.com/group/nirvana-and-hole

Yahoo! Groups: nirvanafan
http://groups.yahoo.com/group/nirvanafan

FAQs

The Internet Nirvana Fan Club: FAQ
http://nirvanaclub.com/nfc_faq.htm

Galleries

AtPictures.Com: Nirvana
www.atpictures.com/nirvana

NirvanaFreak.Net: Pictures
www.netacc.net/~extreme/pics2.html

The Internet Nirvana Fan Club: Galleries
http://nirvanaclub.com/pics.htm

Vladislav Bajev's Nirvana Pictures Archive
http://nirvanaclub.com/pictures

Links

Mosiqa Top 100 Nirvana Sites
www.top.mosiqa.com/nirvana

Top 25 Nirvana Sites
http://nirvana25.hypermart.net/top/index.html

Lyrics

The Internet Nirvana Fan Club: Lyrics
http://nirvanaclub.com/lyrics

News

Nirvana Freak.Net: News
www.netacc.net/~extreme/news.html

The Internet Nirvana Fan Club: News
http://nirvanaclub.com/news.html

Reference

All Music Guide: Nirvana
http://allmusic.com/cg/x.dll?p=amg&sql=1NIRVANA

Rock on the Net: Nirvana
www.rockonthenet.com/artists-n/nirvana_main.htm

The Complete List of Nirvana Songs
http://nirvanaclub.com/text/songs.txt

The Internet Nirvana Fan Club: Facts & Information
http://nirvanaclub.com/facts

Wall of Sound: Nirvana
http://wallofsound.go.com/artists/nirvana

Software

Artist Desktop Themes: Nirvana
http://artistdesktopthemes.com/gb/n/nirvana.dt.1.html

Celebrity Desktop: Nirvana
www.celebritydesktop.com/musicians/nirvana

Downer - A Nirvana Web Site: Downloads
http://members.nbci.com/_XMCM/downr/downloads_index.html

Nirvana for Your PC
http://nirvanaclub.com/compstuff.htm

Top Sites

Downer - A Nirvana Web Site
http://downer.ipfox.com

Heart-Shaped Box Web Page
www.nirvanapage.com

Never Fade Away
http://home.online.no/~olaeik/Nirvana

Nirvana-Rocks.Com
www.nirvana-rocks.com

NirvanaFreak.Net
www.nirvanafreak.net

NirvanaWay
http://nirvana.ipfox.com

NirvanaWeb.Com
www.nirvanaweb.com

The Internet Nirvana Fan Club
http://nirvanaclub.com

The Happening Nirvana Archive
www.digitalnirvana.net/happening

VH1 Fan Club: Nirvana
http://nirvana.vh1.com

Video

The Internet Nirvana Fan Club: Movie Gallery
http://nirvanaclub.com/movies.htm

Webrings

Breed - The Nirvana Webring
http://nav.webring.yahoo.com/hub?ring=breed&list

In The Sun, The Nirvana Webring
http://nav.webring.yahoo.com/hub?ring=kurt07b&list

School - The Nirvana Webring
http://nav.webring.yahoo.com/hub?ring=kurt&list

no doubt

SUPER SINGLES "Simple Kind of Life" | "Ex-Girlfriend" | "New" | "Don't Speak" | "Just a Girl"

E-Mail

nodoubt@nodoubt.com

Official Site

No Doubt
www.nodoubt.com

Articles

Artificially Tragic: News
www.nd-lauren.net/news/news

dotmusic: No Doubt
www.dotmusic.com/artists/NoDoubt

Jam! Showbiz: Music: No Doubt
www.canoe.ca/JamMusicArtistsN/nodoubt.html

Discussion

Yahoo! Clubs: Gwen Stefani
http://clubs.yahoo.com/clubs/gwenstefani

Yahoo! Clubs: No Doubt
http://clubs.yahoo.com/clubs/nodoubt

Yahoo! Clubs: No Doubt's Planet
http://clubs.yahoo.com/clubs/nodoubtsplanet

Yahoo! Groups: No Doubt
http://groups.yahoo.com/group/no_doubt

Yahoo! Groups: stefanig
http://groups.yahoo.com/group/stefanig

Ecards

Let's Get Back: No Doubt Postcards
www.geocities.com/letsgetbackforever/postcards.html

Galleries

AtPictures.Com: Gwen Stefani
www.atpictures.com/gwen

Links

Mosiqa Top 100 No Doubt Sites
www.top.mosiqa.com/nodoubt

No Doubt Top Sites
www.topsitelists.com/run/nodoubt/topsites.html

Lyrics

NoDoubtOnline.Com: Lyrics
www.musicfanclubs.org/nodoubt/Lyrics/Index.html

Merchandise

No Doubt Direct - The Official Store
http://nodoubtdirect.com

Reference

All Music Guide: No Doubt
http://allmusic.com/cg/x.dll?p=amg&sql=1NO|DOUBT

Rock on the Net: No Doubt
www.rockonthenet.com/artists-n/nodoubt_main.htm

Wall of Sound: No Doubt
http://wallofsound.go.com/artists/nodoubt

Software

No Doubt Obsessed: Downloads
www.geocities.com/rulez6969/downloads.htm

Top Sites

AllFans.Org: No Doubt
http://nodoubt.allfans.org

Artificially Tragic
www.nd-lauren.net

Got Doubt?
http://gotdoubt.cjb.net

Let's Get Back
www.geocities.com/letsgetbackforever

Little Bit of No Doubt
www.angelfire.com/mn/aynsley/nodoubt.html

No Doubt Obsessed
http://jump.to/obsessed

No Doubt Universe
www.nduniverse.com

NoDoubtOnline.Com
www.nodoubtonline.com

Simply Saturn
www.all.at/nodoubt

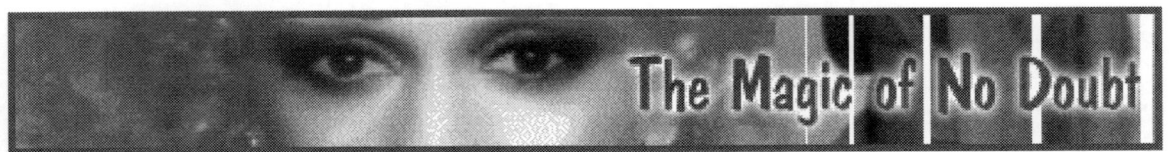

The Magic of No Doubt
www.tstonramp.com/~dkayatta

Tragically Pink
www.angelfire.com/nj3/pink/enter

VH1 Fan Club: No Doubt
www.vh1.com/fanclubs/main/1003.jhtml

Video

MTV.Com: No Doubt
http://no-doubt.mtv.com

Wallpapers

Let's Get Back: Wallpapers
www.geocities.com/letsgetbackforever/wallpapers.html

Webrings

No Doubt -WORLD-
http://nav.webring.yahoo.com/hub?ring=ndworld&list

Spider Webs - A No Doubt Webring
http://nav.webring.yahoo.com/hub?ring=gwen&list

The High Postin' No Doubt Ring
http://nav.webring.yahoo.com/hub?ring=no_doubt&list

oasis

Super Singles "Champagne Supernova" | "Wonderwall" | "Supersonic"

Official Site

Official Oasis Web Site
www.oasisinet.com

Articles

Canoe: Oasis News Archive
www.canoe.ca/JamOasis/home.html

dotmusic: Oasis
www.dotmusic.com/artists/Oasis

Jam! Showbiz: Music: Oasis
www.canoe.com/JamOasis

Underneath the Sky: Articles
www.musicfanclubs.org/oasis/articles.html

Audio

Underneath the Sky: Audio
www.musicfanclubs.org/oasis/sounds.html

Discussion

Yahoo! Clubs: Oasis
http://clubs.yahoo.com/clubs/oasis

Yahoo! Clubs: Oasis Official Club
http://clubs.yahoo.com/clubs/oasisofficialclub

Yahoo! Clubs: Oasis Official Fans Club
http://clubs.yahoo.com/clubs/oasisofficialfansclub

Yahoo! Clubs: Standing on Oasis
http://clubs.yahoo.com/clubs/standingonoasis

Yahoo! Groups: Oasis
http://groups.yahoo.com/group/oasis

FAQs

Oasis FAQ
www.geocities.com/SunsetStrip/Underground/3284/contents.html

Galleries

PopFolio: Oasis
www.popfolio.com/oasis.htm

Links

Oasis Fan Sites
http://64.33.72.188/fans/fansites.html

The Master Plan: Links Database
www.the-masterplan.com/tmp/scripts/links/dclinks.cgi

The Top 100 Oasis Sites
www.topsitelists.com/start/top50oasis/topsites.html

Lyrics

Underneath the Sky: Lyrics
www.musicfanclubs.org/oasis/lyrics.html

News

Entertainment Sleuth: Oasis
http://e.sleuth.com/details.asp?Entity=5853

Reference

All Music Guide: Oasis
http://allmusic.com/cg/x.dll?p=amg&sql=1OASIS

Rock on the Net: Oasis
www.rockonthenet.com/artists-o/oasis_main.htm

Wall of Sound: Oasis
http://wallofsound.go.com/artists/oasis

Software

Artist Desktop Themes: Oasis
http://artistdesktopthemes.com/gb/o/oasis.dt.1.html

Celebrity Desktop: Oasis
www.celebritydesktop.com/musicians/oasis

Oasis Font
http://64.33.72.188/downloads/index.html

Top Sites

100% Oasis
http://listen.to/cyberoasis

Oasis Central
www.oasiscentral.com

The Mad Ferret
www.oa515.com

The Master Plan
www.the-masterplan.com

The Oasis
www.theoasis.co.uk

Underneath the Sky
www.musicfanclubs.org/oasis

Where Did It All Go Wrong?
www.wherediditallgowrong.com

Video

The Mad Ferret: Videos
www.oa515.com/vids.htm

Underneath the Sky: Video Clips
www.musicfanclubs.org/oasis/vidclips.html

Webrings

M-M-Mad For It!! The Crazy Side of Oasis
http://nav.webring.yahoo.com/hub?ring=madforit&list

The Be Here Now Oasis Ring
http://nav.webring.yahoo.com/hub?ring=megring&list

The Where Did It All Go Wrong? Oasis Ring
http://nav.webring.yahoo.com/hub?ring=oasis1234&list

O-Town

SUPER SINGLE "Liquid Dreams"

Official Site

O-Town Official Site
www.o-town.com

Discussion

Yahoo! Clubs: otown
http://clubs.yahoo.com/clubs/otown

Yahoo! Clubs: O-Town Central
http://clubs.yahoo.com/clubs/otowncentral

Yahoo! Clubs: O-Town Heaven
http://clubs.yahoo.com/clubs/otownheaven

Yahoo! Clubs: O-Town Official Club
http://clubs.yahoo.com/clubs/otownofficalclub

Yahoo! Groups: O-Town Bands Party
http://groups.yahoo.com/group/O-Town_Bands_Party

Yahoo! Groups: O-Town-Fans
http://groups.yahoo.com/group/O-Town-Fans

Merchandise

Signature Superstars: O-Town
www.signaturessuperstars.com/artists/pop/otown/index.html

News

Entertainment Sleuth: O-Town
http://e.sleuth.com/details.asp?Entity=6112

Reference

All Music Guide: O-Town
http://allmusic.com/cg/x.dll?p=amg&sql=10|TOWN

Top Sites

Click2Music: O-Town
www.click2music.com/otown

O-Town Central
www.otowncentral.net

O-Town on the Net
www.efanguide.com/~otown

Optimum O-Town
www.expage.com/0town

The Unofficial O-Town Fan Page
http://devoted.to/OTown

Webrings

O-Town
http://nav.webring.yahoo.com/hub?ring=otown&list

O-Town Band
http://nav.webring.yahoo.com/hub?ring=otownband&list

Official Site | **pearl jam**

pearl jam

SUPER SINGLES "Even Flow" | "Jeremy" | "Given to Fly" | "Last Kiss"

Official Site

Pearl Jam Synergy
www.sonymusic.com/artists/PearlJam

Articles

Canoe: Pearl Jam News Archive
www.canoe.ca/JamMusicPearlJam/home.html

dotmusic: Pearl Jam
www.dotmusic.com/artists/PearlJam

Jam! Showbiz: Music: Pearl Jam
www.canoe.ca/JamMusicArtistsP/pearljam.html

Discussion

Yahoo! Clubs: Faithful Pearl Jam Club
http://clubs.yahoo.com/clubs/faithfullpearljamclub

Yahoo! Clubs: Pearl Jam Club
http://clubs.yahoo.com/clubs/pearljamclub

Yahoo! Clubs: pearljam
http://clubs.yahoo.com/clubs/pearljam

Yahoo! Groups: Pearl Jam
http://groups.yahoo.com/group/Pearl_Jam_

Yahoo! Groups: Pearl-Jam
http://groups.yahoo.com/group/Pearl-Jam

Links

Links to Pearl Jam Sites
http://members.tripod.com/~pugskank/pjlinks.html

Lyrics

The Pearl Jam Network: Song Archive
www.pearljamnetwork.com/archive/index.shtml

The Sky I Scrape - A Pearl Jam Lyrical Database
www.eden.rutgers.edu/~sgh

Merchandise

Pass It Around - The Pearl Jam Trader's Page
www.freespeech.org/passitaround

Pearl Jam Official Store
http://pearljamdirect.com

News

Entertainment Sleuth: Pearl Jam
http://e.sleuth.com/details.asp?Entity=4903

Five Horizons - A Pearl Jam Fanzine
www.fivehorizons.com

Reference

All Music Guide: Pearl Jam
http://allmusic.com/cg/x.dll?p=amg&sql=1PEARL|JAM

Rock on the Net: Pearl Jam
www.rockonthenet.com/artists-p/pearljam_main.htm

Wall of Sound: Pearl Jam
http://wallofsound.go.com/artists/pearljam

Software

Celebrity Desktop: Pearl Jam
www.celebritydesktop.com/musicians/pearl_jam

Top Sites

All Those Yesterdays
www.pearljam.hispeed.com

Dirty Frank's Pearl Jam Page
http://members.tripod.com/~pugskank/pearljam.html

EvenFlow.Org
www.evenflow.org

Pearl Jam - Ten Club
www.tenclub.net

Pearl Jam Vault
www.pauserecord.com/john/pjvault

The Pearl Jam Network
www.pearljamnetwork.com

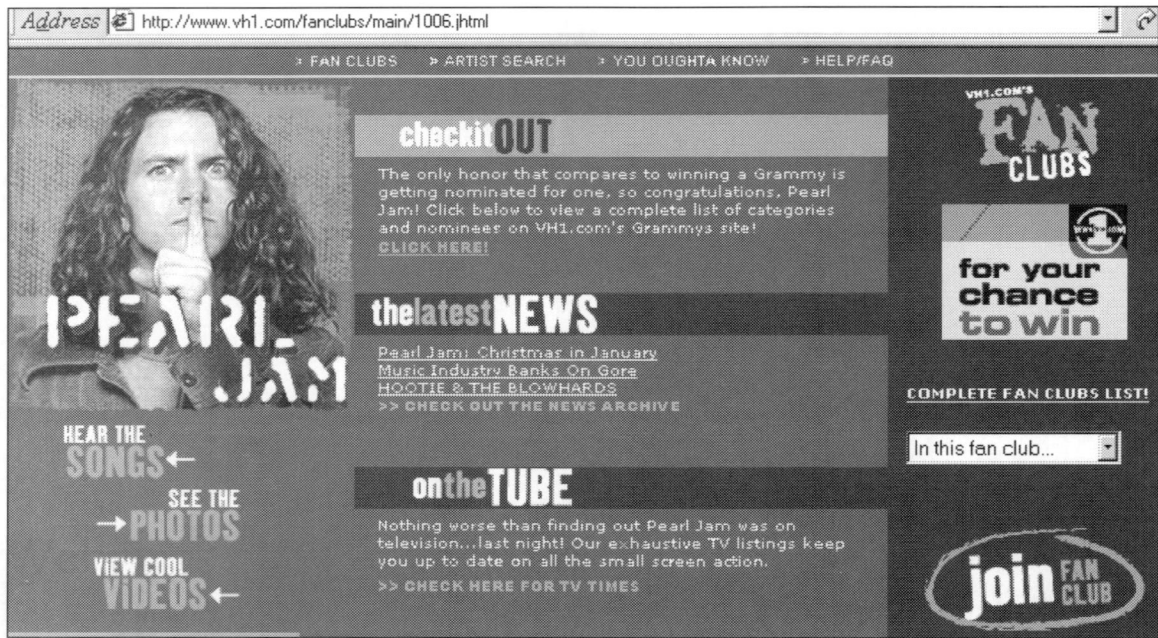

VH1 Fan Club: Pearl Jam
http://pearl-jam.vh1.com

Webrings

Dirty Frank's Pearl Jam Webring
http://nav.webring.yahoo.com/hub?ring=dirtyfrank&list

Pink

SUPER SINGLES "There Ya Go" | "Most Girls" | "You Make Me Sick"

E-mail

fanmail@pinkspage.com

Official Site

Pink's Page
www.pinkspage.com

Articles

Pink News: Articles
www.pinknews.f2s.com/newarticles.htm

Discussion

Pink News: Message Board
http://forumcities.com/messageboard/robindeangel.html

Yahoo! Clubs: Absolutely Pink
http://clubs.yahoo.com/clubs/absolutelypink

Yahoo! Clubs: Official Pink Club
http://clubs.yahoo.com/clubs/officialpinkclub

Yahoo! Clubs: Passionately Pink
http://clubs.yahoo.com/clubs/passionatelypink

Yahoo! Clubs: Pink's Split Personality Clique
http://clubs.yahoo.com/clubs/pinkssplitpersonalityclique

Yahoo! Groups: Pink Fans
http://groups.yahoo.com/group/Pink_Fans

Yahoo! Groups: Think Pink
http://groups.yahoo.com/group/Think-Pink

FAQs

Here She Comes: FAQ
www.angelfire.com/oh3/justtobeclose/faq.html

Galleries

Here She Comes: Pictures
www.angelfire.com/rnb/Pink/mainpic.html

Nabou.com: Celebrities: Pink: Photo Galleries
www.nabou.com/celebrities/pink/photo_galleries/index.html

Pink News: Gallery
www.pinknews.f2s.com/newgallery.htm

Lyrics

AllLyrics.Net: Pink
www.alllyrics.net/p/pink

Here She Comes: Lyrics
www.angelfire.com/oh3/justtobeclose/pinklyrix.html

It's a Pink Thing: Lyrics
www.angelfire.com/rock/Kandi/lyricsmain.html

News

Here She Comes: News
www.angelfire.com/oh3/justtobeclose/pinknews.html

Pink News
www.pinknews.f2s.com

Reference

All Music Guide: Pink
http://allmusic.com/cg/x.dll?p=amg&sql=1PINK

Rock on the Net: Pink
www.rockonthenet.com/artists-p/pink.htm

Wall of Sound: Pink
http://wallofsound.go.com/artists/pink

Software

Pink Connections: Downloads
http://oberon.spaceports.com/%7Epink/downloads.html

Top Sites

Always Pink
www.always-pink.com

Can't Take Me Home
http://canttakemehome.fanspace.com/frames.html

Here She Comes
www.angelfire.com/rnb/Pink

It's a Pink Thing
www.angelfire.com/rock/Kandi/pinkpage.html

Nabou.com: Celebrities: Pink
www.nabou.com/celebrities/pink

Paint the World Pink
www.geocities.com/genienabottle2000/PinkPage1.html

Pink Connections
http://oberon.spaceports.com/%7Epink

Pink News
www.pinknews.f2s.com

Pink's Nest on the Web
www.pinksnest.com

Pink's Private Show
www.geocities.com/pinks_private_show

PinksDaBomb
http://pinksdabomb.tripod.com

PinkFans.Com
www.pinkfans.com

Planet Pink
http://members.dencity.com/4pink/index.html

Video

GetMusic.Com: Pink
www.getmusic.com/pop/pink

MTV.Com: Pink
http://pink.mtv.com

Wallpapers

Nabou.com: Celebrities: Pink: Wallpaper
www.nabou.com/celebrities/pink/wallpaper/index.html

Red Hot Chili Peppers

SUPER SINGLES "Otherside" | "Californication" | "Scar Tissue" | "Soul 2 Squeeze" | "Aearoplane" | "Give It Away" | "Higher Ground" | "Love Rollercoaster" | "Suck My Kiss" | "Warped"

Official Site

redhotchilipeppers online
www.redhotchilipeppers.com

Articles

dotmusic: Red Hot Chili Peppers
www.dotmusic.com/artists/RedHotChiliPeppers

Jam! Showbiz: Music: Red Hot Chili Peppers
www.canoe.ca/JamMusicArtistsR/redhotchilipeppers.html

Audio

Warped: Audio
http://users.northnet.com.au/~generic/peppers/AudVid.html

Discussion

Yahoo! Clubs: Anthony Kiedis
http://clubs.yahoo.com/clubs/anthonykiedis

Yahoo! Clubs: Red Hot Chili Peppers
http://clubs.yahoo.com/clubs/redhotchilipeppers

Yahoo! Clubs: The Red Hot Chili Peppers Official Club
http://clubs.yahoo.com/clubs/theredhotchilipeppersoc

Yahoo! Groups: Red Hot Chili Peppers Mailing List
http://groups.yahoo.com/group/redhotchilipeppers

Ecards

Behind the Sun: Greeting Cards
http://pub36.bravenet.com/postcard/post.asp?usernum=3048763903

E-Mail Services

fun2mail.com: Red Hot Chili Peppers Fan (yourname@redhotchilipeppersfan.com)
www.redhotchilipeppersfan.com

Galleries

PopFolio: Red Hot Chili Peppers
www.popfolio.com/redhotchilipeppers.htm

Lyrics

Mattias' Red Hot Place: Lyrics
http://hjem.get2net.dk/rhcp/lyrics.html

The RHCP Pierre's Page
http://funkydream.free.fr/parole.html

Merchandise

Red Hot Chili Peppers Direct - The Official Store
http://chilipeppersdirect.com

News

Entertainment Sleuth: Red Hot Chili Peppers
http://e.sleuth.com/details.asp?Entity=5763

Planet of Yertle the Turtle: News
http://home6.swipnet.se/~w-61895/rhcp/news.htm

Reference

All Music Guide: Red Hot Chili Peppers
http://allmusic.com/cg/x.dll?p=amg&sql=1RED|HOT|CHILI|PEPPERS

Rock on the Net: Red Hot Chili Peppers
www.rockonthenet.com/artists-r/redhotchilipeppers_main.htm

Wall of Sound: Red Hot Chili Peppers
http://wallofsound.go.com/artists/redhotchilipeppers

Top Sites

Anthony Kiedes Universe
www.kiedis.net

Behind the Sun
http://fly.to/behindthesun

Give It Away
www.thefunkymonks.com

Mattias' Red Hot Place
http://fly.to/rhcp

Muthaland - A Red Hot Chili Peppers Site
www.rpi.net.au/~mutha

Parallel Universe: Red Hot Chili Peppers
www.geocities.com/aeropeppers/rhcp.html

Planet of Yertle the Turtle
http://come.to/rhcp

Red Hot Chili Peppers - Unofficial Site
www.redhotchilipeppers.org.uk

Red Hot Chili Peppers Circus
www.geocities.com/Vienna/Studio/1528/main.htm

The Chilean Brotherhood (Spanish)
www.geocities.com/latapiat

The Red Hot Page
http://redhotpage.hem.netlink.se

VH1 Fan Club: Red Hot Chili Peppers
www.vh1.com/fanclubs/main/1012.jhtml

Warped
http://users.northnet.com.au/~generic/peppers

Video

MTV.Com: Red Hot Chili Peppers
http://red-hot-chili-peppers.mtv.com

The Chilean Brotheroood: Video
www.geocities.com/latapiat/videos.htm

Webrings

Red Hot Ring
http://nav.webring.yahoo.com/hub?ring=rhcp&list

Ricky Martin

SUPER SINGLES "Livin' La Vida Loca" | "Cup of Life" | "She Bangs" | "She's All I Ever Had"

Official Site

Ricky Martin Official Fan Club
www.rickymartinfanclub.net

RickyMartin - Official Site
www.rickymartin.com

Articles

dotmusic: Ricky Martin
www.dotmusic.com/artists/RickyMartin

Jam! Showbiz: Music: Ricky Martin
www.canoe.ca/JamMusicArtistsM/martin_ricky.html

Audio

Ricky Martin Vuelve: Music
http://rickymartinmanagement.com/english/music/musicframe.htm

Discussion

Yahoo! Clubs: Pix of Ricky Martin
http://clubs.yahoo.com/clubs/pixofrickymartin

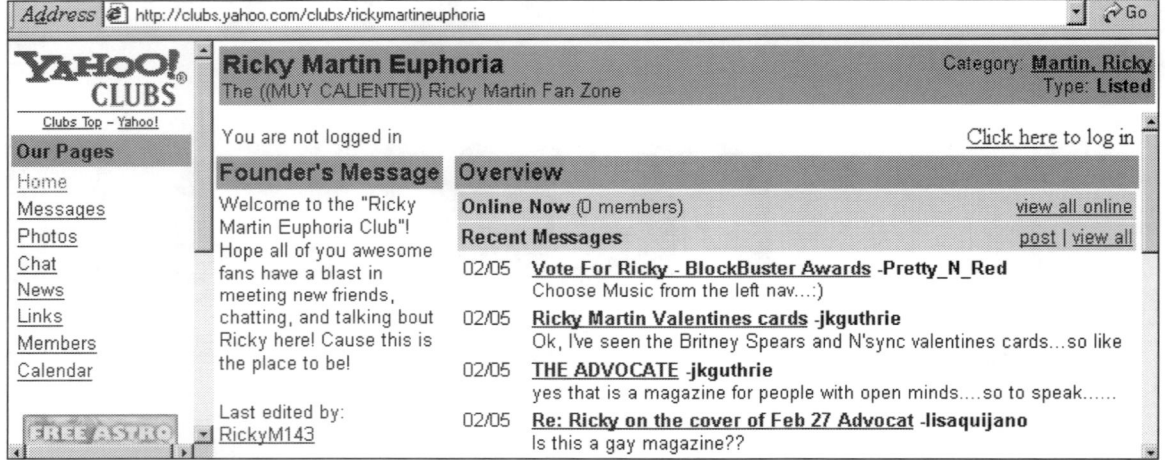

Yahoo! Clubs: Ricky Martin Euphoria
http://clubs.yahoo.com/clubs/rickymartineuphoria

Yahoo! Clubs: Sweet Ricky Martin
http://clubs.yahoo.com/clubs/sweetrickymartin

Yahoo! Clubs: The Ricky Martin Club
http://clubs.yahoo.com/clubs/therickymartinclub

Yahoo! Groups: Ricky Martin Luvers
http://groups.yahoo.com/group/Ricky_Martin_Luvers

Galleries

A List Celebrities: Ricky Martin
www.the-alist.org/RickyMartin

Absolute Pictures: Ricky Martin
www.absolutepictures.com/m/martin_ricky

AtPictures.Com: Ricky Martin
www.atpictures.com/ricky

Nabou.com: Celebrities: Ricky Martin: Photo Galleries
www.nabou.com/celebrities/ricky_martin/photo_galleries/index.html

Ricky Martin - Sizzling & Seductive
www.rmsizzling.com

Ricky Martin Vuelve: Gallery
http://rickymartinmanagement.com/english/gallery/photo_gallery.htm

Links

FanGuide Top Ricky Martin Sites
www.fanguide.com/autorankm/ricky

Mosiqa Top 100 Ricky Martin Sites
http://topsites.mosiqa.com/ricky

Lyrics

Erica's Ricky Martin Fan Site: Lyrics
www.angelfire.com/wi/rickymartin2000/lyrics.html

Nabou.com: Celebrities: Ricky Martin: Lyrics
www.nabou.com/celebrities/ricky_martin/lyrics/index.html

Merchandise

Ricky Direct - The Official Store
http://rickydirect.com

News

Abstracts.Net: Ricky Martin
www.abstracts.net/ricky-martin

Entertainment Sleuth: Ricky Martin
http://e.sleuth.com/details.asp?Entity=2846

Mr. Showbiz Celebrities: Ricky Martin
http://mrshowbiz.go.com/people/rickymartin

Ricky Martin Vuelve: News
http://rickymartinmanagement.com/english/news/newsframe.htm

Reference

All Music Guide: Ricky Martin
http://allmusic.com/cg/x.dll?p=amg&sql=1RICKY|MARTIN

Internet Movie Database: Ricky Martin
http://us.imdb.com/Name?Ricky+Martin

Rock on the Net: Ricky Martin
www.rockonthenet.com/artists-m/rickymartin_main.htm

Wall of Sound: Ricky Martin
http://wallofsound.go.com/artists/rickymartin

Yahoo! Web Celeb: Ricky Martin
http://features.yahoo.com/webceleb/ricky

Software

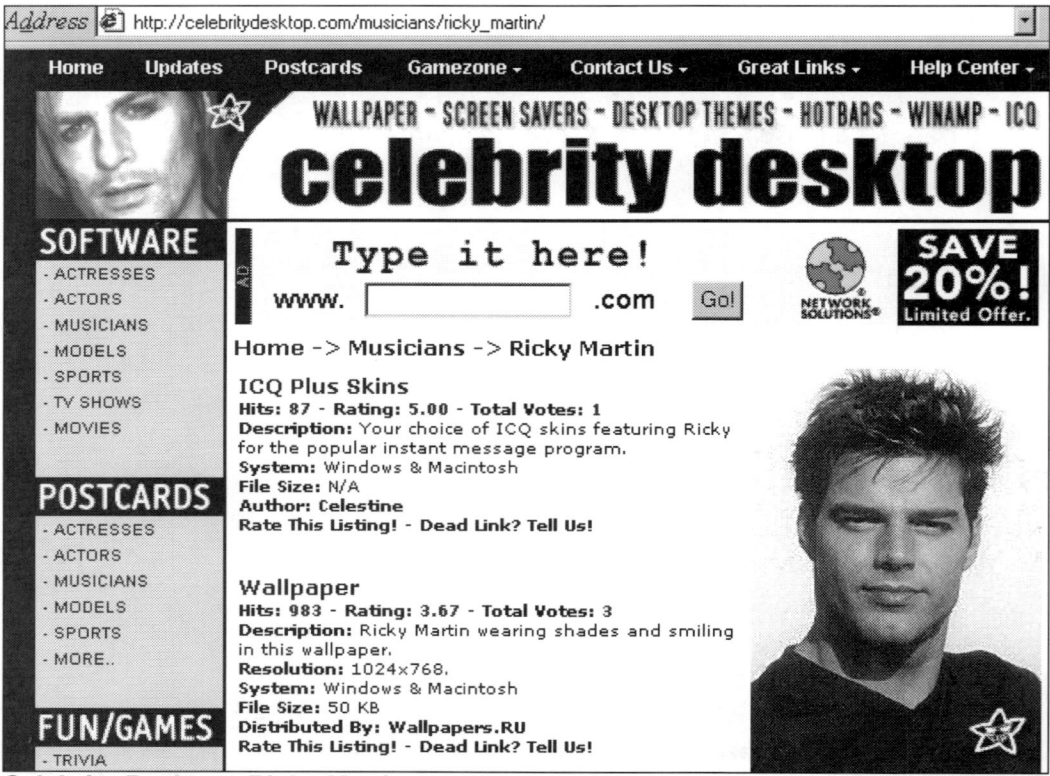

Celebrity Desktop: Ricky Martin
www.celebritydesktop.com/musicians/ricky_martin

Cinema Desktop Themes: Ricky Martin
www.cinemadesktopthemes.com/st/m/ricky_martin.dt.1.html

Top Sites

All About Ricky
http://members.nbci.com/sapphire00

Erica's Ricky Martin Fan Site
www.angelfire.com/wi/rickymartin2000

Nabou.com: Celebrities: Ricky Martin
www.nabou.com/celebrities/ricky_martin

Ricky Martin - East Coast Style
www.geocities.com/rmecs

Ricky Martin Fan Club
www.rickymartinfanclub.com

Ricky Martin Net
www.rickymartin.com.mx

Ricky Martin Vuelve
http://rickymartinmanagement.com

VH1 Fan Club: Ricky Martin
www.vh1.com/fanclubs/main/501085.jhtml

Vuelve - A Ricky Martin Fan Site
www.fansites.nl/ricky

Video

Nabou.com: Celebrities: Ricky Martin: Multimedia
www.nabou.com/celebrities/ricky_martin/multimedia/index.html

Wallpapers

Nabou.com: Celebrities: Ricky Martin: Wallpaper
www.nabou.com/celebrities/ricky_martin/wallpaper/index.html

Webrings

The Ricky Martin Fan Ring
http://nav.webring.yahoo.com/hub?ring=rickymartinfans&list

The Ricky Martin Webring
http://nav.webring.yahoo.com/hub?ring=rickymartin&list

SANTANA

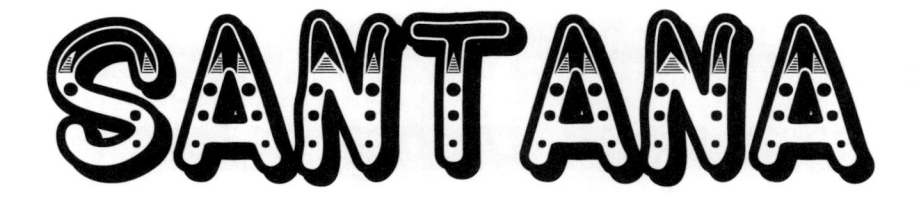

SUPER SINGLES "Smooth" | "Maria Maria"

Official Site

Santana
www.santana.com

Articles

Jam! Showbiz: Music: Santana
www.canoe.ca/JamMusicArtistsS/santana.html

Discussion

Santana Café
http://polycafe.com/santana/santanacafe.htm

Yahoo! Clubs: Santana
http://clubs.yahoo.com/clubs/santana

Yahoo! Groups: Santana4Life
http://groups.yahoo.com/group/Santana4Life

E-Mail Services

fun2mail: Santana Fan (yourname@santanafan.com)
www.santanafan.com

Galleries

Santana Photo Gallery
www.santanaphotogallery.com

Lyrics

Santana World: Lyrics
http://members.home.nl/voshege/lyricspage.htm

News

Entertainment Sleuth: Santana
http://e.sleuth.com/details.asp?Entity=5165

Reference

All Music Guide: Santana
    http://allmusic.com/cg/x.dll?p=amg&sql=1CARLOS|SANTANA

Internet Movie Database: Carlos Santana
    http://us.imdb.com/Name?Carlos+Santana

People Magazine Profiles: Carlos Santana
    http://people.aol.com/people/pprofiles/csantana

Rock on the Net: Santana
    www.rockonthenet.com/artists-s/santana.htm

Wall of Sound: Santana
    http://wallofsound.go.com/artists/santana

Software

Artist Desktop Themes: Santana
http://artistdesktopthemes.com/gb/s/santana.dt.1.html

Celebrity Desktop: Santana
www.celebritydesktop.com/musicians/santana

Top Sites

Santana Pa Ti
www.geocities.com/miguelzv

Santana World
www.come.to/santanaworld

Santanamigos
http://members.aol.com/santanamigos

The Music of Carlos Santana
www.charlie-heavner.com/cshome.htm

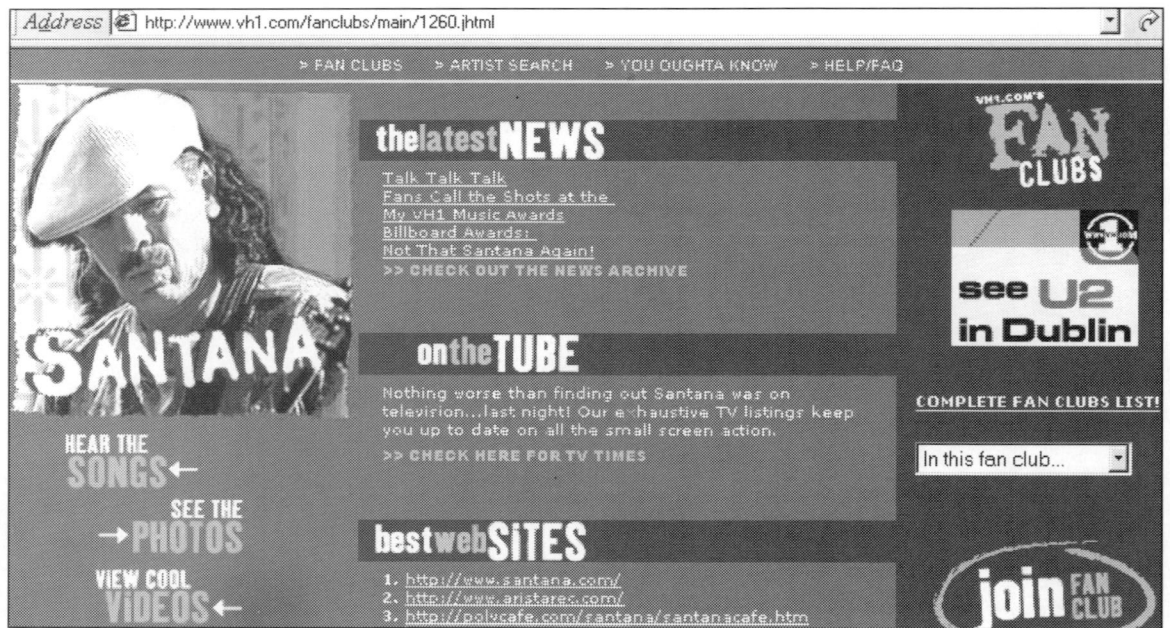

VH1 Fan Club: Santana
http://santana.vh1.com

Sarah McLachlan

SUPER SINGLES "Angel" | "Building a Mystery" | "I Will Remember You" | "Adia"

Official Site

SarahMcLachlan.Com
www.sarahmclachlan.com

Articles

Canoe: Sarah McLachlan News Archive
www.canoe.ca/JamMusicSarahMcLachlan/home.html

Esther's Sarah McLachlan Page: Interviews & Reviews
www.best.com/~donh/sarah/views.html

Jam! Showbiz: Music: Sarah McLachlan
www.canoe.com/JamMusicSarahMcLachlan

Discussion

Sarah McLachlan Music Newsgroup
alt.music.s-mclachlan

Yahoo! Clubs: Angela's Sarah McLachlan Club
http://clubs.yahoo.com/clubs/angelassarahmclachlanclub

Yahoo! Clubs: Mandy's Sarah McLachlan Café
http://clubs.yahoo.com/clubs/mandyssarahmclachlancafe

Yahoo! Clubs: Sarah McLachlan
http://clubs.yahoo.com/clubs/sarahmclachlan

Yahoo! Groups: sarahboots
http://groups.yahoo.com/group/sarahboots

E-Mail Services

SarahFan.Com: E-Mail (yourname@sarahfan.com)
http://mail.bigmailbox.com/users/sarahfancom

FAQs

The Fumbler FAQ
www.uncg.edu/~wlestes/fumblerfaq.html

Galleries

PopFolio: Sarah McLachlan
www.popfolio.com/mclachlan.htm

Links

Mosiqa Top 100 Sarah McLachlan Sites
www.top.mosiqa.com/sarah

Lyrics

SarahFan.Com: Lyrics
www.sarahfan.com/lyrics.shtml

News

Entertainment Sleuth: Sarah McLachlan
http://e.sleuth.com/details.asp?Entity=4944

Mr. Showbiz Celebrities: Sarah McLachlan
http://mrshowbiz.go.com/people/sarahmclachlan

Reference

All Music Guide: Sarah McLachlan
http://allmusic.com/cg/x.dll?p=amg&sql=1SARAH|MCLACHLAN

Internet Movie Database: Sarah McLachlan
http://us.imdb.com/Name?Sarah+McLachlan

Rock on the Net: Sarah McLachlan
www.rockonthenet.com/artists-m/sarahmclachlan_main.htm

Wall of Sound: Sarah McLachlan
http://wallofsound.go.com/artists/sarahmclachlan

Software

Celebrity Desktop: Sarah McLachlan
www.celebritydesktop.com/musicians/sarah_mclachlan

Top Sites

Angel of Hope - Sarah McLachlan
www.redrival.com/angelofhope

Esther's Sarah McLachlan Page
www.best.com/~donh/sarah

Heaven Holds a Sense of Wonder
www.intothefire.com/heaven

Holding on to Ecstasy
http://members.aol.com/DEREKMAN

IntoTheFire.Com
www.intothefire.com

Morning Smiles
   http://intothefire.com/smiles

SarahFan.Com
   www.sarahfan.com

Sea of Walking Dreams
   www.aquezada.com/sarah

Sweet Surrender
   http://surrender.e-vapor.net

The Great Divide
   http://members.aol.com/greatdivide1

VH1 Fan Club: Sarah McLachlan
   http://sarah-mclachlan.vh1.com

Wallpapers

Sweet Surrender: Wallpapers
   http://surrender.e-vapor.net/wallpaper/index.html

Webrings

Surfacing Ring
   http://nav.webring.yahoo.com/hub?ring=smclachlan&list

The Sarah McLachlan Webring
   http://nav.webring.yahoo.com/hub?ring=sarahm&list

Witnesses to Our Goddess - Where Angels Wander - A Sarah McLachlan Webring
   http://nav.webring.yahoo.com/hub?ring=surfacingshrine&list

Savage Garden

SUPER SINGLES "Crash & Burn" | "Truly Madly Deeply" | "I Knew I Loved You"

Official Site

Savage Garden
www.savagegarden.com

Articles

dotmusic: Savage Garden
www.dotmusic.com/artists/SavageGarden

Jam! Showbiz: Music: Savage Garden
www.canoe.ca/JamMusicArtistsS/savage_garden.html

Savage Garden - Superstars & Cannonballs: Articles
http://members.nbci.com/_XMCM/ymkktx/SandC/Articles/articles.htm

Savage Garden Central: Articles
www.savage-garden.net/articles/index.htm

Audio

Savage Garden Central: Multimedia
www.savage-garden.net/multimedia/index.htm

Savage Media
http://savagemedia.cjb.net

Discussion

Savage Garden Central: Mailing Lists
www.savage-garden.net/mailing_lists.htm

Savage Garden Central: Message Board
http://members.boardhost.com/savagegarden

Yahoo! Clubs: Darren & Daniel
http://clubs.yahoo.com/clubs/darrenanddaniel

Yahoo! Clubs: Savage Garden
http://clubs.yahoo.com/clubs/savagegarden

Yahoo! Clubs: Savage Garden Fever
http://clubs.yahoo.com/clubs/savagegardenfever

Yahoo! Clubs: Unofficial Savage Garden Fan Club
http://clubs.yahoo.com/clubs/unofficalsavagegardenfanclub

Yahoo! Groups: Savage Garden
http://groups.yahoo.com/group/savage_garden

Yahoo! Groups: Savage-Garden
http://groups.yahoo.com/group/savage-garden

Ecards

Savage Garden Online: Greeting Cards
http://redrival.com/sgonline/greet.htm

Ultimately Savage Garden: Greeting Cards
http://pub36.bravenet.com/postcard/post.asp?usernum=3051657671

E-Mail Services

Savage Garden Central: Free E-Mail (yourname@savage-garden.net)
www.savage-garden.net/email/index.htm

Galleries

Savage Garden - Superstars & Cannonballs: Pictures
http://members.nbci.com/_XMCM/ymkktx/SandC/PICTUREG/pictures.htm

Savage Garden Central: Picture Gallery
www.savage-garden.net/images/index.htm

Stojanka's Savage Garden Dominion: Gallery
www.geocities.com/stojothecat/pics.html

Links

Chained to Savage Garden Links
http://savagelinks.cjb.net

Mosiqa Top 100 Savage Garden Sites
http://topsites.mosiqa.com/savage

Lyrics

Savage Land: Lyrics
www.angelfire.com/wy/savage/lyrics.html

Stojanka's Savage Garden Dominion: Lyrics
www.geocities.com/stojothecat/lyrics_menu.html

News

Savage Garden Central: News
www.savage-garden.net/news/index.htm

Reference

All Music Guide: Savage Garden
http://allmusic.com/cg/x.dll?p=amg&sql=1SAVAGE|GARDEN

Rock on the Net: Savage Garden
www.rockonthenet.com/artists-s/savagegarden_main.htm

Wall of Sound: Savage Garden
http://wallofsound.go.com/artists/savagegarden

Software

Artist Desktop Themes: Savage Garden
http://artistdesktopthemes.com/gb/s/savage_garden.dt.1.html

Celebrity Desktop: Savage Garden
www.celebritydesktop.com/musicians/savage_garden

Savage Garden Online: Downloads
http://redrival.com/sgonline/download.htm

Top Sites

A Cosmopolitan Savage Garden
http://fly.to/acsg

Cassandra's Truth
www.savagegarden1.com

Ericsson's Savage Garden World
http://listen.to/savage

Karli's Savage Paradise
www.geocities.com/madly_ng

Katherine's Savage Garden Page
http://savagekat.virtualave.net

Miki's Savage Garden Site
http://go.to/MikiSavage

Riley's Savage Garden Home Page
http://members.aol.com/Graviton13

Top Sites — Savage Garden

Running Out of Words
www.angelfire.com/ok3/sillything

Savage Dreams
http://clix.to/fisky

Savage Garden Central
www.savage-garden.net

Savage Garden Official Fanzine Site
www.savagegardenfan.com

Savage Garden Online
http://redrival.com/sgonline

Savage Garden Scrapbook
www.savagegarden.musicpage.com

Savaged Land
www.angelfire.com/wy/savage/index.html

Stojanka's Savage Garden Dominion
http://welcome.to/my_garden

The Garden of Savage Delights
www.angelfire.com/in/gardenofsavagedlites

The Official #SavageGarden Regspage
www.regspage.com

To Savage Garden & Back
www.igs.net/~woodley/2sg&bac.htm

Truly, Madly Savage Garden
www.telusplanet.net/public/fchomiak/SGWebpage.htm

Ultimately Savage Garden
www.geocities.com/SunsetStrip/4253/index2.html

Video

Ericsson's Savage Garden World: Videos
http://w1.550.telia.com/~u55004318/videos.htm

MTV.Com: Savage Garden
http://savage-garden.mtv.com

Savage Garden Online: Videos
http://redrival.com/sgonline/video.htm

Savage Media
http://savagemedia.cjb.net

Webrings

Addicted to Savage Garden
http://nav.webring.yahoo.com/hub?ring=addicted2savage&list

Savage Garden Webring
http://nav.webring.yahoo.com/hub?ring=savagegarden&list

Savashitos Webring
http://nav.webring.yahoo.com/hub?ring=a1769997&list

Tangled Web Around Savage Garden
http://nav.webring.yahoo.com/hub?ring=sav_gar&list

The Savage Garden Universe
http://nav.webring.yahoo.com/hub?ring=savage33&list

Shania Twain

SUPER SINGLES "That Don't Impress Me Much" | "You're Still the One" | "From This Moment On"

Official Site

Shania Twain's Official Site
www.shania-twain.com

Articles

Canoe: Shania Twain News Archive
www.canoe.ca/JamCountryTwain/home.html

dotmusic: Shania Twain
www.dotmusic.com/artists/ShaniaTwain

Longshot: Articles
www.shania.org/articles.html

The Shania Files: Articles
http://shfilez.virtualave.net/art/articles.html

www.shania-twain.co.uk: Articles
www.shania-twain.co.uk/starticles.html

Audio

Everything Shania: Multimedia
www.everythingshania.com/media

Stwain.Com: Multimedia
www.stwain.com/multimedia

TwainThis' Shania World: Multimedia
http://pluto.spaceports.com/~grappler/shania/multi.htm

Discussion

Shania Twain US Online Fan Club: Message Board
www.shania-twain.org/cgi-bin/Ultimate.cgi

Shania.Net: Fan Chat
www.shania.net/fanchat

Shania.Net: Forums
www.shaniaforums.com

Yahoo! Clubs: Euphoria Shania
http://clubs.yahoo.com/clubs/euphoriashania

Yahoo! Clubs: Shania Mania
http://clubs.yahoo.com/clubs/shaniamania

Yahoo! Clubs: Shania Twain Internet Fan Club
http://clubs.yahoo.com/clubs/shaniatwaininternetfanclub

Yahoo! Groups: Shania
http://groups.yahoo.com/group/Shania

Galleries

A List Celebrities: Shania Twain
www.the-alist.org/ShaniaTwain

Absolute Pictures: Shania Twain
www.absolutepictures.com/t/twain_shania

Beautfiul Celebrities: Shania Twain
www.beautifulcelebrities.com/shania_twain_pics.html

Shania.Net: Photo Gallery
www.shania.net/photogallery

Links

Mosiqa Top 100 Shania Twain Sites
www.top.mosiqa.com/shania

Lyrics

TwainThis' Shania World: Lyrics
http://pluto.spaceports.com/~grappler/shania/lyrics.htm

Merchandise

Shania Twain Store
www.shaniatwainstore.com

News

Abstracts.Net: Shania Twain
www.abstracts.net/shania-twain

Entertainment Sleuth: Shania Twain
http://e.sleuth.com/details.asp?Entity=4461

Stwain.Com: News
www.stwain.com/news

Reference

All Music Guide: Shania Twain
http://allmusic.com/cg/x.dll?p=amg&sql=1SHANIA|TWAIN

Internet Movie Database: Shania Twain
http://us.imdb.com/Name?Shania+Twain

People Magazine Profiles: Shania Twain
http://people.aol.com/people/pprofiles/celebhomepage/0,3371,100,00.html

Rock on the Net: Shania Twain
www.rockonthenet.com/artists-t/shaniatwain_main.htm

Wall of Sound: Shania Twain
http://wallofsound.go.com/artists/shaniatwain

Software

Celebrity Desktop: Shania Twain
www.celebritydesktop.com/musicians/shania_twain

Cinema Desktop Themes: Shania Twain
www.cinemadesktopthemes.com/st/t/shania_twain.dt.1.html

Top Sites

Escape to Shaniaville
http://escape.to/shaniaville

Everything Shania
www.everythingshania.com

Forever Shania
www.bluetears.com/shania

Jake the Snake's Shania Twain Page
http://users.pandora.be/shania.twain

Longshot - Shania Twain Online Fan Club
www.shania.org

Planet Shania
www.geocities.com/Nashville/Opry/6951

Shania Central
www.geocities.com/Nashville/6445

Shania Online
www.shania-online.com

Shania Spotlight
www.shania-spotlight.com

Shania Twain Canada Online Fan Club
www.shania-canada.com

Shania Twain City - European Online Fan Club
www.shaniatwaincity.com

Shania Twain Shrine
www.musicfanclubs.org/shania

Shania Twain US Online Fan Club
www.shania-twain.org

Shania.Net
www.shania.net

Stwain.Com
www.stwain.com

Talon's Shania Twain Page
www.mnsi.net/~talon/shania.htm

The Pages of Shania Twain
http://members.aol.com/azsteves/twain001.htm

The Shania Files
http://shfilez.virtualave.net

The Shania Twain Israeli Site
www.shania-twain.co.il/english.htm

Twain Town
www.geocities.com/Nashville/8691

TwainThis' Shania World
www.twainthis.com

VH1 Fan Club: Shania Twain
http://shania-twain.vh1.com

www.shania-twain.co.uk
www.shania-twain.co.uk

Video

Forever Shania: Multimedia
www.bluetears.com/shania/multi.html

Wallpapers

Shania Heaven
http://members.nbci.com/diabloe76

Shania Twain's Wallpaper World
www.shaniawallpapers.co.uk

ShaniaVille: Wallpapers
http://members.nbci.com/lonewolf279/SHANIAVILLE/wallpaperx.html

TwainThis' Shania World: Wallpaper
http://pluto.spaceports.com/~grappler/shania/wall1.htm

Webrings

Shania Twain
http://nav.webring.yahoo.com/hub?ring=shaniatwain&list

Sheryl Crow

SUPER SINGLES "My Favorite Mistake" | "Everyday is a Winding Road" | "Strong Enough" | "If It Makes You Happy" | "All I Wanna Do"

E-Mail

sherylcrow@igamail.com

Official Site

Sheryl Crow
www.sherylcrow.com

Articles

dotmusic: Sheryl Crow
www.dotmusic.com/artists/SherylCrow

Audio

Sheryl Crow Paradise: Audio/Video
www.sherylcrowparadise.com/audiovideo.html

Discussion

Yahoo! Clubs: Sheryl Crow Hangout
http://clubs.yahoo.com/clubs/sherylcrowhangout

Yahoo! Clubs: Sheryl Crow's Strong Enough Club
http://clubs.yahoo.com/clubs/sherylcrowsstrongenoughclub

Yahoo! Groups: Sheryl Crow
http://groups.yahoo.com/group/sheryl_crow

Galleries

PopFolio: Sheryl Crow
www.popfolio.com/crow.htm

Sheryl Crow Paradise: Galleries
www.sherylcrowparadise.com/pictures/paradisepictures.html

Lyrics

Sheryl Crow Paradise: Lyrics
www.sherylcrowparadise.com/chords.html

Sheryl Crow, Little Superstar: Lyrics
www.multimania.com/sherylcrow/lyrics.htm

Merchandise

Official Sheryl Crow Store
http://sherylcrowdirect.com

News

Entertainment Sleuth: Sheryl Crow
http://e.sleuth.com/details.asp?Entity=977

Mr. Showbiz Celebrities: Sheryl Crow
http://mrshowbiz.go.com/people/sherylcrow

Yahoo! Groups: scnews
http://groups.yahoo.com/group/scnews

Reference

All Music Guide: Sheryl Crow
http://allmusic.com/cg/x.dll?p=amg&sql=1SHERYL|CROW

Internet Movie Database: Sheryl Crow
http://us.imdb.com/Name?Sheryl+Crow

People Magazine Profiles: Sheryl Crow
http://people.aol.com/people/pprofiles/scrow

Rock on the Net: Sheryl Crow
www.rockonthenet.com/artists-c/sherylcrow_main.htm

The Sheryl Crow Discography
www.sherylcrow.org

Wall of Sound: Sheryl Crow
http://wallofsound.go.com/artists/sherylcrow

Software

Celebrity Desktop: Sheryl Crow
www.celebritydesktop.com/musicians/sheryl_crow

Sheryl Crow's Neighborhood: Miscellaneous Goodies
www.multimania.com/rocksheryl/downloads/main.html

Top Sites

1440 Media/Radio Free Entertainment presents Sheryl Crow
www.radiofree.com/profiles/sheryl_crow

Dedicated to Sheryl Crow
http://home.talkcity.com/ChaplinCt/sherylfan

Home of Sheryl Crow
One stop shopping for everything Sheryl

Home of Sheryl Crow
www.geocities.com/SunsetStrip/Alley/8457/main.html

My/Be Angels Sheryl Crow
http://members.nbci.com/DJCulture/index.html

Sheryl Crow - I Shall Believe
www.geocities.com/SunsetStrip/Club/4768/sherylcrow1.html

Sheryl Crow - If It Makes You happy
www.geocities.com/SunsetStrip/Frontrow/8750/main.html

Sheryl Crow Framed
www.zip.com.au/~mayor/sheryl/main.htm

Sheryl Crow Kicks
www.geocities.com/SunsetStrip/Arena/4617

Sheryl Crow Paradise
www.sherylcrowparadise.com

Sheryl Crow, Little Superstar
www.multimania.com/sherylcrow

Sheryl Crow's Neighborhood
www.multimania.com/rocksheryl

The Australian Sheryl Crow Web Site
http://enterprise.powerup.com.au/~saraaime

The Neighborhood
http://welcome.to/neighborhood

VH1 Fan Club: Sheryl Crow
http://sheryl-crow.vh1.com

Video

Sheryl Crow Paradise: Audio/Video
www.sherylcrowparadise.com/audiovideo.html

Wallpapers

Sheryl Crow Framed: Wallpapers
www.zip.com.au/~mayor/sheryl/wallpapers.htm

Webrings

Ring of Sheryl Crow
http://nav.webring.yahoo.com/hub?ring=scpage&list

Smashing Pumpkins

SUPER SINGLES "Perfect" | "Ava Adore" | "Tonight Tonight" | " 1979" | "Disarm"

Official Site

Smashing Pumpkins
www.smashingpumpkins.com

Articles

dotmusic: Smashing Pumpkins
www.dotmusic.com/artists/SmashingPumpkins

Jam! Showbiz: Music: Smashing Pumpkins
www.canoe.ca/JamMusicArtistsS/smashing_pumpkins.html

Audio

Below Zero: Audio
www.musicfanclubs.org/smashingpumpkins/audio.htm

Netphoria: Smashing Pumpkins Real Audio Collection
www.netphoria.org/realaudio.htm

Smashing Pumpkins Real Audio Archive
www.spraa.org

The Smashing Pumpkins Collection: Audio
www.smashing-pumpkins.net/realaudio/index.html

Discussion

Listessa - Smashing Pumpkins Discussion List
www.spfc.org/online/listessa.html

Smashing Pumpkins Music Newsgroup
alt.music.smash-pumpkins

Yahoo! Clubs: Cherub Penny
http://clubs.yahoo.com/clubs/cherubpenny

Yahoo! Clubs: Smashing Pumpkins
http://clubs.yahoo.com/clubs/smashingpumpkins

Yahoo! Clubs: The Smashing Pumpkins
http://clubs.yahoo.com/clubs/thesmashingpumpkins

Yahoo! Groups: Smashing
http://groups.yahoo.com/group/smashing

Yahoo! Groups: Smashing Pumpkins
http://groups.yahoo.com/group/smashing_pumpkins

FAQs

Smashing Pumpkins FAQ
www.starla.org/faq.html

Galleries

PopFolio: Smashing Pumpkins
www.popfolio.com/smashingpumpkins.htm

The Smashing Pumpkins Images Collection
www.smashing-pumpkins.net/images

Links

The Smashing Pumpkins Search Engine

The Smashing Pumpkins Search Engine
http://blamo.simplenet.com/sp/search.hts

Lyrics

Rotten Apples
www.netphoria.org/rottenapples/sp.htm

Smashing Pumpkins Discography
www.blamo.org/sp/discography.shtml

Songlist
http://www-personal.umich.edu/~brt/sp/alpha.html

Vortex of Lost Souls: Lyrics
www.lost-vortex.com/songlist.htm

News

Entertainment Sleuth: Smashing Pumpkins
http://e.sleuth.com/details.asp?Entity=5741

Netphoria - Your Daily Pumpkins Fix
www.netphoria.org

Reference

All Music Guide: Smashing Pumpkins
http://allmusic.com/cg/x.dll?p=amg&sql=1SMASHING|PUMPKINS

People Magazine Profiles: Smashing Pumpkins
http://people.aol.com/people/pprofiles/celebhomepage/0,3371,103,00.html

Rock on the Net: Smashing Pumpkins
www.rockonthenet.com/artists-s/smashingpumpkins_main.htm

Wall of Sound: Smashing Pumpkins
http://wallofsound.go.com/artists/smashingpumpkins

Software

Below Zero: Fonts
www.musicfanclubs.org/smashingpumpkins/fonts.htm

Celebrity Desktop: Smashing Pumpkins
www.celebritydesktop.com/musicians/smashing_pumpkins

Nowhere
www.geocities.com/SunsetStrip/Club/9725

postsadness - Pumpkins PC Resource
www.progsoc.uts.edu.au/~wormwood/darcy/main.html

The Smashing Pumpkins AMP Adore Page
http://ampdore.2007.org

Top Sites

Below Zero
www.musicfanclubs.org/smashingpumpkins/index.htm

Ground Zero Dime
www.geocities.com/SunsetStrip/Arena/1985

Landslide
http://landslide.2007.org

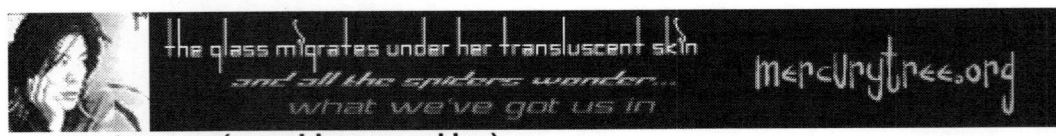

mercurytree.org (smashing pumpkins)
http://mercurytree.org/index2.html

Netphoria - Your Daily Pumpkins Fix
www.netphoria.org

Pumpkin Soup
www.starla.org/pumpkinsoup

Siva - The Smashing Pumpkins Web Site
www.blamo.org

SPFC.org - The Smashing Pumpkins Fan Collaborative
www.spfc.org

The Pumpkingdom
www.nd.edu/~mwinter1

The Slipstream
www.geocities.com/SunsetStrip/Pavilion/2963

The Smashing Pumpkins Collection
www.smashing-pumpkins.net

The Window Paine - A Smashing Pumpkins Site
www.gwsd.com/windowpaine

VH1 Fan Club: Smashing Pumpkins
www.vh1.com/fanclubs/main/1016.jhtml

Vortex of Lost Souls
www.lost-vortex.com

Video

Below Zero: Videos
www.musicfanclubs.org/smashingpumpkins/vidfile.htm

MTV.Com: Smashing Pumpkins
http://smashing-pumpkins.mtv.com

Netphoria: Real Videos
www.netphoria.org/videos/videos.htm

Webrings

Adore - The Smashing Pumpkins Webring
http://nav.webring.yahoo.com/hub?ring=adoresp&list

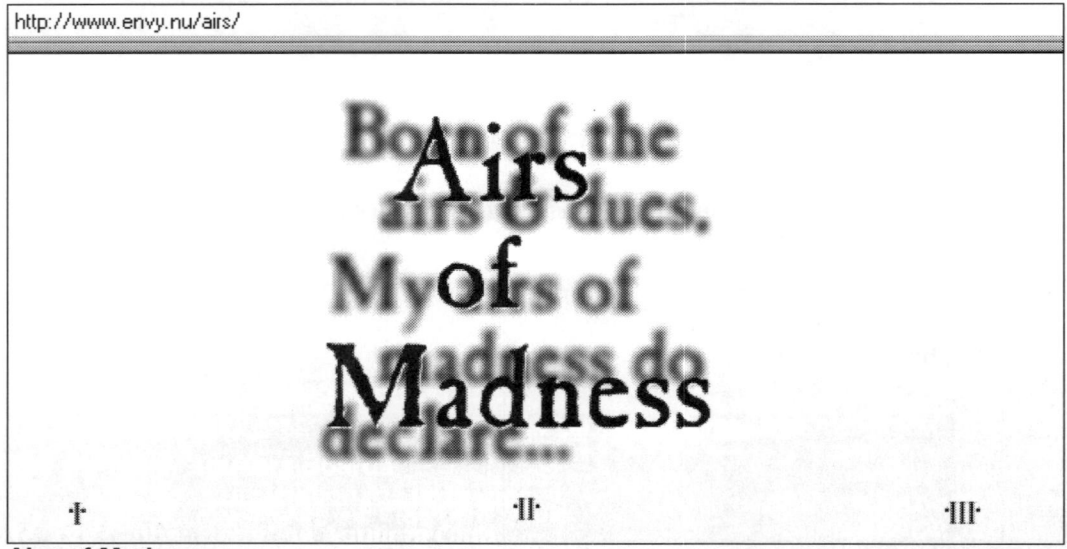

Airs of Madness
www.envy.nu/airs

Smashing Pumpkins Webring
http://nav.webring.yahoo.com/hub?ring=spring&list

SP Mayhem - A Smashing Pumpkins Webring
http://nav.webring.yahoo.com/hub?ring=spmayhem&list

The Smashing Pumpkin Network
http://nav.webring.yahoo.com/hub?ring=spn&list

The Smashing Pumpkins Webring
http://nav.webring.yahoo.com/hub?ring=pumpkinsring&list

sting

SUPER SINGLES "Desert Rose" | "After the Rain Has Fallen" | "Fields of Gold"

Official Site

The Official Sting Web Site
www.sting.compaq.com

Audio

Fuzzy's Sting & Police MIDI Page
www.stingmidi.de

Articles

Jam! Showbiz: Music: Sting
www.canoe.ca/JamMusicArtistsS/sting.html

Discussion

Sting Fan Newsgroup
alt.fan.sting

Yahoo! Clubs: Brand New Day Sting Fan Club
http://clubs.yahoo.com/clubs/brandnewdaystingfanclub

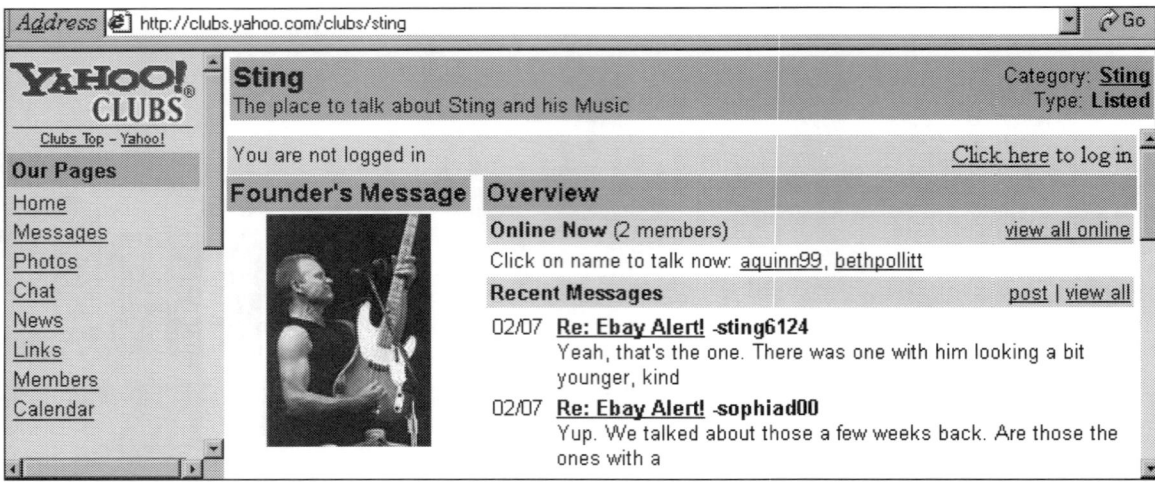

Yahoo! Clubs: Sting
http://clubs.yahoo.com/clubs/sting

Yahoo! Clubs: The Police & Sting
http://clubs.yahoo.com/clubs/thepoliceandsting

Yahoo! Groups: Sting-BrandNewDay
http://groups.yahoo.com/group/Sting-BrandNewDay

FAQs

Sting Etc.: Sting FAQ
www.stingetc.com/sting.html

Sting Us: FAQ
www.stingus.com/faquk/faqstinguk1.htm

Lyrics

Sting Etc.: Sting & The Police Lyrics Library
www.stingetc.com/lyrics/index.html

Stingmania: Lyrics
www.stingmania.com/Texty/Texty.htm

Synchronisite: Lyrics
www.geocities.com/BourbonStreet/5646/lyrics.html

Merchandise

out of print Sting
http://outofprint.free.fr

News

Entertainment Sleuth: Sting
http://e.sleuth.com/details.asp?Entity=4263

Mr. Showbiz Celebrities: Sting
http://mrshowbiz.go.com/people/sting

Reference

All Music Guide: Sting
http://allmusic.com/cg/x.dll?p=amg&sql=1STING

Rock on the Net: Sting
www.rockonthenet.com/artists-s/sting_main.htm

Wall of Sound: Sting
http://wallofsound.go.com/artists/sting

Software

Celebrity Desktop: Sting
www.celebritydesktop.com/musicians/sting

Top Sites

Sting Etc.
www.stingetc.com

Sting Us
www.stingus.com

Stingchronicity
www.stingchronicity.co.uk

Synchronisite - Greg's Sting Page
www.geocities.com/BourbonStreet/5646

VH1 Fan Club: Sting
http://sting.vh1.com

Webrings

Mercury Rising - A Sting Webring
   http://nav.webring.yahoo.com/hub?ring=goldsting&list

Stone Temple Pilots

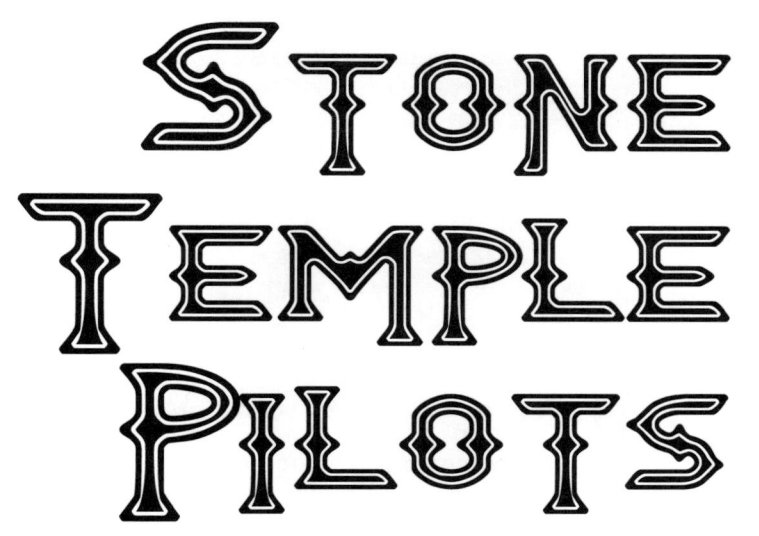

SUPER SINGLES "Sour Girl" | "Vasoline" | "Interstate Love Song" | "Plush"

Official Site

stone temple pilots
www.stonetemplepilots.com

Articles

Jam! Showbiz: Music: Stone Temple Pilots
www.canoe.ca/JamMusicArtistsS/stone_pilots.html

Audio

Pleased to Meet You: Sounds
www.geocities.com/stpdowner/sounds.html

The Motorcade: STP Real Audio
www.geocities.com/oblivion_queen/stprealaudio.htm

Discussion

Stone Temple Pilots Music Newsgroup
alt.music.stone-temple

STP Fan Club
www.geocities.com/stpfanclub Yahoo! Clubs: PLUSH
http://clubs.yahoo.com/clubs/plush

Yahoo! Clubs: Stone Temple Pilots
http://clubs.yahoo.com/clubs/stonetemplepilots

Yahoo! Groups: StoneTemplePilots
http://groups.yahoo.com/group/StoneTemplePilots

Yahoo! Groups: STP
http://groups.yahoo.com/group/stp

Ecards

STP Greetings @ A New Meditation
www.geocities.com/anewmeditation/greetings.html

Where the Birds Can't Sing Along: STP Greetings
http://pages.prodigy.com/KLMV20B/card.htm

Galleries

Diamond Noose: Pictures
www.geocities.com/sharkpilot/pictures.html

Mike's STP Page
http://geocities.com/area51/shadowlands/7697

Nothing 4 Free: Pics
www.fortunecity.com/tinpan/miles/861/nothing4free/pics.html

Lyrics

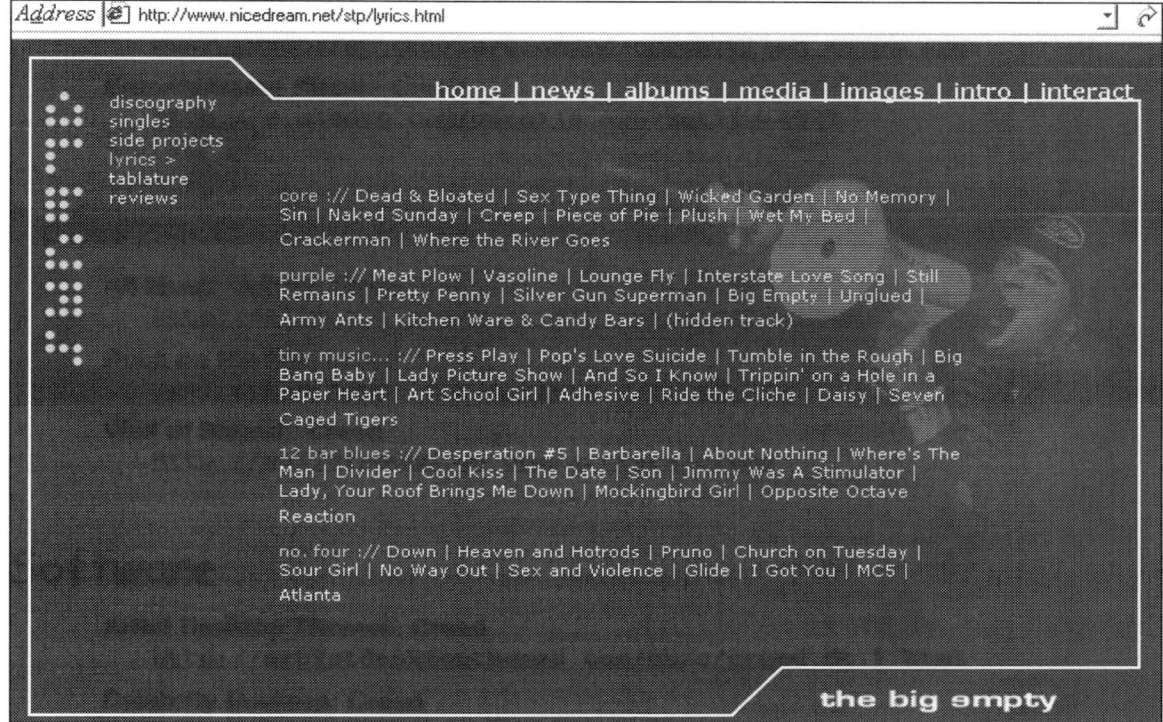

Stone Temple Pilots - The Big Empty: Lyrics
www.nicedream.net/stp/lyrics.html

Merchandise

Official Stone Temple Pilots Store
http://stpdirect.com

STP Classifieds @ A New Meditation
www.geocities.com/anewmeditation/stptrade.html

News

Adhesive & Vasoline
www.adhesiveandvasoline.com

Diamond Noose
www.geocities.com/sharkpilot/DN.html

Entertainment Sleuth: Stone Temple Pilots
http://e.sleuth.com/details.asp?Entity=4914

Reference

All Music Guide: Stone Temple Pilots
http://allmusic.com/cg/x.dll?p=amg&sql=1STONE|TEMPLE|PILOTS

Rock on the Net: Stone Temple Pilots
www.rockonthenet.com/artists-s/stonetemplepilots_main.htm

Wall of Sound: Stone Temple Pilots
http://wallofsound.go.com/artists/stonetemplepilots

Top Sites

A New Meditation
www.geocities.com/anewmeditation

Adhesive & Vasoline
www.adhesiveandvasoline.com

Comatose Commodity
http://come.to/Commodity

Nothing 4 Free
www.fortunecity.com/tinpan/miles/861/nothing4free/home.html

Opposite Octave Reaction
http://members.tripod.com/~scotty_5/index.html

Pleased to Meet You
www.geocities.com/stpdowner

Silvergun Supermen
www.stpilots.com

STP Fan Club
www.geocities.com/stpfanclub

STP Online
www.geocities.com/stponline/index2.html

The Big Empty
www.nicedream.net/stp

The Motorcade
www.geocities.com/stpfreakno_1

The Rose on My Birthday Deathbed
http://fly.to/scottweiland

VH1 Fan Club: Stone Temple Pilots
www.vh1.com/fanclubs/main/1020.jhtml

Where The Birds Can't Sing Along
http://pages.prodigy.com/KLMV20B/birds.htm

Video

Diamond Noose: Videos
www.geocities.com/sharkpilot/video.html

The Motorcade: Videos
www.geocities.com/stpfreakno_1/video.html

Wallpapers

Nothing 4 Free: Wallpapers
www.fortunecity.com/tinpan/miles/861/nothing4free/wallpapers.html

Webrings

Find You In the Dark Webring
http://nav.webring.yahoo.com/hub?ring=stpsilvergun&list

STP the GatheRING
http://nav.webring.yahoo.com/hub?ring=gathering&list

SUGAR RAY

SUPER SINGLES "Falls Apart" | "Every Morning" | "Someday" | "Fly"

Official Site

Atlantic Records' Sugar Ray Site
www.sugar-ray.com

Sugar Ray Online
www.sugarray.com

Articles

Jam! Showbiz: Music: Sugar Ray
www.canoe.ca/JamMusicArtistsS/sugarray.html

Discussion

Yahoo! Clubs: Pictures of Sugar Ray
http://clubs.yahoo.com/clubs/picturesofsugarray

Yahoo! Clubs: Sugar Ray
http://clubs.yahoo.com/clubs/sugarray

Yahoo! Groups: RPMFLYS
http://groups.yahoo.com/group/RPMFLYS

E-Mail Services

fun2mail.com: Sugar Ray Lover (yourname@sugarraylover.com)
www.sugarraylover.com

Galleries

PopFolio: Sugar Ray
www.popfolio.com/sugarray.htm

Links

Top 50 Sugar Ray Sites
www.topsitelists.com/bestsites/sugarraysites/topsites.html

Lyrics

Sugar Ray Online: Lyrics
www.sugarrayonline.com/pages/music/music.html

SugarRayFans.Com: Lyrics
www.sugarrayfans.com/lyrics/lyrics.html

Merchandise

Official Sugar Ray Store
http://sugarraydirect.com

News

Entertainment Sleuth: Sugar Ray
http://e.sleuth.com/details.asp?Entity=5238

SugarRayFans.Com: News
www.sugarrayfans.com/news/news.html

Reference

All Music Guide: Sugar Ray
http://allmusic.com/cg/x.dll?p=amg&sql=1SUGAR|RAY

Rock on the Net: Sugar Ray
www.rockonthenet.com/artists-s/sugarray_main.htm

Wall of Sound: Sugar Ray
http://wallofsound.go.com/artists/sugarray

Yahoo! Web Celeb: Sugar Ray
http://features.yahoo.com/webceleb/sugarray

Software

Celebrity Desktop: Sugar Ray
www.celebritydesktop.com/musicians/sugar_ray

Top Sites

Brennan's Sugar Ray Fan Page
www.angelfire.com/music/sugarray3

Fly With Sugar Ray
www.expage.com/flywithsugarray

Jaime's Super Ray Page
http://gurlpages.com/msayersm

Lemond & Brownies
http://lemonade_and_brownies.homestead.com/Main.html

My Sugar Ray Journal
http://gurlpages.com/s.a._jcfan/journal.html

Sugar Ray
http://gurlpages.com/sugar_1459/index.html

Sugar Ray - Snug Harbor
www.sugarray.sexypage.net

Sugar Ray Kix Ass
www.angelfire.com/punk/sugarray

Sugar Ray Machine
http://clix.to/sugarraymachine

Sugar Ray Snug Harbor
www.angelfire.com/ca5/sugarray

SugarRayFans.Com
www.sugarrayfans.com

The Dome's Sugar Ray Site
www.angelfire.com/ca/sugarray/index.html

VH1 Fan Club: Sugar Ray
http://sugar-ray.vh1.com

Webrings

The Sugar Ray Webring
http://nav.webring.yahoo.com/hub?ring=rpm&list

Toni Braxton

SUPER SINGLES "He Wasn't Man Enough" | "Unbreak My Heart" | "You're Makin' Me High"

Articles

Jam! Showbiz: Music: Toni Braxton
www.canoe.ca/JamMusicArtistsB/braxton_toni.html

Audio

Toni Braxton - Sweet, Soft & Sensual: Audio
www.musicfanclubs.org/tonibraxton/audio.htm

Discussion

Yahoo! Clubs: Toni Braxton
http://clubs.yahoo.com/clubs/tonibraxton

Yahoo! Clubs: Toni Braxton Palace
http://clubs.yahoo.com/clubs/tonibraxtonpalace

Yahoo! Clubs: Tribute to Toni Braxton
http://clubs.yahoo.com/clubs/tributetotonibraxton

Yahoo! Groups: tonibraxton
http://groups.yahoo.com/group/tonibraxton

Ecards

Toni Braxton Greeting Cards
www.geocities.com/toni_braxton_online/tbogc.html

Galleries

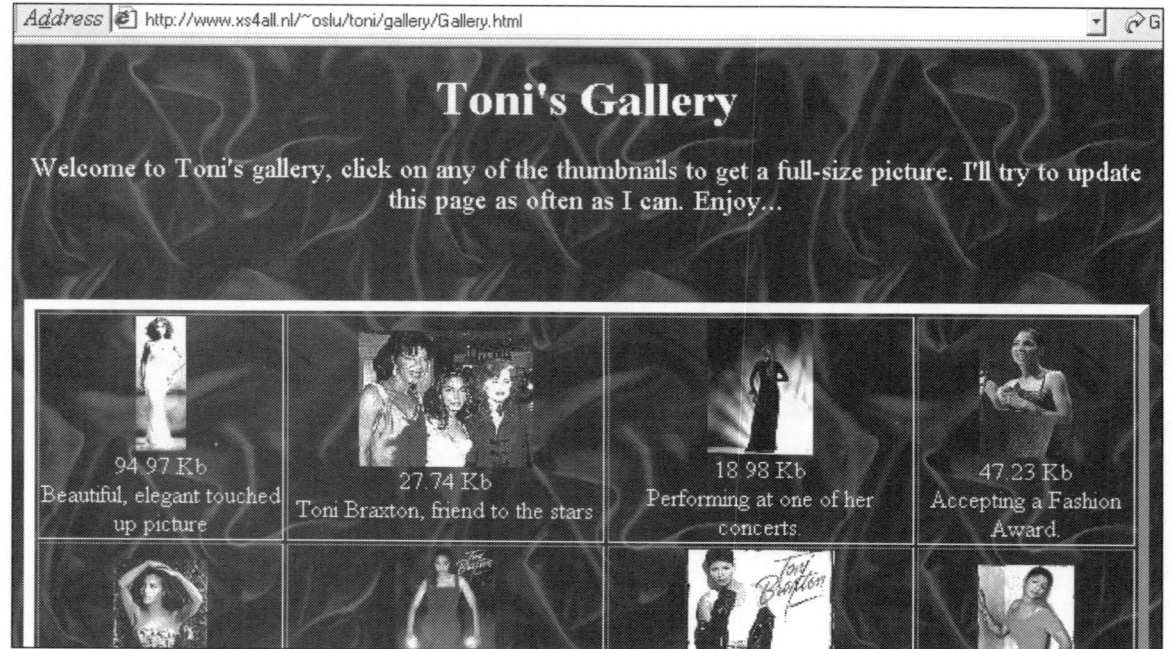

Toni Braxton: Toni's Gallery
www.xs4all.nl/~oslu/toni/gallery/Gallery.html

Toni Braxton - Sweet, Soft & Sensual: Pictures
www.musicfanclubs.org/tonibraxton/pictures.htm

Lyrics

Toni Braxton - Sweet, Soft & Sensual: Lyrics
www.musicfanclubs.org/tonibraxton/Lyrics.htm

News

Entertainment Sleuth: Toni Braxton
http://e.sleuth.com/details.asp?Entity=5101

Reference

All Music Guide: Toni Braxton
http://allmusic.com/cg/x.dll?p=amg&sql=1TONI|BRAXTON

Internet Movie Database: Toni Braxton
http://us.imdb.com/Name?Toni+Braxton

People Magazine Profiles: Toni Braxton
http://people.aol.com/people/pprofiles/celebhomepage/0,3371,97,00.html

Rock on the Net: Toni Braxton
www.rockonthenet.com/artists-b/tonibraxton_main.htm

Wall of Sound: Toni Braxton
http://wallofsound.go.com/artists/tonibraxton

Software

Celebrity Desktop: Toni Braxton
www.celebritydesktop.com/musicians/toni_braxton

Cinema Desktop Themes: Toni Braxton
www.cinemadesktopthemes.com/st/b/toni_braxton.dt.1.html

Toni Braxton - Sweet, Soft & Sensual: Tools
www.musicfanclubs.org/tonibraxton/tools.htm

Top Sites

Braxton Bytes
http://braxtonbytes.com

Braxtonism
http://tonibraxton.cjb.net

Click2Music: Toni Braxton
www.click2music.com/tonibraxton

Toni Braxton
www.xs4all.nl/~oslu/toni/main.htm

Toni Braxton - Sweet, Soft & Sensual
www.musicfanclubs.org/tonibraxton

Toni Braxton Forever
www.tonibraxtonforever.com

Toni Braxton Online
www.geocities.com/toni_braxton_online

Toni's Secrets
www.geocities.com/tonis_secrets

ToniBraxtonOnline.De
www.tonibraxtononline.de

Videos

Toni Braxton - Sweet, Soft & Sensual: Videos
www.musicfanclubs.org/tonibraxton/videos.htm

Wallpapers

Toni Braxton Forever: Wallpapers
www.tonibraxtonforever.com/wallpapers.html

Webrings

Toni Braxtons' Webring
http://nav.webring.yahoo.com/hub?ring=braxton&list

WESTLIFE

Super Singles "Swear It Again" | "What Makes a Man"

Official Site

Westlife Airlines
www.westlife.co.uk

Articles

dotmusic: Westlife
www.dotmusic.com/artists/Westlife

News from the Westside: Articles
www.efanguide.com/~westlife/articles/index.html

Wet Files: Articles
www.filan.f2s.com/magazine.htm

Audio

Westlife.Org: Audio
www.westlife.org/audio/index.html

Discussion

Into the Westlife World Message Board
www.insidetheweb.com/mbs.cgi/mb770456

Westlife.Org: Forum
www.westlife.org/interact/index.html

Yahoo! Clubs: The Westside Club
http://clubs.yahoo.com/clubs/thewestsideclub

Yahoo! Clubs: Westlife
http://clubs.yahoo.com/clubs/westlife

Yahoo! Clubs: Westlife is My Life
http://clubs.yahoo.com/clubs/westlifeismylife

Yahoo! Clubs: Westlife Official Fan Club
http://clubs.yahoo.com/clubs/westlifeofficialfanclub

Yahoo! Clubs: Westlife's Online Fan Club
http://clubs.yahoo.com/clubs/westlifesonlinefanclub

Yahoo! Groups: westlifepicmixs
http://groups.yahoo.com/group/westlifepicmixs

Yahoo! Groups: WestlifeStreetTeam
http://groups.yahoo.com/group/WestlifeStreetTeam

Yahoo! Groups: westlifeweblist
http://groups.yahoo.com/group/westlifeweblist

Yahoo! Groups: WFU list
http://groups.yahoo.com/group/WFU_list

Ecards

Westlife Canada: Greeting Cards
http://pages.sprint.ca/westlife/GreetingCards.html

Westlife Web: Greeting Cards
http://pub12.bravenet.com/postcard/post.asp?usernum=976031889

E-Mail Services

Westlife Web: Free E-Mail (yourname@westlifeweb.com)
www.westlifeweb.com/email.html

Galleries

Aiko's Westlife Picture Gallery
www.geocities.com/aiko_westlife_picture_gallery

Westlife Web: Pictures
www.westlifeweb.com/pictures.html

Links

Mosiqa Top 100 Westlife Sites
http://topsites.mosiqa.com/westlife

Lyrics

Westlife: Songs & Lyrics
www.westlifeweb.com/songs.html

News

Entertainment Sleuth: Westlife
http://e.sleuth.com/details.asp?Entity=5867

News from the Westside - The Latest in Westlife News
www.westlife-news.com

Wahey: News
www.crosswinds.net/~shortty/8k/westlife/news.html

Westlife.Org: News
www.westlife.org/news.html

Reference

All Music Guide: Westlife
http://allmusic.com/cg/x.dll?p=amg&sql=1WESTLIFE

Software

Artist Desktop Themes: Westlife
http://artistdesktopthemes.com/gb/w/westlife.dt.1.html

Celebrity Desktop: Westlife
www.celebritydesktop.com/musicians/westlife

Top Sites

All About Westlife
www.geocities.com/hk_westlife

All That I Want is Westlife & Westlife Fans United Canada
www.westlife.ipfox.com

east2westlife
www.geocities.com/westlife2000_ca

Get Wild With Westlife
http://clix.to/westlife

Just Westlife
http://fate.nu/westlife

My Westlife
http://members.nbci.com/mywestlife

The Westlife Guys
www.geocities.com/westlife_guys

The Wild Side of Westlife
www.angelfire.com/pop/wildsideofwestlife/mainpage.html

Wahey - It's Westlife
http://welcome.to/wahey

West R The Best!
http://go.to/westrthebest

Westlife 360
www.westlife360.com

Westlife Canada
http://pages.sprint.ca/westlife

Westlife Dreams
www.westlifedreams.co.uk

Westlife Exclusive
http://fly.to/westlifex

Westlife Web
www.westlifeweb.com

Westlife World
www.westlife-world.com

Westlife Zone
www.westlifezone.de

Westlife.Org - Absolute Westlife
www.westlife.org

Westlife4Ever
http://go.to/westlife4ever

Wet Files
www.filan.f2s.com

Worldwide Westlife Web Site
www.worldwidewestlife.co.uk

TV Schedule

Westlife.Org: TV Appearances
www.westlife.org/tv.html

Video

Westlife Web: Videos
www.westlifeweb.com/videos.html

Westlife.Org: Videos
www.westlife.org/videos.html

Wallpapers

Wet Files: Wallpapers
www.filan.f2s.com/wallpaper.htm

Webrings

The Westlife Craic Ring
http://nav.webring.yahoo.com/hub?ring=wlcraic&id=9&list

The Westlife Webring
http://nav.webring.yahoo.com/hub?ring=westlife&id=127%20id&list

Whitney Houston

SUPER SINGLES "My Love Is Your Love" | "I Learned from the Best" | "It's Not Right, But It's Okay" | "Queen of the Night" | "So Emotional"

Official Site

Arista Records: Whitney Houston
www.aristarec.com/aristaweb/WhitneyHouston

Articles

dotmusic: Whitney Houston
www.dotmusic.com/artists/WhitneyHouston

Jam! Showbiz: Music: Whitney Houston
www.canoe.ca/JamMusicArtistsH/houston.html

Discussion

Yahoo! Clubs: Anna's Whitney Houston Club
http://clubs.yahoo.com/clubs/annaswhitneyhoustonclub

Yahoo! Clubs: HottWhitney Houston Club
http://clubs.yahoo.com/clubs/hottwhitneyhoustonclub

Yahoo! Groups: Whitney
http://groups.yahoo.com/group/whitney

Whitneys' Shrine Newsletter
http://members.sigecom.net/nippy83/newsletter.html

Ecards

A Shrine to Whitney Houston - Greeting Cards
http://members.sigecom.net/nippy83/cardpickup.html

Galleries

A Shrine to Whitney Houston: Galleries
http://members.sigecom.net/nippy83/pictures.html

Links

Mosiqa Top 100 Whitney Houston Sites
http://topsites.mosiqa.com/whitney

Lyrics

A Shrine to Whitney Houston: Lyrics
http://members.sigecom.net/nippy83/lyrics.html

News

A Shrine to Whitney Houston: News
http://members.sigecom.net/nippy83/today.html

Entertainment Sleuth: Whitney Houston
http://e.sleuth.com/details.asp?Entity=2086

Reference

All Music Guide: Whitney Houston
http://allmusic.com/cg/x.dll?p=amg&sql=1WHITNEY|HOUSTON

Internet Movie Database: Whitney Houston
http://us.imdb.com/Name?Whitney+Houston

People Magazine Profiles: Whitney Houston
http://people.aol.com/people/pprofiles/celebhomepage/0,3371,89,00.html

Rock on the Net: Whitney Houston
www.rockonthenet.com/artists-h/whitneyhouston_main.htm

Wall of Sound: Whitney Houston
http://wallofsound.go.com/artists/whitneyhouston

Software

A Shrine to Whitney Houston: Screensavers
http://members.sigecom.net/nippy83/screensavers.html

Celebrity Desktop: Whitney Houston
www.celebritydesktop.com/musicians/whitney_houston

Cinema Desktop Themes: Whitney Houston
www.cinemadesktopthemes.com/st/h/whitney_houston.dt.1.html

Top Sites

A Shrine to Whitney Houston
www.whitneys-shrine.uni.cc

Classic Whitney
www.classicwhitney.com

Inside of Whitney
www.inside-whitney.com

VH1 Fan Club: Whitney Houston
http://whitney-houston.vh1.com

Whitney Houston - A Divine Voice
www.whitney-voice.com

Whitney Houston Illustrated
http://whfan.free.fr

Whitney Houston Online
www.whitney-houston.com

Whitney Houston Worship Page
www.whitney-fan.com

Wonderful World of Whitney
http://whitneyhouston.freeservers.com

TV Schedule

A Shrine to Whitney Houston: TV Guide
http://pub11.bravenet.com/classified/show.asp?usernum=919942149

Video

Click2Music: Whitney Houston
www.click2music.com/whitney

Webrings

The Voice - A Whitney Houston Web Ring
http://nav.webring.yahoo.com/hub?ring=whitneyh&list

Whitney Houston Web Ring
http://nav.webring.yahoo.com/hub?ring=whitneyhouston&list

will smith

SUPER SINGLES "Will 2k" | "Wild Wild West" | "Miami" | "Getting Jiggy Wit It"

Official Site

willsmith.com
www.willsmith.com

Articles

dotmusic: Will Smith
www.dotmusic.com/artists/WillSmith

Discussion

Yahoo! Clubs: Big Willie Style
http://clubs.yahoo.com/clubs/bigwilliestyle

Yahoo! Clubs: Harsh's Will Smith Fan Club
http://clubs.yahoo.com/clubs/harshswillsmithfanclub

Yahoo! Clubs: Will Smith's Official Club
http://clubs.yahoo.com/clubs/willsmithsofficialclub

Yahoo! Groups: Will Smith
http://groups.yahoo.com/group/will_smith

Galleries

Absolute Pictures: Will Smith
www.absolutepictures.com/s/smith_will

AtPictures.Com: Will Smith
http://atpictures.com/will

Will Smith Page: Pictures Gallery
http://members.nbci.com/willsmithp/pictures.htm

Lyrics

Will Smith Page: Lyrics
http://members.nbci.com/willsmithp/lyrics.htm

News

Entertainment Sleuth: Will Smith
http://e.sleuth.com/details.asp?Entity=4146

Mr. Showbiz: Will Smith
http://mrshowbiz.go.com/people/willsmith

Reference

All Music Guide: Will Smith
http://allmusic.com/cg/x.dll?p=amg&sql=1WILL|SMITH

BoxOfficeMojo: Will Smith
www.boxofficemojo.com/willsmith.html

Internet Movie Database: Will Smith
http://us.imdb.com/Name?Will+Smith

People Magazine Profiles: Will Smith
http://people.aol.com/people/pprofiles/celebhomepage/0,3371,87,00.html

Rock on the Net: Will Smith
www.rockonthenet.com/artists-s/willsmith_main.htm

Yahoo! Web Celeb: Will Smith
http://features.yahoo.com/webceleb/smith

Wall of Sound: Will Smith
http://wallofsound.go.com/artists/willsmith

Software

Celebrity Desktop: Will Smith
www.celebritydesktop.com/actors/will_smith

Cinema Desktop Themes: Will Smith
www.cinemadesktopthemes.com/st/s/will_smith.dt.1.html

Top Sites

Come & Get Jiggy With Wil's Page
http://expage.com/page/GetJiggy

EWS Music Presents Will Smith
www.ewsonline.com/music/will

Getting' Jiggy Wit' It
www.angelfire.com/ak/jiggyman

Mike's Will Smith Page
http://webhome.globalserve.net/mpasini

The Will Smith Fan Page
www.geocities.com/twsfp

The Will Smith Fan Site
www.musicfanclubs.org/willsmith

VH1 Fan Club: Will Smith
http://will-smith.vh1.com

Will Smith Page
http://come.to/willsmith

Will Smith's Big Willie Style Page
www.angelfire.com/ok/nitroglis

WSonline
www.geocities.com/WSonline

TV Schedule

TV Now: Will Smith
www.tv-now.com/stars/smith.html

Video

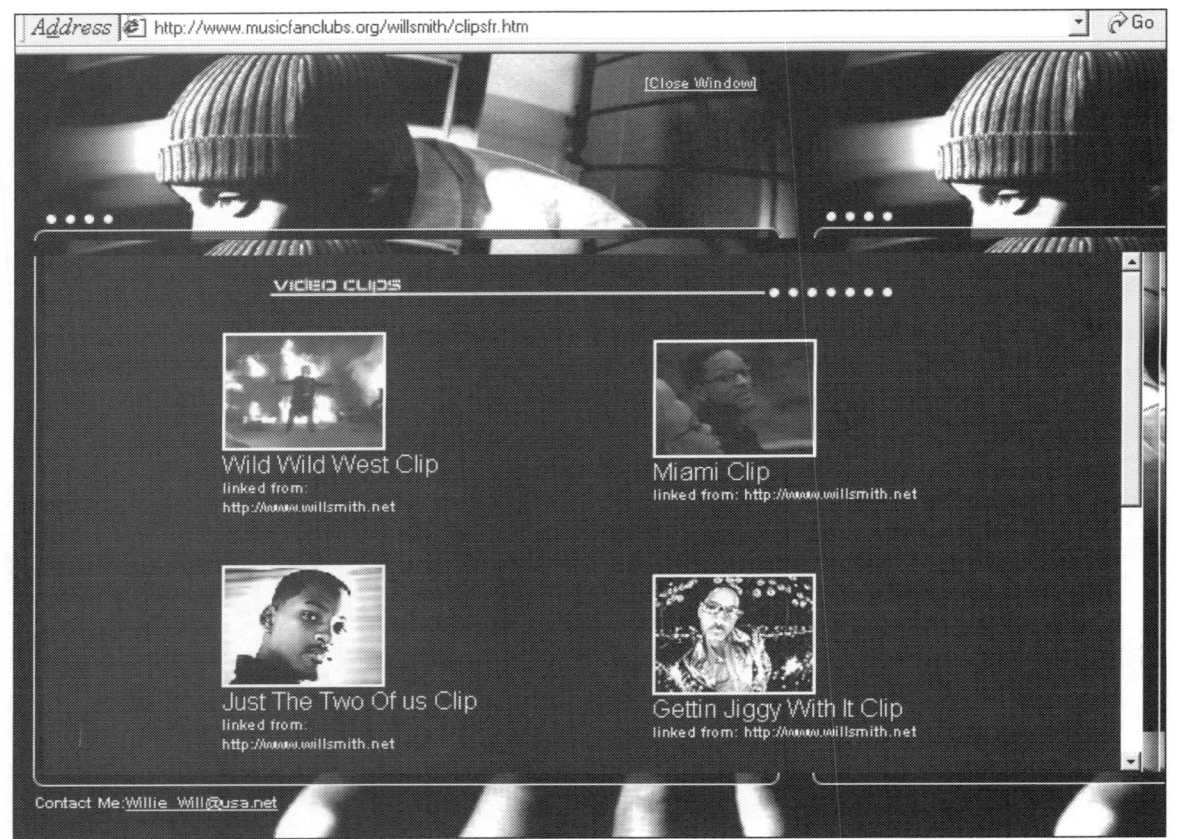

The Will Smith Fan Site: Videos
www.musicfanclubs.org/willsmith/clipsfr.htm

Webrings

Will Smith's Fans Union
http://nav.webring.yahoo.com/hub?ring=wsunion&list

Official Sites of Other Musicians

From A Tribe Called Quest to the Wu-Tang Clan -- they're all here! Over 300 official sites for famous musicians are listed here, so you can find out who Nelly Furtado is, get the latest info on Garbage, discover new artists, and keep up with old favorites. Sites are listed alphabetically by first name. For fan-based sites, see the next chapter - More Music Resources.

10,000 Maniacs
   www.maniacs.com

3 Doors Down
   www.3doorsdown.com

311
   www.311music.com

3LW
   www.3lw.com

5ive
   www.5ive.co.uk

A Tribe Called Quest
www.tribecalledquest.com

Aaron Carter
www.aaroncarter.com

ABBA
www.abbasite.com

AC/DC
www.elektra.com/retro/acdc

Ace of Base
www.aceofbase.com

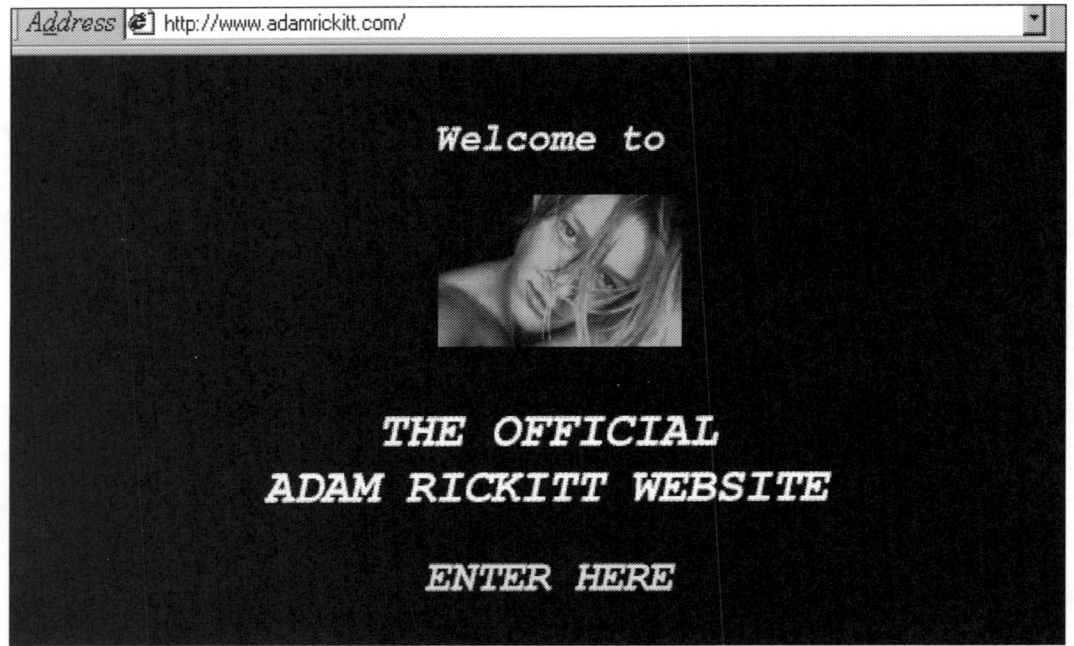

Adam Rickitt
www.adamrickitt.com

Aerosmith
www.aerosmith.com

Aimee Mann
http://aimeemann.com

Air Supply
www.airsupplymusic.com

Alabama
www.thealabamaband.com

Alan Jackson
www.alanjackson.com

Alice Deejay
www.alicedeejay.com

Alice in Chains
www.aliceinchains.com

Amanda
www.maverick.com/amanda

Amber
www.amber-mcc.com

Andreas Johnson
www.andreas-johnson.com

Anita Doth
www.anitadoth.com

Ann Nesby
www.annnesby.com

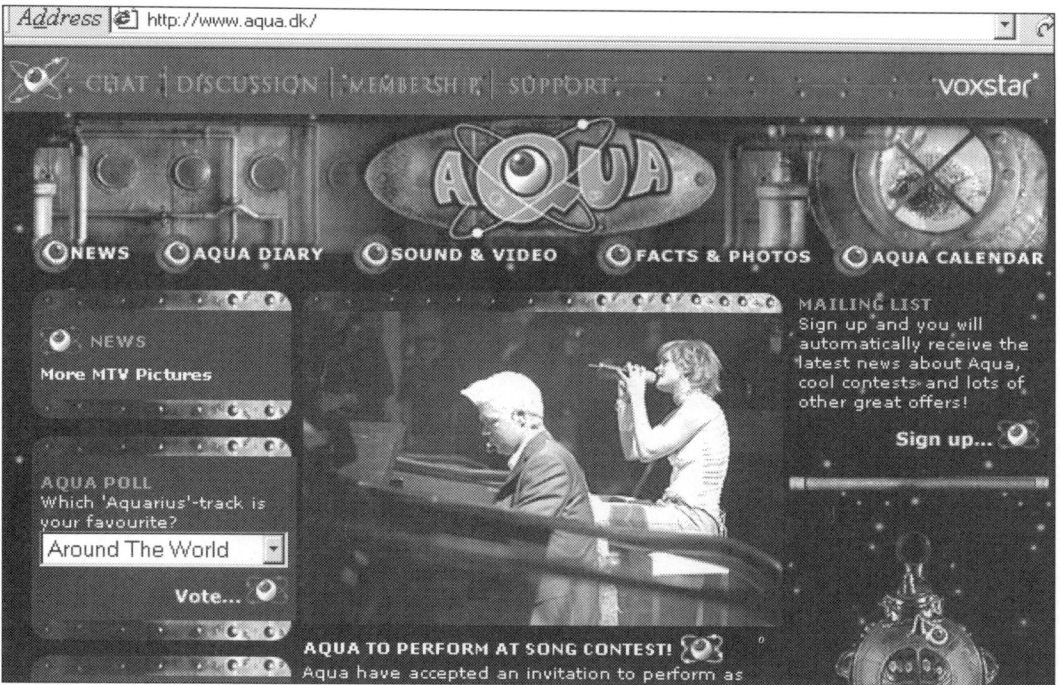

Aqua
www.aqua.dk

Aretha Franklin
www.aristarec.com/aristaweb/ArethaFranklin

Atomic Kitten
http://c3.vmg.co.uk/atomickitten

B*Witched
www.b-witched.com

Bad Religion
www.badreligion.com

Barenaked Ladies
www.barenakedladies.com

Basement Jaxx
www.astralwerks.com/basementjaxx

Beastie Boys
www.beastieboys.com

Beatles
www.thebeatles.com

Beck
www.beck.com

Ben Folds Five
www.benfoldsfive.com

Beth Orton
www.bethorton.com

Bette Midler
www.bettemidler.com

Bif Naked
www.bifnaked.com

Billie Myers
www.billiemyers.net

Billie Piper
http://c3.vmg.co.uk/billie

Billy Idol
www.billyidol.com

Billy Joel
www.billyjoel.com

Black Crowes
www.blackcrowes.com

Blaque
www.blaque.net

Blessed Union of Souls
www.blessidunion.com

Bloodhound Gang
www.bloodhoundgang.com

Blues Traveler
www.bluestraveler.com

Bob Dylan
www.bobdylan.com

Be sure to check out upcoming Bon Jovi tour dates here!

Bon Jovi
www.bonjovi.com

Bone Thugs-N-Harmony
www.bonethugsnharmony.com

Bonnie Raitt
www.bonnieraitt.com

Boyz II Men
www.boyziimen.com

Brian Wilson
www.brianwilson.com

Brooks & Dunn
www.brooks-dunn.com

Bryan Adams
www.bryanadams.com

BT
www.btmusic.com

Bush
www.getmusic.com/alternative/bush

Busta Rhymes
www.busta-rhymes.com

Cake
www.cakemusic.com

Cardigans
http://cardigans.com

Carly Simon
www.carlysimon.com

Cassius
http://the-raft.com/cassius.html

Charlotte Church
www.charlottechurch.com

Chemical Brothers
www.astralwerks.com/chemical

Chris Isaak
www.chrisisaak.com

Cibo Matto
www.cibomatto.com

Clint Black
www.clintblackfans.com

Coldplay
www.coldplay.com

Collective Soul
www.collectivesoul.com

Common
www.okayplayer.com/common

Counting Crows
www.countingcrows.com

Cranberries
www.cranberries.com

Crazy Town
www.crazytown.com

Cure
www.thecure.com

Cypress Hill
www.cypressonline.com

Da Brat
www.dabrat.com

Daft Punk
www.virginrecords.com/daft_punk

Dandy Warhols
www.dandywarhols.com

D'Angelo
www.okayplayer.com/dangelo

Danii Minogue
www.dannii.com

Danny Tenaglia
www.dtenaglia.com

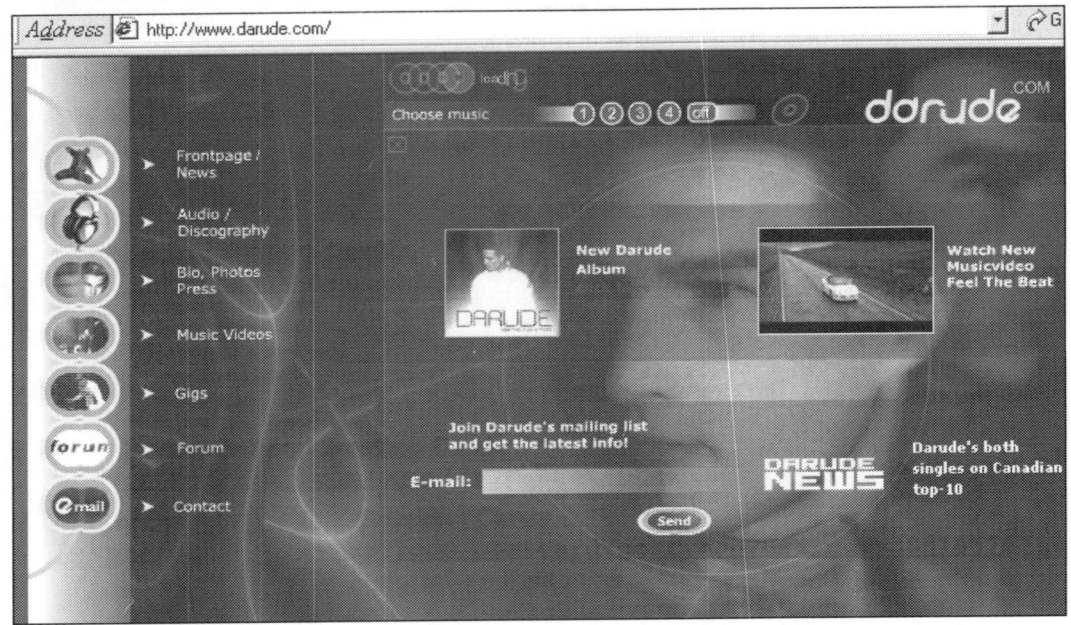

Darude
www.darude.com

Dave Hollister
www.davehollister.com

Dave Matthews Band
www.davematthews.com

David Bowie
www.davidbowie.com

David Lee Roth
www.davidleeroth.com

David Sylvian
http://eden.vmg.co.uk/davidsylvian

Days of the New
www.daysofthenew.com

De La Soul
www.tommyboy.com/dela/index.html

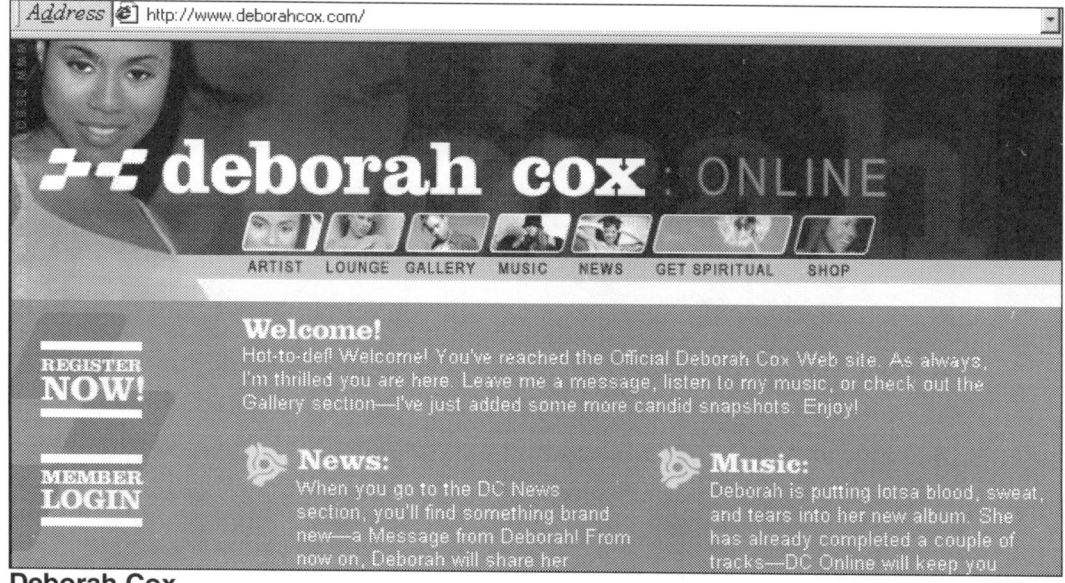

Deborah Cox
www.deborahcox.com

Dee Snider
www.deesnider.com

Def Leppard
www.defleppard.com

Deftones
www.deftones.com

Depeche Mode
www.depechemode.com

Dido
www.didomusic.com

Dilated Peoples
www.okayplayer.com/dilatedpeoples

DMX
www.defjam.com/dmx

Dolly Parton
http://sonynashville.com/DollyParton

Doors
www.thedoors.com

Dr. Dre
www.dre2001.com

Dream
www.thedreamsite.com

Dru Hill
www.druhill.net

Duncan Sheik
www.duncansheik.com

Duran Duran
www.duranduran.com

Dwight Yoakam
www.wbr.com/nashville/dwightyoakam

Edwin
www.edwinonline.com

Eiffel 65
www.eiffel65.net

Elton John
www.eltonjohn.com/flash_index.asp

Enya
www.enya.com

Erasure
www.erasure.com

Eric Clapton
www.repriserec.com/ericclapton

Erykah Badu
www.erykahbadu.com

Evan & Jaron
www.evanandjaron.com

Eve
www.ruffryders2000.com/eve

Everclear
www.everclearonline.com

Everlast
http://everlastmusic.com

Fastball
http://208.218.3.144/Bands/Fastball/flash.html

Fat Boy Slim
www.astralwerks.com/fbs

Femi Kuti
www.femikutimusic.com

Field Mob
www.fieldmob.com

First Love
www.firstlovemusic.com

Front Line Assembly
www.frontlineassembly.com

Garbage
www.garbage.com

Garth Brooks
www.capitol-nashville.com/garth.html

George Michael
www.aegean.net

Gloria Estefan
www.gloriafan.com

Godsmack
www.godsmack.com

Goldfinger
www.goldfingermusic.com

Grateful Dead
www.gratefuldead.com

Green Day
www.greenday.com

Groove Armada
www.groovearmada.com

Guns N' Roses
www.gnronline.com

Harry Connick Jr.
www.hconnickjr.com

Hole
www.hole.com

Hootie & The Blowfish
www.hootie.com

Hooverphonic
www.hooverphonic.com

Ice Cube
www.icecube.com

Indigo Girls
www.indigogirls.com

Insane Clown Posse
www.insaneclownposse.com

Insolence
www.insolence.com

Iron Maiden
www.ironmaiden.com

Ja Rule
www.defjam.com/artists/jarule/jaintro.html

Jamie O'Neal
www.jamieoneal.com

Jamiroquai
www.jamiroquai.co.uk

Jane's Addiction
www.janesaddiction.com

Jay-Z
www.defjam.com/artists/jayz/jayz.html

JazzyFatNastees
www.okayplayer.com/jazzyfatnastees

Jennifer Day
www.jenniferday.com

Jimi Hendrix
www.jimi-hendrix.com

Jimmy Flowers
www.mp3.com/jimmyflowers

Jo Dee Messina
www.jodeemessina.com

Joan Osborne
www.joanosborne.com

Jocelyn Enriquez
www.jocelynenriquez.com

Joe
www.joescrib.com

Joey McIntire
www.joeymcintyre.com

Johnny Cash
www.johnnycash.com

Jordan Knight
www.jordanknight.com

Joy Enriquez
www.joyenriquez.com

Judds
http://mercurynashville.com/thejudds

Julian Lennon
www.julianlennon.com

k. d. lang
www.kdlang.com

K-Ci & Jo-Jo
www.kciandjojo.com

Kelis
  www.kelis.com
Kenny G
  www.kennyg.com
Kid Koala
  www.kidkoala.com
Kid Rock
  www.kidrock.com
KISS
  www.kissonline.com
Korn
  www.korn.com
Kristine W
  www.kristinew.com
Kula Shaker
  www.kulashaker.co.uk
Kylie Minogue
  www.kylie.com
Laurent Garnier
  www.laurentgarnier.com
Led Zeppelin
  www.atlantic-records.com/Led_Zeppelin

Lee Ann Womack
www.leeannwomack.com

Limp Bizkit
www.limpbizkit.com

Linkin Park
www.linkinpark.com

Lisa Loeb
www.lisaloeb.com

Lisa Stansfield
www.aristarec.com/aristaweb/LisaStansfield/index.html

Lit
www.litlounge.com

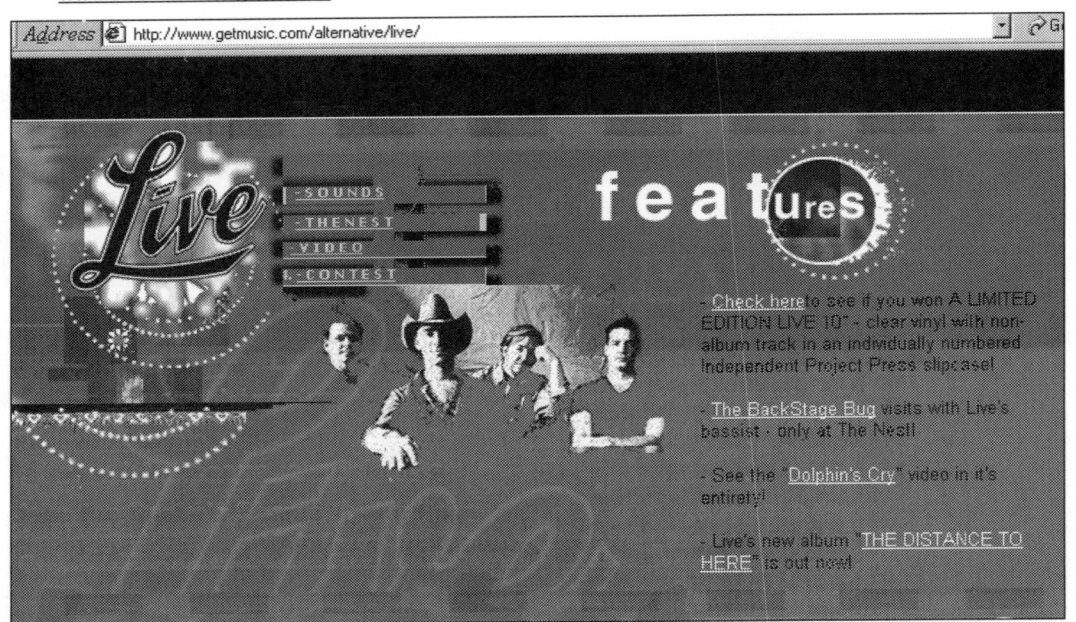

Live
www.getmusic.com/alternative/live

LL Cool J
www.llcoolj.com

Lonestar
www.lonestar-band.com

Lorrie Morgan
www.lorrie.com

Lou Reed
www.loureed.org

Lucy Nation
www.maverick.com/thelucynation

Mansun
www.mansun.com

Marilyn Manson
www.marilynmanson.com

Mark Wahlberg
www.markwahlberg.com

Martina McBride
www.martina-mcbride.com

Mary J Blige
www.mjblige.com

Mauro Picotto
www.mauropicotto.com

Megadeth
www.megadeth.com

Melissa Etheridge
www.melissaetheridge.com

Meredith Brooks
www.meredithbrooks.com

Meshell Ndegeocello
www.meshell.net

Michael Fredo
www.michaelfredo.com

Michael Jackson
www.mjnet.com

Mikaila
www.mikaila.com

Mirwais
www.mirwaisonline.com

Missy Misdemeanor Elliot
www.elektra.com/retro/missy/index.html

MJ Cole
www.mjcole.com

Moby
www.moby.v2music.com

Modjo
www.modjo.com

Moffats
www.themoffatts.com

Monifah
www.monifah.net

Monkees
www.monkees.net

Montell Jordan
www.defsoul.com/montelljordan

Moody Blues
www.moodyblues.co.uk

Motley Crue
www.motleycrue.com

Mudvayne
www.mudvayne.com

Muse
www.maverick.com/muse

MXPX
www.mxpx.com

Mya
www.myamya.com

Mystikal
www.mystikalonline.com

Nas
www.sonymusic.com/artists/Nas

Natalie Cole
www.natalie-cole.com

Natalie Imbruglia
www.natalie-imbruglia.co.uk

Natalie Merchant
www.nataliemerchant.com

Neil Young
www.neilyoung.com

Nelly
www.nelly.net

Nelly Furtado
www.whoanelly.com

Nickelback
www.nickelback.com

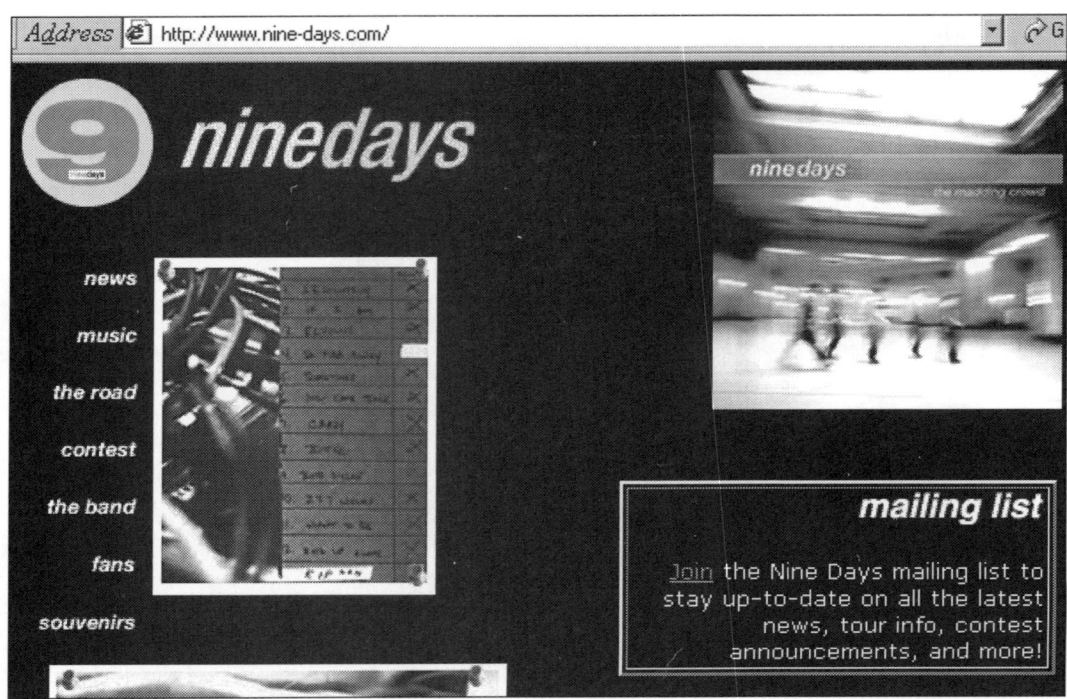

Nine Days
www.nine-days.com

Nine Inch Nails
www.nin.com

No Authority
www.noauthority.com

Offspring
www.offspring.com

Oleander
www.oleander.net

Olive
www.maverick.com/olive

Orbital
www.loopz.co.uk

Our Lady Peace
www.ourladypeace.com

Outkast
www.outkast.com

Papa Roach
www.paparoach.com

Pat Benatar
www.benatar.com

Paula Cole
www.paulacole.com

Peter Gabriel
www.petergabriel.com

Phish
www.phish.com

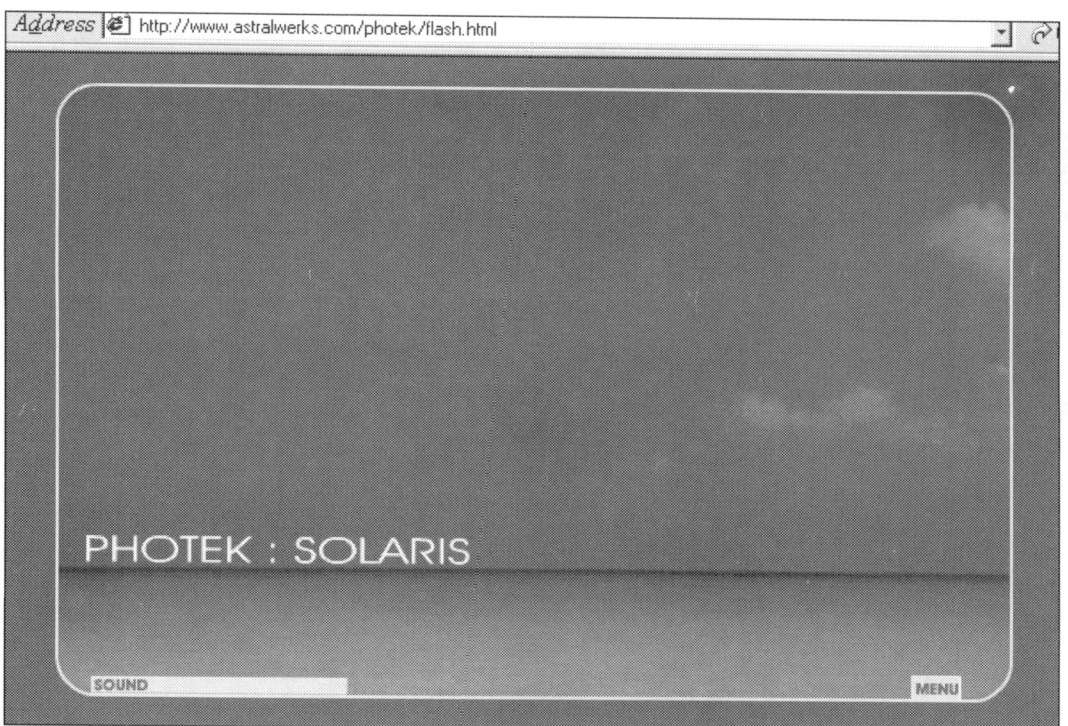

Photek
www.astralwerks.com/photek

Phunk Junkeez
www.phunkjunkeez.com

PJ Harvey
www.pjharvey.net

Porno for Pyros
www.wbr.com/pornoforpyros

Primus
www.primussucks.com

Prince
www.npgonlineltd.com

Puff Daddy
www.puffdaddy.com

R Kelly
www.r-kelly.com

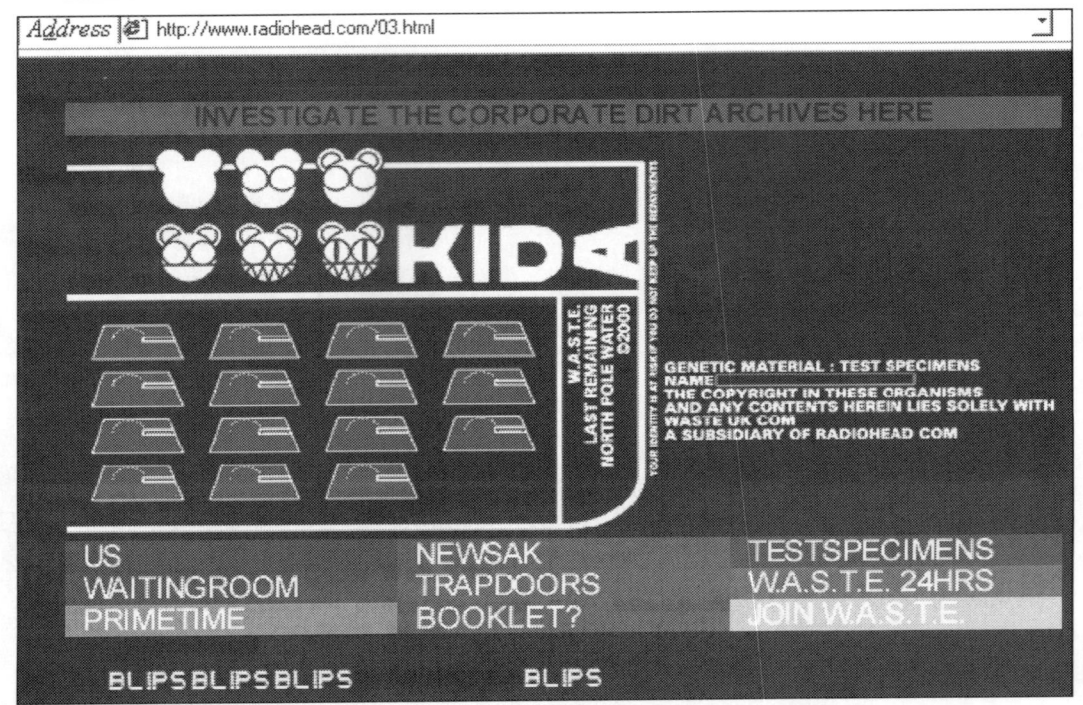

Radiohead
www.radiohead.com

Rage Against the Machine
www.ratm.com

Rammstein
www.rammstein.com

Ramones
www.officialramones.com

Reba McEntire
www.reba.com

REM
www.remhq.com

Rob Zombie
www.robzombie.com

Robbie Williams
www.robbiewilliams.com

Rolling Stones
www.the-rolling-stones.com

Roni Size
www.ronisize.com

Roots
www.okayplayer.com/theroots

Ruff Ryders
www.ruffryders2000.com

S Club 7
www.sclub-usa.com

Sade
www.sade.com

Samantha Mumba
www.samanthamumba.com

Sash!
www.sash.co.uk

Save Ferris
www.saveferris.com

Seal
www.wbr.com/seal

Seven Mary Three
http://7m3.com

Shawn Colvin
www.shawncolvin.com/flashsplash.html

SheDaisy
www.shedaisy.com

Sheena Easton
www.sheenaeaston.com

Silverchair
www.chairpage.com

Sinead O'Connor
www.sinead-oconnor.com

Sisqo
www.sisqo.com

Sister Hazel
www.sisterhazel.com

Sixpence None the Richer
www.sixpence-ntr.com

Smashmouth
www.smashmouth.com

Snoop Dogg
www.bigsnoopdogg.com

Solar Twins
www.maverick.com/solartwins

Sonic Youth
www.sonicyouth.com

Soul Decision
   www.souldecision.com
Soundgarden
   http://imusic.artistdirect.com/soundgarden
Spice Girls
   http://c3.vmg.co.uk/spicegirls
Staind
   www.staind.com
Steps
   www.steps-us.com
Stevie Nicks
   www.nicksfix.com
Sublime
   www.hallucinet.com/sublime
Tal Bachman
   www.talbachman.com
Talib Kweli & Hi-Tek
   www.okayplayer.com/talibkweli
Tantric
   www.maverickrc.com/tantric

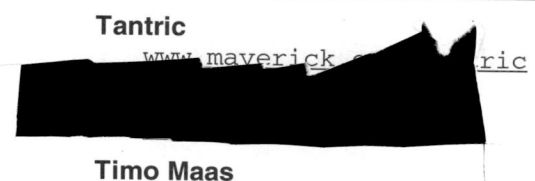

Timo Maas
   www.timomaas.com

Tina Turner
www.tina-turner.com

Toadies
www.thetoadies.com

Toby Keith
www.tobykeith.com

Tom Petty
www.tompetty.com

Tom Waits
www.tomwaits.com

Tonic
www.tonic-online.com

Tool
www.toolband.com

Tori Amos
www.toriamos.com

Towa Tei
www.towatei.com

Travis
www.travisonline.com

Trisha Yearwood
www.mca-nashville.com/trishayearwood

Tupac Shakur
www.tupacshakur.com

U2
www.u2.com

Uncle Kracker
www.unclekracker.com

Usher
www.aristarec.com/aristaweb/Usher

Utada Hikaru
www.toshiba-emi.co.jp/hikki

Van Halen
www.van-halen.com

Vanessa Daou
www.vanessadaou.com

Vanessa-Mae
www.vanessa-mae.com

Venga Boys
www.vengaboys.com

Verve Pipe
www.theververpipe.com

Vince Gill
www.vincegill.com

Vitamin C
www.vitamincfan.com

Voodoo Glow Skulls
www.voodooglowskulls.com

Wallflowers
www.the-wallflowers.com

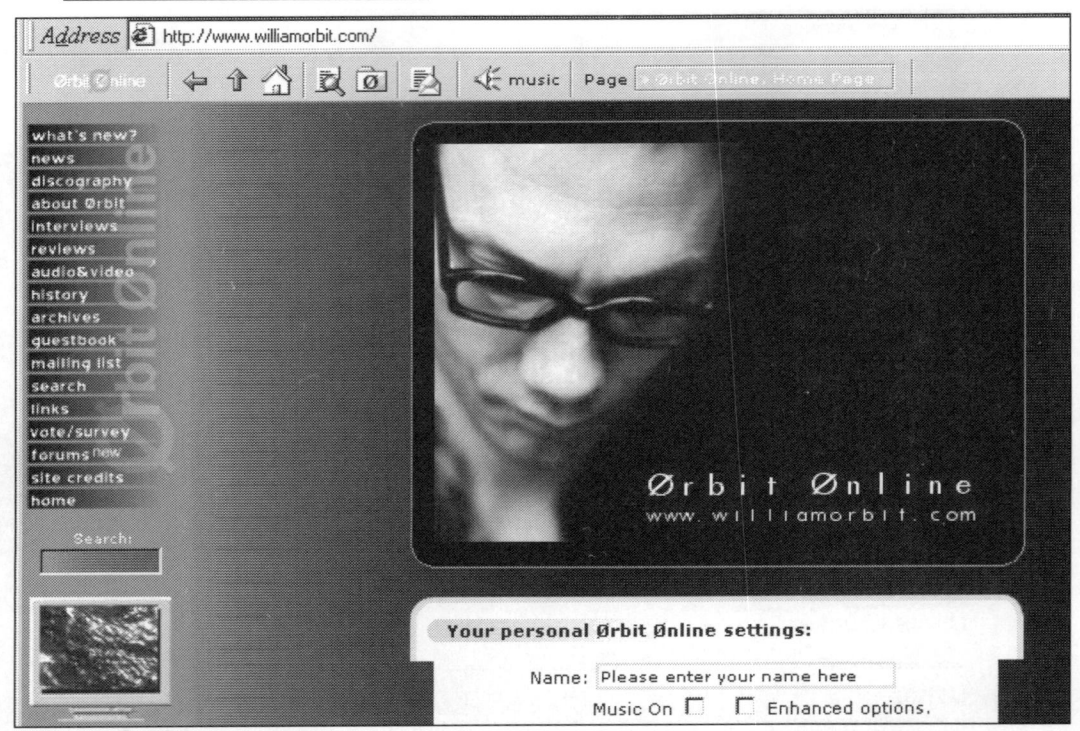

William Orbit
www.williamorbit.com

Willie Nelson
www.willienelson.com

Wu-Tang Clan
www.sonymusic.com/labels/loud/home/wutang_the_w.html

Articles | **Music Resources**

More Music Resources

The sites presented in this chapter will help you find web pages for artists other than those listed in this book. For example, VH1 has Fan Clubs for other artists, including the Rolling Stones, Vertical Horizon, Soundgarden, Joni Mitchell, U2 and even Weird Al. Even the most obscure artist probably has a Yahoo! Club or Group devoted to him or her. There is no limit to the kinds of things you'll find on the Web in connection with a music celeb. Use these sites as a starting point to create your own link collection devoted to your favorite pop star.

Articles

dotmusic
www.dotmusic.com

Discussion

eFGForum.Com
www.efgforum.com/cgi-bin/Ultimate.cgi?action=intro

Yahoo! Clubs: Music: Artists
http://dir.clubs.yahoo.com/music/artists

Yahoo! Groups: Music: Artists
http://dir.groups.yahoo.com/dir/Music/Artists

Ecards

Celebrity Postcard
www.celebritypostcard.com

E-Mail Services

Fun2Mail.Com
www.fun2mail.com

Fan Site Hosting

Music Fan Clubs
www.musicfanclubs.org/webmasters

Galleries

A List Celebrities
www.the-alist.org

Absolute Pictures
www.absolutepictures.com

AnthemPop
www.anthempop.com

AtPictures.Com
www.atpictures.com

Beautiful Celebrities
www.beautifulcelebrities.com

Ditto.Com
www.ditto.com

PopFolio
www.popfolio.com

Links

FanGuide
www.fanguide.com

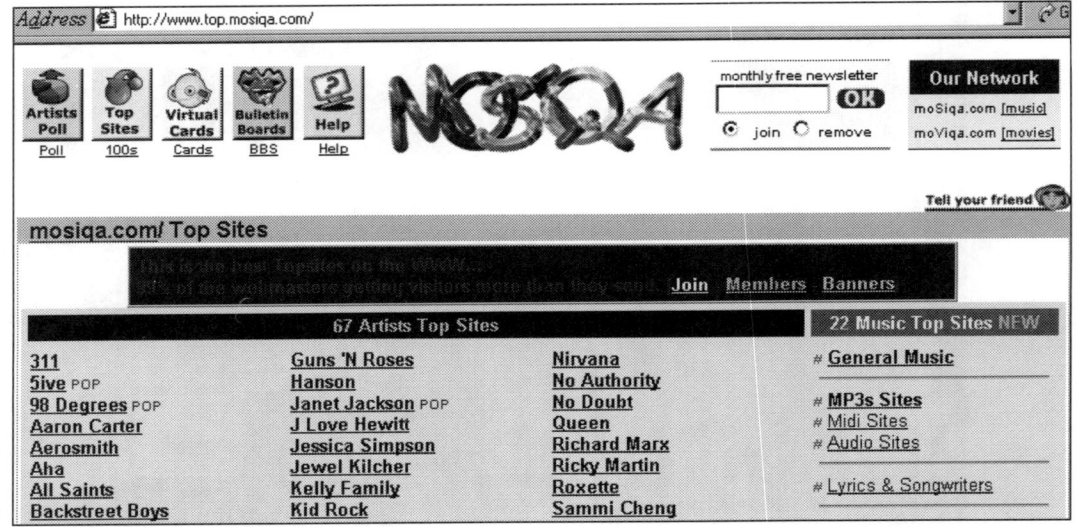

Mosiqa Top 100
www.top.mosiqa.com

Lyrics

AllLyrics.Net
www.alllyrics.net

Lyrics World
www.lyricsworld.com

Lyrix Engine
www.lyrixengine.com

Merchandise

Artist Direct
www.artistdirect.com

CDNow
www.cdnow.com

Signature Superstars
www.signaturesuperstars.com

News

Ananova
www.ananova.com

Abstracts.Net
www.abstracts.net

Billboard
www.billboard.com

Entertaindom: Music
www.entertaindom.com/pages/music/music.jsp

Entertainment Sleuth
http://e.sleuth.com

Jam! Showbiz: Music
www.canoe.com/JamMusic

MTV News
http://news.mtv.com

Mr. Showbiz
http://mrshowbiz.go.com

PeopleNews
www.peoplenews.com

WorldPop
www.worldpop.com

Real Audio

Friskit
www.friskit.com

Real Audio Music
www.angelfire.com/sd/TMOD2

Xtreme Music Place
www.xtrememp.com

Reference

All Music Guide
www.allmusic.com

Clipland - Music Video Database
www.clipland.com

Internet Movie Database
www.imdb.com

People Magazine Profiles
http://people.aol.com/people/pprofiles

Rock on the Net
www.rockonthenet.com

UBL @ Artist Direct
http://ubl.artistdirect.com

Wall of Sound
http://wallofsound.go.com

Software

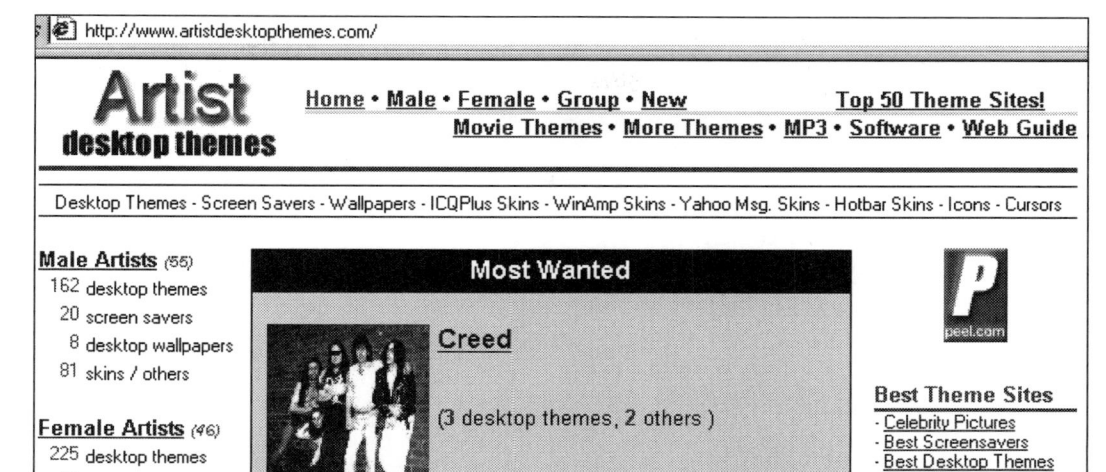

Artist Desktop Themes
www.artistdesktopthemes.com

Celebrity Desktop
www.celebritydesktop.com

Cinema Desktop Themes
www.cinemadesktopthemes.com

Top Sites

AllFans.Org
www.allfans.org

AllStarz.Org
www.allstarz.org

VH1 Fan Clubs
www.vh1.com/fanclubs

Tour & Ticket Information

Aloud.com
www.aloud.com

Pollstarr
www.pollstar.com

TV Schedule

MusicStation: RockOnTV
www.musicstation.com/rockontv

TV Now: Stars on TV
www.tv-now.com/stars/stars.html

Video

Clipland - Music Video Database
www.clipland.com

Launch.Com
www.launch.com

MTV.com
www.mtv.com

Vidnet: Music
http://music.vidnet.com

Webrings

Bomis
www.bomis.com

Yahoo! Webrings
www.webring.com

Listening to Internet Radio

Have you heard the Internet? Find out what you need to know before listening to online radio and how to take over the airwaves yourself!

The Players

Most people who regularly surf the Internet already have streaming audio players installed on their computers. Nonetheless, here is a list of the most common players as well as web sites where you can download them. Real Player and Windows Media Player will not play files designed for each other, so we've also listed the propriety file extensions of each player.

Whether other players, such as WinAmp (<u>www.winamp.com</u>), will work with a particular Internet Radio Service is uncertain; the only way to know is to try it out. Regardless, if you download these two players, you'll be able to listen to all of the Internet radio services discussed here.

- **Real Player**
    <u>www.real.com</u>
    File extensions include .rm and .ra
- **Windows Media Player**
    <u>www.windowsmedia.com</u>
    File extensions include .wma

Internet Radio Services

Internet radio services offer stations (also known as channels) of audio. The stations are broadcast 24 hours a day using streaming audio technology. However, not all Internet radio services are the same.

Here we discuss the most prominent Internet radio services that broadcast music. For Internet radio services that broadcast talk shows, sound bytes and other audio programs, try www.eyada.com, www.broadcastamerica.com, www.voquette.com, www.npr.org and www.givemetalk.com.

All of the Internet Radio Services profiled offer free, 24-hour broadcasts, very few commercial interruptions and a large selection of channels. Broadband access is recommended, but even with cable or DSL connections, surfing the Web while listening will often cause the player to buffer (i.e. slow and distort the transmission).

When it comes to Internet Radio Services, there is no leader of the pack. Rather there are four strong contenders with a variety of features, and there is no reason you can't be a listener of all of them. To help you understand what's available, we've reviewed each of the four and compiled a feature comparison chart.

Internet Radio Service Feature Comparison

		SERVICE			
		Live365	NetRadio	SonicNet	Spinner
FEATURES	Buy Music*	♪	♪	♪	♪
	Custom Station	♪		♪	
	Pause			♪	♪
	Rate Songs		♪		♪
	Skip Songs			♪	
	Song Information	♪	♪	♪	♪
	Station Presets	♪	♪		
	Volume	♪	♪	♪	♪
	# of Stations**	26,000+	120+	40+	150+

*The ability to buy the music that you are currently listening to.
**Live365 stations are user-created; others are service-created.

Live365
www.live365.com

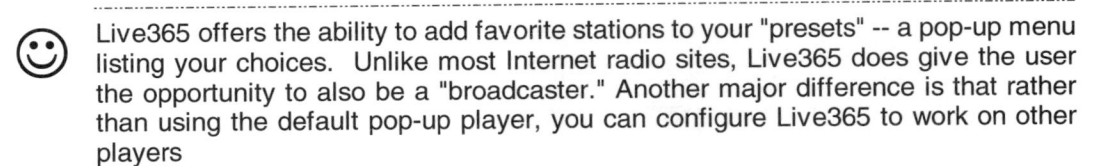

☺ Live365 offers the ability to add favorite stations to your "presets" -- a pop-up menu listing your choices. Unlike most Internet radio sites, Live365 does give the user the opportunity to also be a "broadcaster." Another major difference is that rather than using the default pop-up player, you can configure Live365 to work on other players

☹ Most of Live365's channels have been designed by users, so they are not as specific nor easy to find as those of other online radio services. Although they don't offer a pause button, there is a mute button directly beneath the volume control.

Sample Channels: 80s Live On, Alternative Classics, Hypnotic Trance, Meltdown, PhatBeats

Home Page Quote: "At Live365.com, we are revolutionizing radio and the way music is heard throughout the world. You can create your own Internet radio station and listen to thousands of stations created by others."

NetRadio

www.netradio.com

:) NetRadio offers four customizable preset stations. The channels offered by NetRadio are highly specialized and grouped by related categories, making them easy to find. They also offer several talk channels, including comedy and music news.

:(NetRadio's player does not have the ability to skip songs or pause them.

Sample Channels — Alternative Country, Ambient, British Invasion, Celtic, Club Mix, Disco, Drum 'n' Bass, Earthbeat, Electronica, Funk, Industrial, Lounge, Power Hits, Ska, Soundtracks, Swing, Teen Scene, Techno, Trip Hop

Home Page Quote — "More than 2.5 million unique listeners visit several times per month to enjoy NetRadio.com's 100-plus channels of music and information - on demand, 24 hours a day, seven days a week."

SonicNet

www.sonicnet.com

☺ The ability to skip songs is SonicNet's best feature. Because of its affiliation with MTV, SonicNet offers channels that feature MTV playlists. They also offer stations programmed by celebrities, such as Scott Weiland.

☹ SonicNet seems to have a few more station identifications than other Internet radio sites.

Sample Channels Amp (Electronica), Blast (Top 40), Breaks (Drum 'n' Bass), Dirt (Grunge), London (Brit-Pop), MTV TRL Radio (TRL Artists), Neon (Modern Hits), Vinyl (Dance Club Music), Wrangler (Contemporary Country)

Home Page Quote "Sonicnet.com is the home for music created by people who are passionate about music. Our mission is to ignite, inspire, and nurture the passion for music that fans of all genres share."

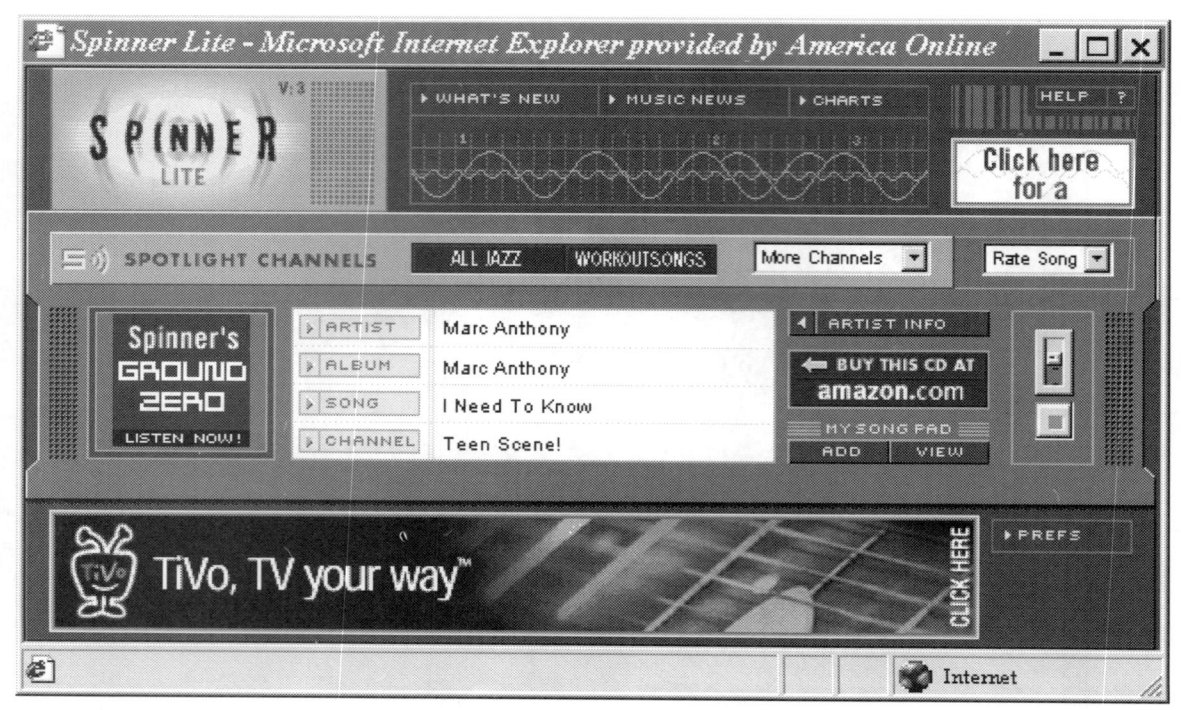

Spinner

www.spinner.com

☺ Spinner has an ever-growing list of stations that are highly specialized and don't have such "cutesy" names, which can make it difficult to identify the type of music played by other services. Spinner's station identification announcements are infrequent -- occurring once or twice an hour. Spinner offers celebrity programmed channels, including one by Madonna.

☹ Spinner's only major fault is the player's inability to skip songs. You can get around this by switching stations when a song you don't like begins to play.

Sample Channels 2 Step Garage, 90's Rock, Brit Pop, Electronica, EuroPop, Metal, MovieScores, NeoJapan, Swing Dance, Teen Scene!, Unplugged, Urban Divas, Workout Songs

Home Page Quote "Spinner.com is the first and largest Internet music service, broadcasting over 22 million songs each week to listeners all over the world. With over 375,000+ songs in rotation on 150+ music channels, Spinner spans an extraordinarily diverse range of musical styles."

More Online Radio

Here are some additional Internet radio sites.

FM Cities
www.fmcities.com
   The stations at FM Cities are customized with local content for major cities.

Friskit
www.friskit.com
   Search for an artist, and Friskit plays what it finds on the 'Net.

Listen.com: Radio
http://radio.listen.com
   Like Spinner and NetRadio, but with a smaller selection of channels.

Yahoo! Internet Life: Radio
www.yil.com/radio
   Spotlights a different online radio service daily.

Be a Broadcaster

Have good taste in music? Want to make your voice heard? Be a broadcaster! Thanks to the Internet, you too can broadcast an audio stream. Some services require that you actually host the stream on your computer, while others will host it for you. Here are some of the best....

Give Me Talk!
www.givmetalk.com
   Broadcast your own talk or variety show; free software available.

Ice Cast
www.icecast.org
   Compatible with WinAmp.

Live 365
www.live365.com
   They offer a variety of options, including the ability to have them host your stuff.

ShoutCast
www.shoutcast.com
   Uses WinAmp technology.

Notes

Notes

Have a Site You Think We Should Add? Spotted a Change?

For review, send details about the site (including its name and URL) to

jflowers@incredibleguides.com

Want to Find Out About Other Titles in This Series?

Visit us on the Web at

www.incredibleguides.com

THE INCREDIBLE INTERNET GUIDES

Find the best web sites on your favorite subject!
Over 1,000 sites categorized and profiled
To save you time!

The Incredible Internet Guide to Comic Books & Superheroes

Wham! Kablam! Kerpow! Now comic book and super hero affectionados can go directly to the web pages of their favorite characters with this desktop companion.
1-889150-15-0 • 400 pgs • Pub Date 2000

The Incredible Internet Guide to Diet & Nutrition

Take the fat out of big search engines and quickly find the best web sites for any kind of diet: weight loss, high performance, vegetarian, adolescent, disease-related, even fad diets!
1-889150-14-2 • 328 pgs • Pub Date 2000

The Incredible Internet Guide to Scandals & Conspiracies

Here's the book that directs you to "scandal laden" web sites to gather information on scandalous affairs, political corruption, financial schemes and other controversial topics.
1-889150-18-5 • 360 pgs • Pub Date 2000

The Incredible Internet Guide for Trekkers

Collectors, gamers, self-enthusiasts, and webmasters will find that this book has something for everyone . . . information on Star Trek characters, actors, chat rooms, message board, newsgroups, and more.
1-889150-11-8 • 360 pgs • Pub Date 1999

THE INCREDIBLE INTERNET GUIDES

The Incredible Internet Guide to Online Investing & Money Management

You can be a "Online money managers" and shop for the best sites for online banking, low cost stock brokers, estate planning and more!
1-889150-16-9 • 384 pgs • Pub Date 2000

The Incredible Internet Guide to Star Wars

We've done the "advanced scouting" by listing all the relevant, interesting sites both alphabetically and by subject — also adding trivia, "found art" and screen captures of cool sites.
1-889150-12-6 • 360 pgs • Pub Date 1999

The Incredible Internet Guide to Howard Stern

Fans can go directly to the sites dedicated to the "King of all Media" that have what they want — images, audio, song parodies, radio transcripts, phony phone calls and more!
1-889150-19-3 • 360 pgs • Pub Date 2000

Facts on Demand Press
PO Box 27869
Tempe, AZ 85285-7869
1-800-929-3811

Address: http://www.incredibleguides.com

Available at Your Local Bookstore
Distributed to the trade by National Book Network, Inc.

Facts on Demand Press

Find It Online

Get the information you need as quickly and easily as a professional researcher. *Find it Online* is a practical, how-to-guide written by a non-techno geek and developed for real people. Learn the difference between search engines and search directories, find people online, cut through government red tape and access the vast amounts of information now available on the Internet.

Alan M. Schlein • 1-889150-20-7 • Pub. Date 2000 • 512 pgs • $19.95

Online Competitive Intelligence

Competitive intelligence on the Internet . . . it's not the wave of the future . . . it's here now! The latest information to keep ahead of the competition is literally at your fingertips. *If* you know where to find it. *Online Competitive Intelligence*, a new title by the nation's leading information professional — Helen P. Burwell, empowers you to find the latest information that major corporations spend thousands of research dollars for — from your own computer.

Helen P. Burwell • 1-889150-08-8 • Pub. Date 1999 • 464 pgs. • $25.95

Public Records Online

How can someone determine which records are available online — who has them and what is available for "free or fee" — without spending time searching endless sources? Use *Public Records Online*. As the only "Master Guide" to online public record searching, *Public Records Online's* second edition details thousands of sites, both government agencies and private sources. This new edition is 80 pages larger, easier to use, and contains:

1-889150-21-5 • Pub. Date 2000 • 460 pgs • $20.95

Available at Your Local Bookstore!

1-800-929-3811 • Facts on Demand Press • www.brbpub.com